"*The Future Leader* isn't just a book, it's a blueprint for great leadership. Backed by unique research, this book is essential reading for leaders and aspiring leaders."

—*Jon Gordon, bestselling author of* The Power of Positive Leadership

"What if you could sit down with the people who actually lead some of the best companies in the world and ask them what really makes a great leader? What if you could tap the wisdom born of experience? Jacob Morgan has enviable access to this wisdom, and he's shared it with all of us. This is one of the best compasses on 21st-century leadership I know."

—*Michael Bungay Stanier, author of the WSJ bestseller,* The Coaching Habit

"Jacob Morgan's book offers a compelling look into the future of leadership—the challenges leaders will face and the mindsets and skills that will be needed to overcome them. Do you want to be a future-ready leader? You need this book!"

—*Horst Schulze, founder and CEO, The Ritz-Carlton Hotel Company*

"*The Future Leader* takes a fresh and original look at a timeless topic. By combining insightful stories from the world's top business leaders with hard data and extensive research, this book will help its readers better understand how to inspire teams and what it really means to be a leader."

—*Barbara Humpton, CEO, Siemens US*

"A fresh and original book that tackles a challenging topic with insightful stories from CEOs along with hard data. It's impossible to read this book and not think differently about leadership and who you are as a leader. A truly must-read!"

—*Garry Ridge, CEO, WD-40 Company*

"*The Future Leader* is an important resource for anyone who wants to make an impact on their organizations—and on the world."

—*Maynard Webb, NYT bestselling author, former chairman of the board of directors at Yahoo!, board member at Salesforce and Visa, founder of Webb Investment Network*

"Finally, a book that looks to the future of leadership and what is needed. Incredible insight for all organizations."

—*Nigel Travis, former CEO of Dunkin' Brands and Papa John's Pizza, principal, Challenge Consulting LLC*

"Based on 140 CEO interviews, this is an important book on an important subject. Jacob Morgan provokes us to think about what leadership is now and what it needs to be in the future."

—*L. David Marquet, bestselling author of* Turn the Ship Around!

"Jacob surveys a massive list of effective CEOs to garner a peek into the attributes of tomorrow's successful leader. This book can help you be that leader."

—*John Venhuizen, CEO, Ace Hardware*

"The imperative to read this book is simple. The world of work is everchanging, and the market continuously demands new types of leaders to guide organizations into the future. This book can help you become the best future leader you can be."

—*Arnold Donald, CEO, Carnival Corporation*

"Jacob has written a book to help you understand how leadership is changing, why it's changing, and what you need to do about it. *The Future Leader* inspires you to rethink what leadership meant in the past and to embrace the skills and mindsets that will be needed to succeed going forward."

—*David Henshall, president and CEO, Citrix*

"There's so much actionable insight in *The Future Leader* that I found relevant to the challenges and opportunities I face every day. Definitely worth reading."

—*Brad Jacobs, chairman and CEO, XPO Logistics*

"Jacob has thoroughly examined how the leaders of some of the biggest brands see their roles and, more importantly, how their actions impact their employees and the world around them. This book offers an opportunity for today's leaders to learn from their peers and for the next generation of leaders to learn from our successes and failures."

—Michel Combes, president and CEO, Sprint

"Do you want to know how to become a great leader? If so, read Jacob Morgan's book!"

—Gerhard Zeiler, chief revenue officer, WarnerMedia

"Being a leader is a tremendous honor and responsibility. You owe it to yourself and to your people to become the best possible leader you can be. You can start by reading this book and putting into practice the ideas that are explored in it. A valuable read!"

—David Novak, CEO of oGoLead, co-founder,
retired chairman and CEO of Yum! Brands, Inc.

"Today's corporate leaders don't start from scratch. They build their leadership practice from the collective experience of those before them and apply that wisdom to drive transformation, build markets, and grow brands. Jacob Morgan's new book provides access to that insight and experience."

—Michael Kneeland, chairman of the board, United Rentals

"This book is different from mainstream leadership books because it is based upon global macroeconomics of life at work. It has real content. The practice of management quit working 30 years ago. This book makes a rare, badly needed, grand contribution to leadership, teams, and human development."

—Jim Clifton, chairman and CEO, Gallup

THE
FUTURE
LEADER

THE
FUTURE
LEADER

9 SKILLS AND MINDSETS TO SUCCEED IN THE NEXT DECADE

JACOB MORGAN

Published by John Wiley & Sons, Inc., Hoboken, New Jersey.
Published simultaneously in Canada.

For general information on our other products and services or for technical support, please
contact our Customer Care Department within the United States at (800) 762-2974, outside
the United States at (317) 572-3993 or fax (317) 572-4002.

Wiley publishes in a variety of print and electronic formats and by print-on-demand. Some
material included with standard print versions of this book may not be included in e-books
or in print-on-demand. If this book refers to media such as a CD or DVD that is not included
in the version you purchased, you may download this material at http://booksupport.wiley.
com. For more information about Wiley products, visit www.wiley.com.

Library of Congress Cataloging-in-Publication Data:

Names: Morgan, Jacob, 1983- author.
Title: The future leader : 9 skills and mindsets to succeed in the next
   decade / Jacob Morgan.
Description: First Edition. | Hoboken : Wiley, 2020. | Includes
   bibliographical references.
Identifiers: LCCN 2019045915 (print) | LCCN 2019045916 (ebook) | ISBN
   9781119518372 (hardback) | ISBN 9781119518303 (adobe pdf) | ISBN
   9781119518389 (epub)
Subjects: LCSH: Leadership. | Organizational change.
Classification: LCC HD57.7 .M663456 2020 (print) | LCC HD57.7 (ebook) |
   DDC 658.4/092—dc23
LC record available at https://lccn.loc.gov/2019045915
LC ebook record available at https://lccn.loc.gov/2019045916

Cover Design: Gerard Allen Mendoza
Cover Image: Lighthouse © Michael Rayback/Shutterstock,
Clouds © markovka/Depositphotos.com

Printed in the United States of America

SKY10034204_042222

To my parents, David and Ella, who have always been my lighthouses, thank you for guiding me. And to my wife, Blake, whose love, support, and encouragement makes everything I do possible.

Contents

Introduction

Thousands of years ago, when mariners and explorers would set sail into uncharted waters, the only way they could find their way back home or to their destination would be to look for a landmark like a pile of rocks during the day, or to look for a fire at night. These not only served to lead sailors to their destinations, but also to warn them of any dangers that might wreck their ships. Perhaps the most famous lighthouse, and one of the Seven Wonders of the World, was the Pharos of Alexandria, which was constructed in the third century BCE. The story is that this structure was over 450 feet tall and survived for 1,500 years before being destroyed by an earthquake.

Throughout history, lighthouses have served as beacons to lead us to our destinations while at the same time helping us avoid any dangers. This is why I chose to use a lighthouse as the cover of this book. I see current and future leaders as lighthouses who guide their employees and organizations to success while steering them away from the rocky shores that might crush them.

Great leaders change the world, or perhaps more aptly, great leaders make the world. They help design the products and services that we use in our personal and professional lives; they create companies that provide jobs so that the people who work there can provide for their families; they fight for social causes and injustices to help make the world a better place; they support charities and non-profits; and they shape the culture, attitude, and behavior of the people who work there, meaning they shape who we are as human beings. It's a tremendous responsibility but an enormous privilege.

In order to create a world we all want to work and live in, we need to make sure that we have the right leaders in place, now and especially in the future. In the context of this book, this means within a business environment, although the concepts here can be applied to any individual in any organization. This is a challenging thing to do because the world of work is changing quickly, and what worked in the past won't work in the future. Wayne Gretzky famously said,

"I skate to where the puck is going to be, not where it has been." I want to help leaders and organizations understand where the puck is going so that they can start moving there now.

Over the past ten years I've written five books, including this one. During that ten-year period I've been fortunate enough to work with hundreds of companies, travel the world, and get my work in front of millions of people. I've shared a lot of ideas and insights during my journey but I still consider myself to be a perpetual learner. Leadership is one of the areas I'm particularly fascinated by.

Every year (during non-pandemic times) I speak at around 40 conferences and events around the world, always on themes and topics related to leadership, the future of work, and employee experience. I started to notice a recurring trend from audience members and from executives that I would advise, meet, or interview. More and more I would get questions not on present-day leadership but on what leadership would look like in the next decade. I certainly had my ideas and theories around this, but I thought this was a rather interesting question to explore. I started digging around and realized that there is almost nothing out there that tackles this and certainly nothing with solid research behind it that actually incorporates the insights from global CEOs and employees.

It seems as though the business world is getting increasingly inundated with present-day leadership strategies and ideas. While some progress has been made toward creating great leaders, there's still a long way to go and things change quickly! Over the past decade, for example, it can be argued that leaders were predominantly obsessed with stock price, diversity and inclusion efforts were nascent, technology (especially artificial intelligence) was nowhere near as advanced or changing as quickly as it is today, hierarchy was being challenged but not to the degree we are seeing now, social media platforms were just getting off the ground, the iPhone was barely in existence, the phrase "employee experience" was rarely muttered, purpose and impact were laughable concepts, workforces weren't as distributed or as diverse as they are today, short-termism was rampant, and the emphasis on physical workspaces beyond the typical cubicle was weak, not to mention that we were dealing with the dramatic impact of the 2008 financial crisis.

Shortly before the financial crisis I had my first job out of college working for a technology company in Los Angeles. I graduated from the University of California, Santa Cruz, with honors and a dual B.A. in business management economics and psychology. I was ready to join the corporate world and took a job that required me to commute three hours a day in bumper-to-bumper traffic. I took the job because I was sold a story of what it was like to work there. A few months into my job I'm doing data entry, cold calling, PowerPoint presentations, and hating my life. One day the CEO yells my name from across the office and tells me he has a very important project for me to work on. Naturally I got excited and thought that after "paying my dues" I'd finally be able to contribute and have an impact. The CEO takes out his wallet, gives me $10 and says, "I'm late for a meeting, I need you to run down to Starbucks and get me a cup of coffee, and by the way get yourself something as well." Ugh! This was one of the last jobs I've ever had working for anyone else and since then I've been passionate about creating organizations where we all want to show up to work. Leaders are a big part of that.

Most of us don't realize how much things have changed over the past decade because we have been "in it," so to speak. Imagine that you boarded a train to go on a very long train ride, one that lasted ten years. While you are aboard the train things appear to remain as is, technologies remain the same, the attire that everyone wears is the same – nothing has changed. But ten years go by and you finally arrive at your destination. When you disembark you can hardly recognize the new world that surrounds you. Our organizations have collectively been on this long train ride. If you never make any stops along your journey to observe the world around you, you will never really see change happening, until one day you appear to be in an entirely new place.

In Ernest Hemingway's novel *The Sun Also Rises*, there is a dialogue between two characters that goes like this: "How did you go bankrupt?" Bill asked. "Two ways," Mike said. "Gradually and then suddenly."

If you take an outside perspective, you quickly realize that leadership from ten years ago is not what it is today, and more importantly, leadership today will not be what it is ten years from now. But since we are so involved with the day-to-day aspects of our lives and careers, we rarely think about this change and what it might look like.

I wasn't sure how to go about answering this question on the future of leadership, so I decided to collect data. I interviewed over 140 CEOs at companies around the world, representing Turkey, France, India, Australia, Japan, Finland, the UK, the United States, Canada, Italy, Brazil, Ireland, Peru, and others. Industries include healthcare, food and beverage, nonprofits, automotive, financial services, equipment rental, software, real estate, and everything in between. The CEOs are from companies such as Mastercard, Best Buy, Unilever, Oracle, Verizon, St. Jude Children's Research Hospital, Philip Morris International, Itau Unibanco, InterContinental Hotels Group, Saint Gobain, ZF Friedrichshafen, Kaiser, Koç Holdings, and many others around the world. With the exception of a few, I held all the interviews either in person or via live one-on-one calls that lasted around 45 to 60 minutes. I specifically wanted to focus on CEOs because these are the ultimate leaders in the business world. They are the ones who are responsible for the decisions the organization makes, and the impact the organization has on the world and on the stakeholders, including employees and customers.

In total these CEOs represent over 7 million people, 35 industries, and 20 countries around the world. There are not many female CEOs out there, so getting them involved with my book was challenging, but I'm proud of how many I was able to include: 23% of all of the CEOs I interviewed were female. For comparison, less than 7% of all of the Fortune 500 CEOs are female (Zillman, 2019), and only 5% of the CEOs on the S&P 500 are female (Catalyst, 2019). In fact, women hold fewer than 5% of CEO positions in the United States and Europe (Edgecliffe-Johnson, 2018). I was fortunate to eclipse all of those numbers by several times.

All of the CEOs were asked a series of 12 questions:

1. What trends will impact the future of leadership?
2. What mindset(s) do you think the leader of the future will need to possess and why? (How should they think?)

3. What skills do you think the leader of the future will need to possess and why? (What should they need to know how to do?)
4. When you think of leaders today and in the next decade, what will be the main differences?
5. Imagine a day in the life of a leader in the next decade. What does that look like?
6. What will be some of the greatest challenges for the leader of the future?
7. Can you can point to any leaders today who illustrate what you think leaders will be like in ten years, and why?
8. Is your company thinking about this issue and/or working on it in some way?
9. Have you thought about what skills you will need to be a leader in another decade?
10. How do you define leadership?
11. Anything else you want to add about the future of leadership?
12. Do you have a leadership hack that has worked well for you? (Tips, techniques, or strategies you use on a regular basis to be a more effective leader.)

Prior to my asking these questions, I also provided context to the CEOs about the book and focusing on leadership over the next decade. All of these interviews were then transcribed and read through in order to pull key pieces of information. In this case I was looking for specific themes and ideas along with common responses to the list of questions. For example, what are the common skills and mindsets that CEOs keep identifying as being crucial to the future of leadership? All of these responses were then coded into a large Google Sheet that allowed me to filter by various criteria such as company size, gender of the CEO, and industry.

LOOK OUT for this image in the book! When you see it, the corresponding section will contain a quote directly from one of the many CEOs that I interviewed.

I also teamed up with LinkedIn, the world's largest professional social network, to survey almost 14,000 of their members around the world who self-identified as full-time employees to see if their perceptions lined up with what CEOs were saying. The survey was statistically significant at 95% confidence. The employees surveyed represented China, Australia, the United States, United Kingdom, India, Austria, Germany, Switzerland, Brazil, and the United Arab Emirates. Here too the employees represented a variety of industries, with company sizes ranging from 50 employees to over 100,000, and seniority levels ranging from individual contributors all the way up to C-level executives. It was extremely comprehensive and global in nature.

The survey used the same 12 questions, with the addition of a few that asked survey respondents to evaluate themselves, their managers, and their senior executives across various areas that CEOs deemed as crucial for the future of leadership. As an example, for the question "What mindset(s) do you think the leader of the future will need to possess and why? (How should they think?)," survey respondents were also asked how they, their managers, and their senior executives were practicing those mindsets. This allowed me to capture a full leadership picture for organizations around the world and to really see if what CEOs were telling me was actually being practiced and how well. Employees were also able to select up to three responses for some of the questions; for example, when identifying the top mindsets for the future leader, they had the option to pick three responses, not just one.

Finally, I interviewed several academics, researchers, and coaches and combed through hundreds of case studies, books, articles, and reports on leadership and the future of leadership to see what else I might be able to learn. I believe this is the most comprehensive and perhaps one of the only projects of this kind specifically devoted to exploring the future leader and the future of leadership through 2030 and beyond. As you go through the book you will find many quotes that came directly from the CEOs I interviewed. I want you to read and hear exactly what the world's top business leaders are telling me, in their own words.

The book is divided into a few core parts, each of which is an essential element for the future leader to understand and master. In Part 1, I define leadership. Part 2 focuses on the trends shaping the future of leadership and the implications of those trends for future leaders. This section also explores the greatest challenges that leaders of the future will be faced with.

Part 3 discusses the most crucial mindsets that leaders of the future must possess in order to lead effectively. Part 4 examines skills that leaders of the future must possess, meaning specific things that leaders of the future need to know how to do. Part 5 looks at how to become the future leader and where to begin the journey.

To accompany this book, I also created two resources you can access. The first is an assessment that will evaluate you on the skills and mindsets outlined in this book which you can find at FutureLeaderSurvey.com. Second, if you want to be coached and mentored personally by me for a full month and get access to the unique leadership hacks from the world's top CEOs, go to LeadershipReset.com. I hope you find them useful!

I specifically wanted to look at the future of leadership over the next ten years because it's not too far out to be unrealistic and it's close enough still to be practical. My hope is that you will read this book and understand what you, your team, and your organization should be working on now in order to be able to lead successfully in the coming years. You don't need to be a leader to apply the concepts in this book, but if you are or want to be a leader, then you absolutely must apply them. Everything in this book is applicable and important in today's business world but will become like air and water in the future.

This book came out around the time COVID-19 was reaching global pandemic proportions and Black Lives Matter protests were sweeping the world. One of the questions I get asked the most around leadership is how these events (and others in 2020) have impacted the research and the findings from the book. They shrunk the timeline!

This book was aimed at being future-focused but what the events of 2020 have done is made The Future Leader into The Present Leader. We need leaders and aspiring leaders to embrace the skills and mindsets explored in this book NOW.

A few years ago, I interviewed two very successful business leaders on my podcast, *The Future of Work With Jacob Morgan*. Both of them were running multi-billion dollar companies and were at the top of their game. Then 2020 happened. One of these executives was since fired from her company because hundreds of employees rose up against her because she didn't take the issues of Black Lives Matter and diversity and inclusion seriously enough. Employees went to the leadership team and gave them an ultimatum, "either she goes, or we go." The executive was promptly let go.

The other executive I interviewed was under the impression that his business and his industry were bullet proof. They were making tons of money and didn't see the need to change, evolve, or adapt new ways of working or doing business. In less than a year, his company filed for bankruptcy.

You can't afford to be passive and assume that you, your company, and your industry are immune to change because as the two examples above show… you're not. Now is the time for action, now is the time for change, and now is the time for you to decide and commit to being the leader we all need and deserve. I strongly believe that with tremendous change also comes tremendous opportunity, if you are willing to seize it. The Future Leader is very much The Present Leader.

Leaders who embrace the skills and mindsets outlined in this book, and help others around them do the same, will find that not only are they able to create organizations where employees actually want to show up to work, but they will also create a world that all of us will be proud to live in. It's time to step off the train.

Jacob Morgan
Alameda, California
April 2021

PART 1

UNDERSTANDING THE ROLE OF THE LEADER

1
The Leadership Gap

How many leaders would you estimate are in your city? How about your country? What about all over the world? If we're going to look at the future leader, then it's important for us to know just how many of these individuals we have now, and how many we might have in the future.

In the United States alone there are roughly 25 million supervisors and managers, people who are responsible for others. This is about 1 in 6 Americans. In the UK this number is around 5 million, which also comes to 1 in 6 people. McKinsey predicts that in 2030 the global workforce will be around 3.5 billion people (McKinsey, 2012). In 2020 the International Labour Organization estimates a workforce that is 45% self-employed, which has actually been decreasing over the past few years (World Bank, 2019). If we assume that 50% of the total workforce will be self-employed by 2030, that leaves us with 1.75 billion employed people (OECD, n.d.). The number of employees per manager or supervisor is referred to as the "span of control," and the suggested number of employees per manager varies from 4 employees per manager to upwards of 20. This means that around the world, there will be roughly between 87,500,000 and 437,500,000 leaders, which is actually a conservative range since many of the self-employed individuals also have full-time jobs. That is a lot of leaders! Leaders help make our world, so we'd better make sure we have the right people in those positions. We all deserve to like (or, dare I say, love) our jobs, and this starts with having the right leaders at the helm of our organizations.

Leaders Today Are Struggling

Unfortunately, most of our leaders are, bluntly speaking, not good. If they were, then we would see that reflected in the data. It doesn't mean they are bad people, but the way that we teach and talk about leadership is extremely antiquated and that's largely what leaders today are familiar with and practice. It's a bit like trying to fly a modern jet when you were only trained on an original Wright Brothers plane. You might get it in the air, but you aren't going to go far.

According to a study conducted by Ultimate Software and the Center for Generational Kinetics, 80% of employees say they can do their jobs without their managers and actually think that their managers are not necessary (Ultimate Software, 2017). Another study by Randstad found that almost half of the 2,257 survey respondents said they could do a better job than their boss (RandstadUSA, n.d.). A second Randstad study conducted in 2018 found that 60% of employees have left jobs or are considering leaving because they don't like their direct supervisors (RandstadUSA, 2018). These numbers alone paint a picture of current leaders that makes them seem nonessential. Let's be honest: we've all felt that way about our leaders at some point during our careers. I certainly have; in fact, there have been several occasions when I would see a leader at work and my inner voice would say, "What do you even do here?"

A Gallup study of over 7,000 Americans concluded that one in two people had actually left a job at some point during their career to get away from their managers in order to improve their overall quality of life (Harter, 2015). Let that sink in for a moment. It's a very somber statistic, yet one that we can all relate to. The same study shows that managers account for at least 70% of the variance in employee engagement scores. Even in the UK, research published by the *Independent* found that nearly half of British workers believe they could do a better job than their boss (Bailey, 2017). Perhaps the more alarming finding was that 13% said that their bosses are dangerously incompetent at their jobs.

Let's also not forget the seminal Gallup study on global engagement, which found that only 15% of employees around the world are engaged in their jobs. According to the study, "employees everywhere don't necessarily hate the company or organization they work for as much as they do their boss. Employees—especially the stars—join a company and then quit their manager" (Clifton, 2017).

An entire book could be written about how leaders around the world are failing us. These are supposed to be the people whom we look up to, admire, and want to emulate? These are the people who are supposed to lead our organizations and help us shape and create the future? While these numbers paint a bleak picture of present-day leadership, the numbers don't look any better when we look toward the future.

In its most recent Global Leadership Forecast report, DDI surveyed over 25,000 leaders around the world and found that only 42% said that the overall quality of leadership inside their organizations was high (DDI, 2018). Perhaps more shocking was that only 14% of organizations have what DDI calls a strong "bench," which is ready-now leaders who can step in to replace those who retire or move on. This means that if a "leadership virus" wiped out all the present-day leaders, we would have nobody to step in to take their place. Even sports teams have talented players on the bench who could step up when someone gets injured, but our companies do not. Perhaps this is because our models of leadership are not changing, meaning we are teaching leaders how to lead in a world that no longer exists.

In another DDI report exploring the "State of Leadership Development," half of the organizations surveyed said their leaders are not skilled to lead their organizations effectively today (DDI, 2015), and 71% said their leaders are not ready to lead their organizations into the future. A study by the Center for Creative Leadership found similar results in their aptly titled study "The Leadership Gap," where the authors state, "Leaders are not adequately prepared for the future. Today's leadership capacity is insufficient to meet future leadership requirements. This finding is consistent across countries, organizations, and levels in the organization" (Leslie, 2015). Finally, in its report "Ready-Now Leaders," the Conference Board in partnership with DDI found that 85% of executives are not confident in their own leadership pipelines. Here are a few more numbers for you to consider (DDI, 2014).

In Deloitte's most recent Millennial survey, which collected 10,000 responses from 36 countries, 71% of millennials said they are expecting to leave their employment in the next two years because they are unhappy with how their leadership skills are being developed (Deloitte, 2019). This is particularly disturbing because there is obviously a new generation of workers who want to step into leadership roles but organizations are not doing enough to make this possible.

Clearly something is wrong with leadership around the world, otherwise these numbers wouldn't be as abysmal as they are globally. Virtually every human indicator is telling us that we have a problem, yet most organizations and current leaders are doing nothing to address it. Just imagine for a moment that you're driving a car and in the middle of your trip the "check engine" light comes on, followed by the tire pressure warning, the low fuel light, and the battery light, all while your car temperature indicator is in the red. Now imagine your whole family is in the car with you. Would you really just keep on driving, hoping to make it to your destination? I would hope not. Yet in the business world we are on cruise control, and the worst part is that we are all sitting in the same car!

It's Time to Change

When I see all of the data presented in this chapter, I feel angry, frustrated, and just sad. We all should. This means that today and in the future we will live and work in a world where we have hundreds of millions of leaders globally who are quite simply bad leaders—unless we do something about it. It's not as though we just have millions of empty global leadership slots. As the numbers above show we actually have lots of people in leadership roles, just not all the right ones. But their days are numbered. I absolutely believe that leadership is a privilege that should be given to those who truly demonstrate the mindsets and skills outlined in this book. Make no mistake: there is a massive leadership gap inside of our organizations that will only continue to grow in the coming years. The organizations able to close this gap are the ones that will continue to exist and thrive in the future, and the individuals who are able to become future leaders are the ones who will lead these organizations. I know it sounds like all leaders are bad, but they aren't. We do have plenty of amazing leaders all over the world and I've interviewed many of them for this book, but we just don't have enough of them. My sincere hope is that this book and the research behind it will help change that but you are the one who has to make that change a reality.

Thankfully, this book will guide you through doing just that by teaching you how to implement the Notable Nine. These are a collection of four mindsets and five skills that the world's top business leaders have identified as being most crucial for future leaders. These Notable Nine are the solution to the leadership crisis that so many organizations and individuals around the world are experiencing. At the end of the book you will also find a path forward for how to become the future leader that we all need and deserve. Let's begin.

2
Three Essential Leadership Questions

In order to talk about the future leader, we must first answer three crucial questions about the present-day leader:

What is leadership and who is a leader?

Should someone be called a leader or a manager?

Is the leader of 2030 really going to be that different from the leader of today? And if so, how?

What Is Leadership and Who Is a Leader?

The hardest question for CEOs to answer by far was, "How do you define leadership?" When I asked this question over the phone I would usually get long pauses or comments like "That's a really good question." But by far the most common response was, "*Hmmm*, nobody's ever asked me that before." In my head I would be shouting, "What?! What do you mean, nobody's ever asked you that, you're leading a multibillion-dollar company with thousands of employees!" But of course, I never actually said that, otherwise it would be a rather short phone call. I thought about this for a while and then it started to make sense. We just take the concept of a leader for granted and assume that we all know what that looks like and who is a great leader. It's a bit like trying to define water; it sounds silly, because after all, we all know what water is, right? But how would you define water to someone who has never seen it? Would you just say it's a clear tasteless liquid? Dozens of liquids are clear and tasteless. Leadership is the same; it's everywhere in some form and we experience it daily, whether at work, playing sports, watching TV, or shopping. It's all around us like air, and as a result we never stop to question what it really is or who a leader is.

Think about it for a moment. How would you define leadership? Is it about doing the right thing? Achieving a certain level of performance or driving business results? Having followers? Inspiring and motivating others? Maybe it's about having a clear vision and aligning people? Or is it just one of those things where you know it when you see it?

Was Hitler a leader? How about Mother Teresa, Abraham Lincoln, Darth Vader, Genghis Khan, Queen Elizabeth I, Elon Musk, Rosa Parks, Jeffrey Skilling, LeBron James, or Al Capone? All of these people, whether good or bad, fictional or real, meet some of the criteria above.

The word "lead" can be traced back to the year 900 and means "to go before or with to show the way." A leader is then someone who does this. With this definition, all of the above individuals can be described as leaders. What separates the people above isn't the fact that they guide others; it's the direction in which they guide others and the path they take. Hitler chose a direction of evil, war, and death. Mother Teresa chose a direction of kindness, service, and gratitude. Many leaders today are on the wrong path. If as leader your responsibility is to show others the way, what does that way look like?

From all of the business leaders I interviewed, I didn't receive a single duplicate answer to my question of how to define leadership. Of course there were some common elements, which will be explored in this book, but the explanations and definitions as a whole were each unique. CEOs assigned different attributes or characteristics to leaders. Some focused on more human qualities like empathy, diversity, and humility, whereas others focused more on business acumen such as achieving goals, knowing how to prioritize, and setting a vision. Of course, other CEOs tried to find a nice blend and balance of both sides.

Here we have over 140 CEOs from the world's top organizations and they all define leadership differently. How can that be?

I learned two things from asking this question. The first surprising thing is that leaders around the world rarely ask themselves what leadership means. Not only that, but this isn't even explored at an organizational level. It's completely taken for granted, or perhaps it's just assumed that everyone knows a good leader when they see one. The second thing I learned is that leadership is defined differently, depending on the leader and the organization. There is no common or universal definition of leadership. This would be completely fine if we all operated purely as individuals, but we don't; we are all part of groups, teams, and/or organizations. This means that the first step to becoming or to creating a great leader is to define what leadership means and how it comes to life inside your organization (and/or your personal life).

How CEOs Define Leadership

Consider for a moment how the following CEOs define leadership.

Judy Marks is the CEO of Otis Elevator and leads a team of over 70,000 employees around the world. According to Judy, "I think it's really the ability to drive results, and I'll leave that word *results* fairly generic. My role in terms of leadership is to set the vision and to share it. To create an environment where people can resonate not only with the mission but deliver it. To eliminate obstacles so my team can succeed. I think all of those are part of leadership."

Marissa Mayer is the former CEO of Yahoo! When I met with her, she told me that her definition of leadership is "helping believe in a better tomorrow or a better outcome than you have today."

Mark Hurd was the CEO of Oracle, an information technology and services company with over 137,000 employees globally. We met right after I keynoted their HCM World conference in Dallas, Texas. Sadly, he passed away a few months after we met but the time we spent together left a lasting impression on me. Here's what Mark had to say: "The most basic definition of leadership is you set the destination. You come up with a strategy to get to that destination and do your best to align and supply the resources to make that happen."

Bill Thomas is the global chairman of KPMG, a professional services firm with over 200,000 employees around the world. He defines leadership as: "Thinking hard about the future and setting a vision that best positions your organization to thrive in this new world. Building a diverse leadership team capable of delivering that vision. Communicating both the vision and a shorter-term business plan to your people in a way that makes it relevant and personal to them. Staying connected to the world outside your business to understand the forces shaping not only the market you operate in but the society you serve."

Hans Vestberg is the CEO of Verizon Communications, an American multinational telecommunications conglomerate with over 152,000 employees around the world. Hans believes leadership is: "Ensuring that people have everything they need to achieve the missions of an organization. That's it. All else is footnotes."

Who is right and which leadership definition most resonates with you? All of these CEOs think about and define leadership in their own unique way and that's exactly the point. They are all correct. Judy, Marissa, Mark, Bill, and Hans have clear definitions of leadership, which then impacts the types of people who join their organizations, the culture and the values that are created, and the strategic direction and priorities of the business. The definition of leadership can also change as the leaders who run these organization change. Perhaps the best example of this comes from Microsoft and how it has evolved under the leadership of former CEO Steve Ballmer to current CEO Satya Nadella. Both leaders are genuinely described as successful CEOs from a corporate performance perspective but their styles are radically different.

Ballmer was known for having a temper and while he was a passionate leader, he also had a reputation of being combative and enjoying the spotlight. He's the type many would consider to be a "celebrity CEO." With his larger-than-life personality, he was extremely competitive and encouraged this competition among his employees. Ballmer also believed in stack ranking, which forces employees into a series of performance buckets. For example, 10% of employees would be considered high achievers, 10% underperformers, and 80% average but still valuable. Leaders were forced to have this kind of a team distribution even if they didn't feel any of their employees belonged in that bottom 10%. At one point, Steve Ballmer was the lowest-ranked CEO of any technology company on Glassdoor, with a 39% approval rating. Still, despite all of this, many believe that Satya would not be in a position to succeed as the new CEO of Microsoft had it not been for Ballmer.

When Satya Nadella joined the company, his first letter to employees highlighted the importance that his family plays in his life. Satya famously said he wants to move away from having a "know-it-all" culture to a "learn-it-all" culture. He's a big advocate of diversity and inclusion, collaboration instead of ruthless competition, being open minded, encouraging other perspectives and ideas, and of doing good. Instead of the constant infighting that Microsoft was known for, Satya wanted to create a culture based on empathy. One of his first acts as CEO was to ask his employees to read the book "Nonviolent Communication." At the time of this writing, Satya has a 96% approval rating from employees and the stock price has more than tripled. During Ballmer's tenure Microsoft had a market cap of around $300 billion, and now it's hovering around $900 billion.

We are indeed seeing more of a shift toward collaboration, teamwork, and co-creation. Erik Anderson is the Executive Chairman of Topgolf Entertainment Group, which employs almost 20,000 people. He is also the chairman of Singularity University. He told me, "If you want to thrive inside of your community and your company, then you need to learn how to collaborate instead of compete, and you will grow faster. Standing alone and competing all the time is a dangerous strategy, so moving from competition to collaboration and co-creation is crucial."

What Are Your Leadership Filters?

The worst thing you and your organization can do is not have a clear definition of what leadership is and what it means to be a leader. Even if you're not sure if your leadership definition is perfect, you have to start somewhere and then improve. I am an avid chess player, and in chess it is said that having a bad plan is better than having no plan at all.

This is why many organizations have leaders who are admired and loved and other leaders who are hated and avoided. It's because each of these leaders got to their position as a result of varying definitions and ideas of leadership from those who promoted them.

But if there was a shared vision of what leadership is and who a leader is, then the chances of this happening would dramatically decrease. Another crucial aspect here is making sure that your organization has filters in place so the right leaders end up in positions where they are responsible for other people. Filters will range quite a bit, depending on the organization. Here are just a few to consider:

◆ Meeting business and/or financial goals
◆ Positive reviews from peers and managers
◆ Supporting and building up other team members
◆ Collaborating across teams and geographies
◆ A strong moral and ethical compass
◆ Promoting and helping create a diverse and inclusive environment
◆ Ability to engage, empower, and inspire others
◆ Constantly delivering great quality work

Think of this like an organizational sifter. You want to make sure that your filters only let the right people in.

Facebook is one of the few organizations that has actually tied employee bonuses and compensation to progress on social issues and focusing on social good. Traditionally, employees were evaluated based on eligible earnings, individual bonus target, individual performance, and company performance. Social good includes things like eliminating hate speech, creating a more transparent company, and helping small businesses. Because Facebook has made this a core part of their filter system, the types of leaders they attract and grow are the ones who care about and focus on these issues, as opposed to being purely motivated by the mighty dollar (Hamilton, 2019). It's no coincidence that in my previous book on employee experience, Facebook was ranked number one out of 252 organizations.

IBM launched an intensive future of leadership program designed to attract, identify, develop, and promote candidates who are best suited for leadership roles. Through a series of assessments powered by technology, IBM has identified the skills and mindsets that are required to be a successful leader at the company. These included things like situational judgment, cognitive ability, exploration, and having a growth mindset. In other words, they identified and created their IBM leadership filters to go beyond the usual performance metrics. The digital assessments are in the form of a video narrative that explores the day in the life of a first-line manager at a made-up company. Each part of the assessment takes place at different points in the manager's day and asks the candidate to make certain decisions. Based on those decisions IBM is able to measure against their desired skills and mindsets (IBM, n.d.).

Does your organization know what it means to be a leader and has it identified the required skills and mindsets for the future leader? For most organizations, the answer here is no. If you don't have a clear grasp of these things, then how can you expect to lead in the future?

If the filters in your organization are purely based on the ability to meet goals and deadlines and bring in money, then those are the types of people who will end up in leadership roles. This is typical in many industries such as finance. I'll never forget when I interned for Morgan Stanley over 18 years ago. The vice president who actually hired me was promoted to his position because he brought in a lot of new business. A few weeks into my internship he was let go because some of the deals fell through and he wasn't able to bring new ones into the firm. This was common across all of the leaders I worked with there; these people were getting promoted for the wrong reasons and it's thanks to this internship that I realized I never wanted a career in finance.

If the filters are geared more toward the human side of business with an emphasis on coaching and mentoring others, then those are the types of people who will end up in leadership roles. What kinds of people do you want at the helm of your company and what filters do you have in place to make sure that those are the people who are actually getting there?

Define Leadership

But what is leadership? Who is a leader? I don't believe there is a standard definition but if I were to start from something and then mold it, it would blend together both business acumen and humanity. I encourage you to start with and manipulate this to make it work for you and your organization.

A leader is someone who has the ability to see that something can be better than it is now, is able to rally people to move toward that better vision, can come up with a plan to create that vision, and can work toward making that vision a reality while putting people first.

Jim Kavanaugh is the CEO of World Wide Technology, a technology service provider with over 5,000 employees, headquartered in Missouri (by the way, St. Louis is one of the chess capitals of the world!). He has been ranked as one of the top CEOs by Glassdoor and his company has been recognized as a great place to work for several years.

Jim has great advice for current and future leaders:

As a leader, you must be willing to dig into the details but you also need to be able to step back and look at things from a 30,000-foot view. If you're someone sitting on top of a mountain or you're an eagle looking out over things and surveying what's going on, you have a good view of what's happening. Ask yourself what are the most important things relative to your organization? What are you trying to accomplish? How do you want people to behave? What do you want to deliver? And how do you make an impact?

Leader or Manager?

What makes someone a manager, and what makes someone a leader? This too was something I explored in a previous book, *The Future of Work,* but it's worth quickly addressing here. Some people say that the distinction between managers and leaders is purely semantic, whereas others stand firm that these are two completely separate types of people. We typically assume that managers are the ones who are responsible for people, making decisions and executing on them, delegating, building teams, enforcing control, and the like. Leaders, on the other hand, are the ones whom we believe to be visionaries. These are the people who inspire, motivate, and encourage others; they challenge the status quo; they see a better world and are determined to build it. But why are these two different and separate people? Shouldn't anyone who is responsible for others be able to excel at both of these areas? I firmly believe that anyone inside of an organization can be a leader but that managers *must* be leaders.

The words we use at work and in life matter a great deal, which is why we should stop using the word "manager" altogether. It has turned into a word with a negative connotation and meaning, so why use it? Do you want to be managed? Do you want to work for a stereotypical manager like the one we see portrayed in films like *Office Space*? Nobody wants to be managed and in fact many don't even want to be called a manager anymore.

Anyone can become a leader; it's a matter of understanding whom you are leading. For example, you can lead yourself, you can lead a small team or function, a department, or an entire organization. But with this comes a caveat. This isn't simply a name change or a title change. This is a skill and mindset change and if you are not able to embrace the skills and mindsets outlined in this book, then you have no business being a leader of people. If you are currently sitting in a leadership position and find that you don't possess the skills and mindsets outlined here, then it's your job and responsibility to learn and practice them, or you won't be a leader for much longer. It's a tough-love approach but it's also the only approach. There is no place for bad leaders in the future of work.

A recent research report by Deloitte surveyed over 5,000 knowledge workers in the United States, and 72% stated, "We need a new definition of what a 'leader' is in today's world" (Deloitte, June 2018). Imagine how much this number will increase over the next decade.

Is the Leader of 2030 Really That Different Than the Leader of Today?

Organizations are no longer just places where employees show up to get a paycheck and do a job. That is the world that most leaders are used to. Organizations are financial planners, health and wellness centers, caterers, learning centers, daycares, career counselors, life advisors, places where we have fun and make friends, charities, and more. We are seeing the integration of work and life and, for many of us, we actually spend just as much time, if not more, at work as we do at home. This isn't the type of organization most leaders are used to but it's the one we are all becoming a part of.

The world and business are changing quickly, which forces us to ask two important questions. Will leadership in the next decade really be that different than it is today, and if so, how?

Of the CEOs I interviewed, a small handful said leadership will change so drastically that it will be unrecognizable, and a slightly larger group said that leadership will stay pretty much the same as it is now. The vast majority of CEOs, however, said that leadership will be based on a set of fundamental existing principles and ideas such as vision and being able to execute on that vision, but that future leaders will need to build on top of these things with a new arsenal of skills and mindsets. That's exactly what this book is about.

Tim Ryan is the chairman of PwC in the United States and overseas, a workforce of over 55,000 employees. When we spoke about the future of leadership and if it's changing, he said, "It's changing before our very eyes. I would actually submit that what made a great leader 50 years ago or 25 years ago will not likely make a great leader 10 years from now."

Make no mistake, being a leader in the future is the hardest job that will exist, and if you embark on this journey, it will be one of the greatest challenges of your professional career but also the most rewarding.

Shawn Riegsecker is the CEO of Centro, a digital advertising software company with around 700 employees. We talked at length about this and he gave me this gem:

There's no shortcut to being a great leader. In fact, getting there will take time and you will likely face ups and downs along your journey. In order to get what you want, you must do those things that give you the confidence to do just a little bit more the next day. Nobody likes failure. Failure simply represents a challenge and a learning opportunity, not something to avoid. I believe the greatest point of growth occurs when you get uncomfortable and push yourself outside of your comfort zone. You must put your toes on the edge of "comfortable" and step into uncertainty to make a real difference in your life.

It's natural to resist change and to be a bit scared and uncomfortable, but as Shawn said, that's where true growth happens. If you're willing to push yourself to become a great future leader, then read on.

3
The Impact of a Leader

Who is a leader you admire, respect, and want to emulate? You probably thought of a leader that you have never met, someone who is running a big successful company. Now imagine for a moment that this leader (whom you have never met) is running a big successful company and treats employees poorly. The leader pays them low wages, berates them on calls and meetings, forces them to work unreasonable hours, and quite frankly treats them like cogs. Imagine that this leader's organization was hurting the environment or local communities. What if the leader was using shady business practices to inflate the numbers? What if this leader didn't fight for any social causes? What if this leader was just simply mean? Would you still consider this person a leader even though the business was making a ton of money? Would you want to work for this kind of person?

How Great and Bad Leaders Influence You and Your Organization

For almost all of the CEOs I interviewed and for most people in general, the perception of a successful leader is based on someone who makes money and grows a business. For some, that's good enough, but for those of us who want to be future leaders and put people first, this should be unacceptable. This was specifically called out when I interviewed Abraham Schot, the CEO of Audi, the automotive company, with over 90,000 employees. He told me, "Leadership is about walking the extra mile and solving problems that others cannot solve. Foremost, leadership is about caring for people and not only for numbers."

A few CEOs I interviewed mentioned they admire family members, past leaders who mentored them to success, and leaders of charitable or religious organizations that they were a part of. We need to change our perception of who a leader is and why; it's not just about money.

Leaders help shape the world and have a profound impact on all of our lives, especially if we work with them. You have likely experienced the impacts of working with both great and terrible leaders, as have I. When you work for a terrible leader you feel like a cog; you don't want to show up to work and when you do, you try your best to avoid seeing him or her. Bad leaders make you doubt yourself; they suck the soul and meaning right out of your body, and they can quite literally ruin your life while you work for them, but they make the business a lot of money.

Bad leaders make you feel drained and uninspired, and you may argue more with your spouse, feel depressed, or perhaps overwork yourself to the point of burnout, which means no time to eat healthy, exercise, or take time for yourself or your family. I worked for several of these leaders when I first joined the corporate world and the worst part of my day was when my alarm clock woke me up at 6:30 a.m. and I knew that it was time for me to face the "soul-sucking CEO," a term from Garry Ridge, the CEO of WD-40 Company. These bad leaders are toxic to the organization and to the individual employees. Like weeds, they must be plucked from our organizations without mercy or they must adapt. Life is too short to work with these types of people and it's especially too short to be led by these types of people.

Toxic Leaders

The University of Manchester's Business School did a 1,200-participant study to explore the impact of leaders. You won't be shocked to learn that employees who worked for a toxic boss had lower rates of job satisfaction. However, the scarier statistic is that the effects of a toxic boss spill over into the personal lives of employees. The study found that employees working for a narcissistic or psychopathic boss were more likely to experience clinical depression. These bosses also lack empathy and self-awareness. The same study also found that employees who work for this kind of boss are more likely to become overly critical of one another, take credit for other people's work, and behave more aggressively toward their fellow employees. The behavior of a toxic boss was also found to spread like wildfire inside organizations. This means that if you have bad leaders at your company, unless you make a drastic change, the behaviors and actions of those toxic leaders will become the norm, like a virus. A very recent study of over 400,000 Americans actually found that bad bosses may be giving employees heart disease. Bad leaders can literally kill you (De Luce, 2019).

Perhaps this explains why the business world is having such a hard time fixing this issue. A 2018 study by Korn Ferry that explored stress at work found that the largest percentage of respondents say their boss is the biggest stressor at work (Korn Ferry, 2018). The one person at the company who is supposed to have your back, support you, and encourage you is your biggest cause of stress? That is not acceptable. A study done by Zenger Folkman, a leadership development firm, found that uninspiring leaders have only 9% overall leadership effectiveness. The average engagement of direct reports is only 23%, and 47% of direct reports are thinking about quitting (Zenger, 2015).

There's no easy way around this. If you have bad leaders at your organization whom you can't train or coach, get them out of your company or at least out of leadership positions. Getting rid of these types of leaders won't just save your organization; it will save the lives of the people who work there. How can we possibly justify having bad leaders? The money isn't worth it. I recently did some advisory work for a large insurance company in Latin America that was replacing over 30% of their leaders because they were not willing or able to adapt to the changing needs of the organization. Tough? Yes. But necessary if this organization wants to remain in business in the coming years and if it wants to preserve the health of the people who work there.

GREAT LEADERS

Great leaders, on the other hand, have the exact opposite effect. When you work for a great leader you are excited to show up to work. You constantly feel like you are learning and growing and that you have a true coach and mentor who has your back. You are more confident in your abilities and are willing to bring more of yourself to the organization. Sometimes, work might not even feel like work. The Zenger Folkman study mentioned earlier found that good leaders can actually double company profits. Not only is toxic leadership contagious but so is good leadership! The research also found that if you are a good boss, you probably work for a good boss. If you're a high-level manager doing a subpar job, then not only are you eroding the engagement of the people who work directly for you, but you're also eroding the engagement of the people who work for them. It's a trickle-down effect. But the exact opposite is also true: if you're doing a great job, you increase the engagement of those working for you and those working for them. If bad leaders should be plucked mercilessly, then great leaders should be planted relentlessly and given every opportunity, resource, incentive, and encouragement to grow.

I recently had the opportunity to sit down with Marissa Mayer, the former CEO of Yahoo! I met her in Palo Alto, which is not too far away from where I live. We talked for an hour in her office, which was filled with all sorts of memorabilia from her career. During our discussion she told me:

> When you're leading an organization, you have to take into account that people are always the most important thing in the company. How you recruit those people, how you motivate them, how you task them with the overall mission and what you want to accomplish, is the core of leadership.

A recent study called "Leadership, Job Satisfaction and Organizational Commitment in Healthcare Sector: Proposing and Testing a Model" found that the leadership behavior of managers accounted for a 28% variance in employee job satisfaction and a 20% variance in an employee's organizational commitment (Mosadeghrad and Ferdosi, 2013). Development Dimensions International (DDI), a global leadership consulting firm, conducted a study with almost 15,000 participants around the world and found that the difference in the impact of a top-performing leader and an average performing leader is 50%. When looking at financial performance, organizations with the highest-quality leaders were 13 times more likely to outperform their industry competitors (Tanner, 2018). These organizations also had higher employee retention and engagement rates up to three times that of their competitors.

We Need More Great Leaders

It's clear that the impact of leaders is significant. It's the difference between happiness and misery, a thriving organization or one that is barely above water, life and death. Now is the time for action.

Wolf-Henning Scheider is the CEO of ZF Friedrichshafen, a German manufacturing company with 150,000 employees around the world. They provide products for cars such as transmissions, clutches, and brakes. Brands like Audi, Bentley, Toyota, Rolls-Royce, BMW, and Dodge all use their products. Wolf-Henning told me, "We can't only hire superstars. We also have to create them and enable them. It's a huge leadership task and I see it as the number one priority."

Unfortunately, a poll from Monster.com found that only 19% of employees in the United States consider their boss to be a mentor or someone they can learn from and know has their back, and 76% of respondents said they currently have or recently had a toxic boss (Kaufman, 2018). These figures are not much better around the world. In the UK, for example, two out of every three workers has experienced working with a bad boss, according to Glassdoor (Di Toro, 2017).

Leaders can make or break your organization, and leaders can make or break the people who work there. It's time to start asking the tough questions. What kind of a leader do you want to be, what kinds of leaders does your organization want to have, and how do you create and enable them? Don't leave this to chance and don't assume that this will just get taken care of by another department like HR. This is everyone's responsibility, especially yours.

Chris McCann, the president and CEO of 1-800-flowers.com, echoed this sentiment: "If you feel you have motivated or inspired someone to do more, then you've acted as a leader." These are the types of people we need more of.

PART 2

TRENDS AND CHALLENGES SHAPING FUTURE LEADERS

4

Artificial Intelligence and Technology

Why do so many CEOs think that leadership will be different in the next ten years? What are the trends causing them to believe that a new set of skills and mindsets will be required to lead? In this and the next few chapters, I will explore the trends that are shaping the future of leadership through 2030 and beyond (Figure 4.1). Current and future leaders must be aware of all of these trends and the implications that these trends will create.

Artificial intelligence and technology was by far the number-one trend that CEOs and employees across all levels identified as most impacting the future of leadership. During the CEO interviews, these discussions were usually more focused specifically on artificial intelligence. This was also the number-one trend identified by individual contributors, managers, and senior executives in the LinkedIn survey.

Our obsession with creating something better, stronger, faster, and smarter than us started many years ago. Our earliest encounter with some kind of AI appeared in the Greek story of Jason and the Argonauts, whose first mention appears in 800 BCE. According to the story, Jason was supposed to be king of a land called Iolkos but instead his uncle, King Pelias, sat on the throne. In order to reclaim his kingdom, Pelias told Jason to retrieve the Fleece of the Golden Ram.

6 Trends Shaping the Future of Leadership

FIGURE 4.1 SIX TRENDS SHAPING THE FUTURE OF LEADERSHIP.

Jason assembled a team of heroes and adventurers and their journey began. On their way home after retrieving the fleece they were swept off course to a small island near what is now modern-day Greece. On this island Jason encountered the giant automaton Talos, whom he was able to defeat by removing a small pin near Talos's heel that caused his ichor, or life blood, to drain out. In Jewish folklore we hear the story of Golem, who came to the aid of the Jewish people, and in Islam the alchemist Jabir ibn Hayyan wrote of Takwin, or the creation of synthetic life. Of course, more recently we have been introduced to the likes of HAL from *2001: A Space Odyssey* and to Skynet from

The Terminator. But these are just more modern versions of ideas that came from stories, myths, and legends from thousands of years ago. Now the big question for us is what happens when these things actually become reality?

In PwC's 22nd Annual Global CEO Survey, which includes responses from 1,378 CEOs around the world, 42% agree that AI will have a larger impact than the internet and 21% of CEOs strongly agree with that statement, and for good reason. PwC also estimates $15.7 trillion in global GDP gains from AI by 2030 (PwC, 2019).

Since the beginning of the modern business world, we have created organizations perfectly suited for artificial intelligence, bots, and software: environments where employees show up at the same time every day, wear the same uniform, do the same job over and over, and where they are told to not ask questions and to just "do their jobs." The problem is that decades ago these technologies didn't exist, so instead we used the next best thing: humans. Today, we finally have the technologies that are able to take the jobs designed for them to begin with. This is a monumental reality for us to deal with because it challenges the foundation on which today's organizations were built.

Are the Machines Going to Take Over?

We must now ask what jobs will humans do, how will they do them, and why? We have always assumed that artificial intelligence will have the greatest impact on routine jobs, such as number crunching or data entry. Most of the studies on the future of work and automation already highlight this. However, one of the roles that will be most affected is leadership.

Almost every single one of the CEOs I interviewed was optimistic about the impact that artificial intelligence and technology will have on leadership and on the future of work. This is because technology will free up our time and resources and allow us to focus on the people inside of organizations. This is really what leadership is all about. But this comes with a caveat of embracing new technology, not running from it, which is in stark contrast to the many reports we have seen over the past few years touting the destruction and elimination of jobs. Many of the studies and reports predict anywhere from a few million to several billion jobs being eliminated. It's as if we're going to be living out a scene from *The Walking Dead* where we all just walk around with pitchforks.

There is a large gap between what research says versus what the world's top leaders tell me. It's true that some areas will see an impact as a result of automation, but I believe the vast proportion of this impact will be felt more around how jobs are changing as opposed to how they are being eliminated. We have to remember that automating a job or a task isn't the same thing as replacing a person.

Christian Ulbrich is the CEO of JLL, one of the world's largest commercial real estate firms, with almost 100,000 employees around the world. He was one of the many CEOs I interviewed who expressed this view. "We will succeed in the digital era only if we engage with enthusiasm and welcome the ideas and opportunities that digital tools, data analysis, and new technologies will bring."

Automating a Job Is Not Replacing a Human

Another issue we need to address when it comes to AI and jobs is making sure that whatever new jobs we do create are jobs worth having. In other words, job creation is useless if the jobs are all soul-sucking! Thankfully what we have largely seen thus far is organizations using AI to heavily automate routine functions while upskilling employees to focus more on human roles. Take the case of Accenture, which automated over 17,000 employees yet didn't replace a single worker. How could this be? The automated jobs were in the realm of finance and instead of these employees crunching numbers, they were upskilled and retrained to be more like strategic advisors to help Accenture's clients understand what the numbers actually mean and what actions to take based on those numbers. The actual calculation and tabulation of the numbers was being done by AI and bots.

McDonald's is another organization relying heavily on automation by implementing kiosks in many of their retail stores. Their chief people officer told me that instead of automating and losing thousands of employees around the world, the headcount at their stores has either stayed the same or in some cases increased. That's because McDonald's is becoming an experience business and putting a greater emphasis on hospitality, and hospitality requires people. McDonald's customers still say that one of the things they care about most is the warmth and the engagement of the humans who work at their stores. The staff is still there, but they are being utilized in a different way.

These are just two of many examples out there. The point is that the discussions should not focus on humans versus technology; it's about humans working with technology to solve a problem or unlock an opportunity.

What Leaders Do

Great leaders stereotypically focus on two broad responsibilities. The first is decision making. Leaders usually have access to more data and information; they have the authority and the power, and so they make key decisions on things like the strategic direction of the business or on developing new products and services. Decisions are made, and then the rest of the workforce is told about those decisions. In fact, a study by Accenture surveying 1,770 managers from 14 countries found that 54% of their time was spent on administration coordination and control (Accenture, 2016).

Adam Warby is the CEO of Avanade, a technology company with over 36,000 employees around the world. I had the opportunity to spend some time with Adam when I was visiting the UK a few years ago. His comments on leadership and decision making in an era of AI really resonated with me: "I see artificial intelligence and technology as extremely positive for future leaders. It will allow them to have a partner in the decision-making process while allowing them to focus on the most important aspect of leadership, people."

The second typical responsibility of great leaders is getting people to move in the direction of that decision, in other words, engaging, empowering, motivating, and inspiring people. The human aspect of leadership is an area with which many organizations around the world are struggling. Of course, there are several other elements that might fall under these broad buckets.

Bad leaders typically just focus on the decision-making piece; they believe in command and control and just telling other people what needs to get done. In other words, these are the stereotypical "managers."

How AI Will Impact Leadership

We are already seeing the influx of AI inside of our organizations, and in the next decade AI will become the operating system of virtually every organization in existence. In most cases today, AI is already able to make better and more accurate decisions than humans while also analyzing and considering more data and information. This doesn't mean we should simply hand over the decision-making reigns to technology and just assume that what it says is always correct and best for our organizations and our people. But it does mean that technology will be a huge aide in the decision-making process and will help leaders think about and understand various possibilities. However, this also means that if you are a bad leader who just focuses on decision-making and on command and control, then what good are you in the future, or now for that matter? Your value will become marginal at best and nonexistent at worst. If you are a great leader, all of a sudden your value increases tenfold because you are able to rally, motivate, inspire, engage, and coach people. These human qualities will be some of the most important traits of future leaders.

Artificial intelligence will have a few specific impacts on the future of leadership. First, it will make it blatantly clear who the bad leaders are and who the good leaders are. Second, it will force leaders to create a more human organization that is focused on what are typically referred to as "soft skills." Ultimately, it's up to those of you reading this book to take action and to decide what kind of a leader you want to be.

Besides artificial intelligence, all sorts of technologies are entering our lives and our organizations, things like augmented and virtual reality, the internet of things, blockchain, robotics, big data, wearable devices, quantum computing, and dozens of others. All of these technologies are going to change the ways in which we work. For example, virtual reality can help us practice empathy and conflict resolution by putting employees and leaders into immersive virtual situations, something that Walmart is already doing regularly. Blockchain is a platform built on transparency, which means it also has implications for leadership. Blockchain could transform the way HR handles performance reviews, skills assessments, and payments. The internet of things will give leaders more data than they can possibly figure out what to do with. Many leaders around the world are already learning what it's like to lead virtual and globally distributed teams they can't see. Here too, technology will be a critical tool that will change what leaders do, how they do it, and even why they do it.

Like the CEOs I interviewed, I too agree that technology can have a dramatically positive impact on our organizations and on how we lead, but it requires us to seize the opportunity instead of sitting idly by.

 Bill McDermott is the CEO of SAP SE, a technology and software company with around 100,000 employees around the world. He sees enormous potential and possibility in using technology to help us become more human.

"AI and machine learning create so much anxiety, but they also provide incredible opportunity. There can be no fear. We need to be optimistic about the exciting possibilities that result when people and machines work together. Emerging technologies can liberate people from routine and dangerous labor, allowing a shift to higher-value tasks that only humans can do, ultimately making them more effective – happier. In the end, it is a better experience. Machines can't dream. Only people can."

Implications for Leaders

- ◆ Focus on the human side of leadership.
- ◆ Help others understand the impact that AI and technology can have on jobs and careers.
- ◆ Look at the areas where technology can be used to add value to employees as opposed to where it can replace them.
- ◆ Experiment with different technologies on an ongoing basis and get familiar with what they are, what they do, and how they work on a high level.
- ◆ Explore areas where technology can be used to enhance and improve the employee experience.
- ◆ View AI and technology as partners to your organization.

5
Pace of Change

Whether we look at climate change, globalization, technology, demographics, cyber-security, geopolitical issues, competition, or any of the other numerous trends shaping our lives and organizations, it's clear that change happens quickly and happens all the time. We will experience more change in the coming decades than we have experienced in the past hundreds of years.

This was the second top trend impacting the future of leadership as identified by all of the CEOs I interviewed and by all of the people surveyed. Change is a constant. But it's not change itself that the world's top business leaders are concerned with; it's how quickly change happens, and the pace is only increasing! This change is being fueled by many variables such as technological progress, changes in customer and employee demands and expectations, competition, and globalization. It feels as though we're on a treadmill and our trainer keeps telling us to up the speed. The question then becomes, how fast can we truly go?

 The pace of change is aptly summarized from a conversation I had with David Henshall, president and CEO of Citrix, a computer software company with over 8,500 employees around the world. He stated, "Both the rate and the pace of change have been accelerating and will continue to do so in the foreseeable future. As a result, disruption can come from anywhere and from any size company.

This speed changes everything from how we lead to how we create products to how we service customers. Leaders must understand and accept that this is the new world they will have to lead in. The only way to succeed in this world is by challenging the status quo."

If this were 1971 and you wanted to store 1 gigabyte of data (the rough equivalent of 230 songs), you would have to pay $250 million. Today, you can actually get several GB of storage for free. Remember the Apollo 13 and 14 space missions from the 1970s? Those were powered by the Apollo Guidance Computer, which was less powerful than the electronic toaster sitting in your kitchen. The computers on earth that were used to communicate with the lunar landers and run computations were the size of a car and cost over $3.5 million. Assuming you have a somewhat recent smartphone in your pocket right now, it is powerful enough to simultaneously guide 120,000,000 Apollo-era spacecraft to the moon (Puiu, 2019). It's scary to think what we're going to be carrying around in the next five, ten, and twenty years.

According to commercial real estate company Cushman & Wakefield, property built today with a lifespan of 50 years will face technology 30 million times more powerful than today, 11-year-olds will see a 64-fold increase in computing power by the time they finish high school, and an executive moving from graduation to management over 20 years will face technology 500,000 times more powerful than the day they started work (Cushman, 2018). Also consider that solar and wind energy costs have dropped 88% and 69% respectively since 2009 (Lazard, 2018).

Leading in a Future That Doesn't Yet Exist

Dell, in partnership with the Institute for the Future, predicts that 85% of the jobs in 2030 haven't been invented yet (Dell, 2017). CEOs are clearly concerned with how quickly the world is changing and with their organizations' ability to adapt to changes. This applies to all aspects of business, although technology tends to be the big area that organizations focus on. Workplace practices of the past are becoming outdated, technologies over the past few years are obsolete and new ones are emerging rapidly, customer demands are evolving, competition is now coming from all sides with many new incumbents, innovation isn't just about a small R&D team anymore, more data is being generated than we know what to do with, and that's just the tip of the iceberg. On top of all of this, most organizations don't have the right people in place to lead in this new world of work.

There was a time when it was acceptable and even practical to create a detailed five-year company plan. Today that plan is the equivalent of an exercise in creativity. In the 1950s the average lifespan of a company on the S&P 500 was 60 years, almost a full lifetime. In 1965 this shrunk to 33 years, in 1990 to 20 years, and in 2026 it is projected to shrink to 14 years. Forget a lifetime, we're barely talking about becoming a teenager at this point! The Fortune 500 list isn't doing any better. Since its inception in 1955 only 53 companies remain, that's just below 11%. All of the others have either gone bankrupt, merged, or have just dropped off the list. Do you even remember companies like Armour, Esmark, Amoco, RCA, Union Carbide, Bethlehem Steel, or Douglas Aircraft? Probably not, yet all of these organizations were giants of their day.

I recently had the opportunity to work with the leadership team at Royal Caribbean International, which employs over 80,000 people around the world and operates a fleet of over 60 ships globally. I had the chance to sit down with CEO Richard Fain, and when we talked about the pace of change, he told me this:

The pace of change today is slower than it will ever be again. If you look at it from that perspective, you realize that there is very little time to learn about, acclimate to, and promulgate amongst your people, friends, and new processes and new ways of doing things. That puts a lot more pressure on leadership than we've ever seen before. The role of leadership is much more focused on what is coming and getting people throughout the organization to change the paradigm and change it constantly. So I think that has fundamentally changed what the role of a leader is and that will become even more important as we go forward.

Simply put, this means that what has traditionally worked for leaders in the past won't work in the future and what works in the future will change quickly!

In a recent survey of graduates from the 30 top international business schools, the pace of technological and digital advance was ranked as the top threat facing future global business leaders.

I'm an optimist. We can view any change as either a threat or an opportunity. Amy Pressman is the co-founder, board member, and former president of Medallia, a customer experience software company with over 1,000 employees. She put this nicely: "In many ways the change that we go through is good change, but it still creates anxiety for people because our day-to-day may be different. We need to lean into it, embrace it, and not get scared by it."

Implications for Leaders

- ◆ Experiment and test ideas frequently.
- ◆ Be comfortable challenging and not hanging on to the status quo.
- ◆ Embrace uncertainty and don't let fear guide decision-making.
- ◆ Surround yourself with people who are smarter and more capable than you.
- ◆ Give employees at all levels and roles a voice to share ideas, solve problems, and identify opportunities.
- ◆ Build alliances with people and organizations.
- ◆ Revisit your likely outdated workplace policies, procedures, and rules.
- ◆ Focus on improving communication and collaboration across teams and geographies.
- ◆ Pay attention to trends impacting your industry, your company, and your career.
- ◆ Understand that this is the new normal.

6
Purpose and Meaning

Mindy Grossman is the CEO of WW (formerly known as Weight Watchers), which employs around 20,000 people around the world. In our discussion, Mindy echoed what many other CEOs have told me: "Brands of the future are going to have to understand what their purpose and meaning is, no matter what business they're in. Purpose and meaning will be even more valuable in the future."

For decades, the business world has been under the assumption that in order to attract and retain the best people, you simply need to pay them more. This was the greatest lever that organizations could pull, but now it's becoming evident that employees care about more than just making money. A recent study conducted by BetterUp surveyed 2,285 American professionals across 26 industries and found that 9 out of 10 workers would trade money for meaning. How much would they trade? On average 23% of future earnings, which comes to $21,000 per year in order to have work that is always meaningful. The same study showed that employees with meaningful work stay at the company longer, take fewer paid leave days, and are more inspired (BetterUp, 2018). Another survey run, by Imperative, looked at 26,000 LinkedIn members across 40 countries and found that 74% of candidates want a job where they feel like their work matters (Vesty, 2016). Wrike, a work management software company, recently put out a "Happiness Poll" that looked at 4,000 employees in the UK, Germany, France, and the United States and what makes them happy at work and how that impacts the productivity. In the UK, the number-one factor that contributed to employee happiness was doing meaningful work and feeling connected to a purpose (Wrike, 2019).

In August 2019, the CEOs of almost 200 major U.S. organizations, including Amazon, Apple, Boeing, and GM, came together to issue a statement saying shareholder value, something that was long thought to be the purpose of an organization, is no longer their primary concern. Instead, the new purposes of an organization are to invest in employees, deliver value to customers, deal ethically with suppliers, and support outside communities. This is a tremendous shift in how we think about business and how we lead those businesses.

Purpose and meaning are not just "work issues." These are basic human themes that are a part of our very nature. As a species we have constantly asked, "What is the meaning of life?" "What is my purpose?" "Why am I here?" The quest to feel connected and to feel like we have a greater purpose and meaning in life is never ending and it's not something that can be quashed by money.

The words "purpose" and "meaning" are often grouped together. While they are related, it's important for us to understand that they mean different things and to distinguish between them. Employees have a job, that job yields a purpose, as a result of that purpose there is an impact, and from that impact employees will ideally derive meaning. Dr. Paul T.P. Wong, professor emeritus of Trent University, adjunct professor at Saybrook University, and president of the International Network on Personal Meaning, puts this succinctly: the role of purpose is to fulfill a meaning.

Job, Purpose, Impact, Meaning

In the context of business, the job you have quite simply refers to the activities you do, whether that is writing code, selling products or services, helping customers, or the like. The purpose of the job goes one level deeper. You write code because you are trying to design a user-friendly website that customers can easily access; you sell products or services because you want to help the company generate revenue and grow; you help customers because you want to create a great experience for them and inspire loyalty. The impact piece is what actually happens from your purpose. In other words, you help customers because you want to create great experiences for them, but are you? What is the actual impact of the work that you are doing? Purpose is about the potential but the impact is what it really is. If your purpose is to create great experiences but the impact is that you are actually creating worse experiences, then you have an issue. Think of it like two sides of an equation that should at the very least equal each other. The desired state should match the actual state, or better yet the actual state should be greater than the desired state.

Purpose acts as the bridge between the work you are doing and the impact that the work has on customers, other employees, communities, or the world. But do you get meaning from the work you are doing? Meaning is very subjective and unique to each of us and this is often where employees struggle. Meaning is more about why you are personally doing something and the feeling you get from doing it. For the customer service agent, meaning might come from helping people and trying to make their lives a little bit better; for the developer, meaning might come from solving complex problems; for the salesperson, meaning might come from building relationships and the human connection that inherently comes from selling. As you can see, purpose and meaning are not the same thing, even though they are very much tied together.

My job is to write, speak, research, and create content on leadership, the future of work, and employee experience. My purpose is to help create organizations around the world where employees actually want to show up to work each day. Thankfully, this is also the impact I have on organizations and their leaders (or so I'm told). I get a lot of meaning from this, which includes making a positive impact on the lives of employees around the world, working on things I'm genuinely interested in and passionate about, challenging myself, creating my own independent life, and building amazing relationships with the many leaders around the world with whom I work.

Creating Meaningful Work

FIGURE 6.1 CREATING MEANINGFUL WORK.

As shown in Figure 6.1, the job aspect is ideally self-explanatory. Purpose should also be rather commonplace and easy to achieve but unfortunately even here, most people and organizations struggle. This is because we have built organizations to focus on jobs, tasks, and things to keep us busy. Many employees around the world actually have no idea how the work they are doing is impacting anyone or anything; they are simply cogs in a machine. One of the reasons so many employees struggle with meaning is because they don't even understand their purpose.

The research I did for this book made it rather apparent that most employees understand their jobs but struggle with purpose, impact, and meaning. Leaders understand their jobs and often have a more solid grasp on their purpose (since they are now privy to more information, insights, etc.) and the impact they are having, but they too struggle with meaning. Stephen Poor is a partner and chairman emeritus at Seyfarth Shaw LLP, a law firm with almost 1,000 attorneys globally. He told me, "Most leaders I know in organizations have a pretty deep understanding of their particular business, their industry, their competitors, and their clients or customers. Nobody's going to follow somebody who doesn't know what they're talking about." This is, of course, important and for many leaders this is where their purpose comes from, but this is also where many stop. Instead, take this one step further and ask, what does all of this mean to you?

Robert Half researched why employees quit their current jobs, and one of the top responses was to work for another organization with a higher purpose. The only response that ranked higher was going to another organization for more money (Kong, 2018). Another study, conducted by Reward Gateway, found that although 89% of employers say it's critical that employees understand the company's mission, only 25% of employees feel completely informed about the purpose and mission and 32% are completely uninformed (Reward Gateway, 2018). This is very basic stuff. Leaders always want the "low-hanging fruit," and there it is.

A study by E.Y. Beacon Institute and Harvard Business School found that 42% of non-purpose-led companies showed a drop in revenue over a three-year period while 85% of purpose-led companies showed positive growth (Keller, 2015). Not surprisingly, focusing on these things actually impacts the bottom line. In 2018 Mercer surveyed over 7,600 employees around the world and one of the top talent trends they identified was working with purpose (Mercer, 2018).

Purpose and meaning are unique human things that we all desire, crave, and need. The balance of power has dramatically shifted into the hands of employees, and organizations around the world are focusing on creating an employee experience so that employees actually want to show up to work. Employees are saying that they want to be part of an organization where they understand their purpose and can find meaning. A study from BetterUp found that employees produce more, work more, stay at companies longer, and will sacrifice higher pay if they find meaning in their work. Nine of ten workers will also trade money for meaning (BetterUp, 2018). It's a bit disheartening that employees around the world are begging for these human aspects of work and aren't able to get them.

Creating Purpose and Meaning

One of the organizations doing truly pioneering work around purpose and meaning is Unilever, which has around 160,000 employees globally. The company has now put over 34,000 of their employees through an interactive in-person purpose and meaning workshop, with the numbers increasing rapidly. The end goal is to be able to walk away with a purpose statement that can then connect to the purpose of the company as a whole; employees are thus able to truly discover and understand what motivates and drives them. Those who have gone through the workshop include leaders, sales professionals, people on the factory floor, and everyone else in between. In the workshop, employees reflect on their personal and professional experiences, their personal values, and even their childhood memories. I find it amazing and reassuring that organizations like this are helping people understand how and where they fit in the world.

Some might make the argument that purpose and meaning are just reserved for the privileged few who earn a good living and work at a stable company. Unfortunately, most people in the world are barely struggling to put food on the table, let alone worry about any kind of purpose or meaning at work. But that doesn't mean that these people don't deserve to have purpose and meaning as well. We all deserve and need this, whether we are senior executives at global companies, janitors, retail employees, gig workers, or anyone in between. Purpose and meaning should not be a privilege at work; it should be a right for any employee at any level.

Bernard Tyson was the chairman and CEO of Kaiser Permanente, one of America's leading healthcare providers, which employees over 200,000 people. Unfortunately he passed away suddenly right before this book was published. He summarized this concept of standing for something larger than making money.

Companies of the future can no longer think that they can just exist ... significant companies of the future cannot just exist in this little bread box, in this isolated place. We are a part of greater society and a greater society is a part of us. The trend of when and how we engage in the bigger societal issues will continue to be a part of the future of leadership.

Implications for Leaders

- ◆ Differentiate between job, purpose, impact, and meaning; they are not the same thing.
- ◆ Make sure you understand your job, purpose, impact, and meaning first before helping others understand theirs.
- ◆ Focus on storytelling to help employees understand how their work is having an impact.
- ◆ Get to know your employees as individuals to find out what motivates and drives them.
- ◆ When attracting and retaining talent, make purpose, impact, and meaning a core part of your organization.
- ◆ Consider running your own workshops and training sessions focused on purpose, impact, and meaning.

7
New Talent Landscape

"I often say in my business that the competition for talent is fiercer than the competition for customers." That's what Jeffrey Puritt told me. He's the president and CEO of TELUS International, an outsourcing and offshoring company with over 30,000 employees globally.

The Massive Talent Shortage

What talent looks like, where it comes from, and how much talent exists are all factors causing a massive change in the collective workforce. According to research done by Korn Ferry, by 2030 there will be a global talent shortage of around 85 million people, which translates into $8.5 trillion in unrealized annual revenues (Korn Ferry, 2018). ManpowerGroup surveyed 40,000 employers around the world and 45% of them reported difficulty in filling roles today (Manpower, 2018). PwC's CEO survey referenced earlier found that in 2019, one of the top-ten threats for organizations was availability of key skills. It was number three on the list, just one percentage point below policy uncertainty and overregulation (PwC, 2019).

There are several reasons for why this is happening. For starters, fertility rates around the world are declining. In the United States, for example, the number of births is below the required replacement rate for the population, meaning the population could actually start shrinking because more people are passing away and not enough babies are being born to keep the population stable. Western Europe actually has the lowest fertility rate, followed by the UK, Southeast Asia and Oceania, Central Eastern Europe and Central Asia, and North America. This translates into fewer employable people.

Second, we see an aging population. According to the United States Census Bureau, by 2030, 1 out of 5 residents will be of retirement age. By 2035, there will be more people in the United States who are over 65 than under 18 (U.S. Census Bureau, 2018). This is a trend seen in many parts of the world, such as the UK, Australia, Japan, and China. While it's also true that life expectancy is increasing, making it possible for us to work longer, organizations around the world are doing virtually nothing to keep older workers employed. In fact many are "encouraging" their older workers to retire so that cheaper, younger employees can be brought on instead, which is a huge mistake. In old movies, everyone turned to respected elders for advice and guidance, yet inside our organizations it's always the older people we want to get rid of first.

For smart companies there's a tremendous opportunity to tap into that older talent. These are the most experienced and seasoned employees in your organization, the wise sages and counselors, so why would you want them to leave? Instead, build programs that allow them to remain as advisors, coaches, and mentors for the next generation of talent entering your organization.

Next, we see challenges around skills. The optimism from the leaders I interviewed rests on the assumption that human workers will be fluent in the many emerging technologies and related skills that are growing in demand, such as data analytics, cyber-security, augmented and virtual reality, blockchain, artificial intelligence, robotics, and the like. Currently this is not the case.

This skills gap not only exists in office jobs but also in hands-on fields such as manufacturing, welding, machinery, and the like. When I interviewed Barbara Humpton the CEO of Siemens US, which employees over 50,000 employees, she mentioned that they recently had over 1,500 jobs open and while they received over 10,000 applicants to fill those jobs, they weren't able to find enough people with the required skills to take on those roles, which were in hands-on areas.

André Calantzopoulos is the CEO of Philip Morris International, a leading international tobacco company with more than 77,000 employees, which is transforming its business to create a smoke-free future and ultimately replace cigarettes with better alternatives for adult smokers. According to André:

> We're moving from an era of lifetime employment to lifetime employability. If your people don't feel that they are learning and progressing, then they will leave you, and they should! Why would they want to be a part of an organization that is making them obsolete? As a leader it's your job to make sure that doesn't happen. We have to admit that we are not dealing with the same talent landscape we were in the past twenty or even the past ten years where we assumed people will stay forever.

The Need to Upskill and Retrain

In order for a society to have augmentation with technology, as opposed to replacement by technology, there needs to be massive upskilling and reskilling for people around the world. Siemens is overcoming this challenge by bringing back apprenticeships. According to the *Encyclopedia Britannica,* apprenticeships began in the 18th century BCE (thousands of years ago) and were talked about in the Code of Hammurabi of Babylon, where artisans were required to teach their crafts to the next generation.

One of my favorite examples of how an organization is upskilling their knowledge workers comes from PwC. They launched a Digital Fitness app for their employees that evaluates their high-level knowledge across a variety of topics such as artificial intelligence, blockchain, and data analytics. Employees are assessed across four areas: skills, mindsets, behaviors, and relationships. After employees take the assessment, they are granted access to content that helps them improve across all these areas. This might mean reading an article, watching a video, or listening to a podcast. It's an internal library that employees have at their disposal to learn about all the things they need to be successful at PwC and they get nudges to keep learning and growing, improving their digital fitness.

As a part of this they also created a digital accelerator program for thousands of employees across the company that I was fortunate enough to work with them on. These employees are basically like a collective good virus that goes around and infects the rest of the workforce. They are expected to challenge the status quo, offer unique ideas and perspectives, and get the company as a whole to think differently. These digital accelerators spent a few days going through intensive and immersive training and workshops to help and encourage them to think differently. These sessions included things like design thinking and emotional intelligence. This was done in groups with 400–500 employees at a time throughout the year. Lots of organizations are trying to figure out what their strategy is going to be for the future. PwC executives would stand in front of their new "recruits" and say, "You are our strategy for the future." For a professional services team like PwC, billable time is where much of the revenue comes from and typically 90% of an employee's time should be billable. For the almost 2,000 digital accelerators, their billable time dropped to around 60%. For the remaining 30% these employees were encouraged just to spend time learning, exploring, and trying to think of new ideas and ways of doing things. This a tremendous revenue hit to PwC in the short term but a very smart play in the long term. One of the things that really struck me about this program was that during the live events PwC executives would go on stage and say, "If you get back to work after this event and find that as you are trying to challenge the status quo, your managers or team members are giving you pushback, then call or email us, and we will personally fix it." Rarely do you ever hear about executives who are so willing, available, and accessible to help their people. This is how true change happens, when the leaders step up and commit to making it happen and support the people driving the change.

The challenges around skills is also not exclusive to what we would typically classify as "hard skills" either. Things like empathy, self-awareness, communication, and other "soft skills" are just as much in demand and lacking in the workplace. When LinkedIn surveyed 2,000 business leaders, 57% of them said that soft skills are actually more important than hard skills.

The Diversity and Inclusion Imperative

Diversity and inclusion are also critical components of how the talent landscape is changing and is becoming a top priority for senior leaders around the world, and for good reason. In a recent LinkedIn survey of 9,000 talent leaders, 78% said that diversity is extremely important. According to the report, "Diversity used to be a box that companies checked. But today, diversity is directly tied to company culture and financial performance. Our data shows that 78% of companies prioritize diversity to improve culture and 62% do so to boost financial performance." Deloitte's most recent millennial survey also found that millennials and Gen Zers who work for employers perceived to have diversity in the workforce and the senior management teams are more likely to stay at the company for five or more years.

Research done by Alison Reynolds from the UK's Ashridge Business School and David Lewis from the London Business School's Senior Executive Programme found that not only do we recruit in our own image (race, gender, etc.) but we also tend to recruit people who think and behave like we do as well. As a result, we end up with a bunch of like-minded teams, which means low cognitive diversity (Reynolds, 2017). This is a problem because, as we established earlier, the pace of change is one of the top trends driving the future of leadership (and work), which means that there is constantly a high degree of uncertainty. In that environment, teams with low cognitive diversity are not able to approach things differently (for example, analyzing versus experimenting) and they are also not able to see things from unique perspectives or create new options.

Diversity refers to the similarities or differences that we as individuals possess and includes things like age, gender, race, religion, location, and education. Inclusion, on the other hand, is what is done to actually empower these different groups of people inside the organization. In other words, it's not enough just to have a diverse workforce if you aren't able to unlock the potential of that workforce and make them feel like they belong. As a leader, that's your job.

Jeff Dailey is the CEO of Farmers Insurance, which employs around 20,000 people and has over 45,000 exclusive and independent agents. I really love what he told me: "Ultimately the goal of every leader should be to allow everybody to contribute to the best of their possible potential, and to the extent that you're not inclusive, that becomes impossible to do."

California actually became the first state to mandate that all publicly traded companies that have their headquarters in the state have at least one woman on its board by the end of 2019. This will increase by 2021, when companies that have five directors will be required to have two or three women on the board, depending on how large the board is. Companies that don't meet these requirements will face financial penalties.

According to a McKinsey report called "Delivering Through Diversity," "Companies in the top-quartile for gender diversity on their executive teams were 21% more likely to have above-average profitability than companies in the fourth quartile. For ethnic/cultural diversity, top-quartile companies were 33% more likely to outperform on profitability" (McKinsey, 2018).

Mastercard has about 14,000 employees around the world and diversity and inclusion is embedded into the very foundation of how they do business. Ajay Banga, their CEO, explained:

Mastercard believes in being a force for good. We believe that creating inclusive opportunities for all is the way to do business. We believe these things are central to how we succeed as a company. We embed those values throughout everything we do; they're not just words on a poster. We believe that when organizations – public and private – determine that it's in their own interest to do good and operate in ways that are decent and inclusive, we can move toward a healthy, global economy where everyone can thrive. The kind of economy that can produce a better world, with more transparency, greater sustainability, and a legitimate path to prosperity for all people. We have a culture built on purpose, where we get things done and embrace diversity as the key driving innovation and we embrace innovation as fundamental to our survival.

Dow is a material science organization (formerly a part of Dow Chemical) with 40,000 employees globally. They are taking steps to ensure they have the right leaders in place who are promoting diversity and inclusion, which is a major focus for Dow. These leaders are held accountable not only for traditional financial metrics but also for D&I metrics, which are part of the corporate scorecard; it's a component of their evaluation as leaders. When Jim Fitterling, the CEO of Dow Chemical, does his quarterly all-hands meetings and talks about the financial results, he also discusses diversity and inclusion and employee participation in resources groups throughout the organization (Bloomberg, 2019).

Google is one of the few organizations that actually publishes an annual diversity and inclusion report based on their own workforce. This holds Google accountable not only to employees but also to the world at large. When it comes to inclusion efforts, Google currently has over 20 employee resource groups with more than 250 chapters spanning 99 offices and 46 countries. These groups are also led by more than 500 employee volunteers and the groups themselves comprise over 20,000 employees, which is roughly 20% of their workforce. Almost 80% of employees at Google have taken steps to understand their unconscious bias via training and education programs, and over 2,000 employees have taken part in Diversity Core, a program that allows Googlers to spend 20% of their time to come up with ways to make the company more diverse and inclusive. Perhaps the most important statistic is that there are zero statistically significant pay differences among Googlers (Google, n.d.). They are clearly committed not only to building a diverse workforce but also to empowering that workforce to do their best work while making them feel like they belong at Google. Google isn't perfect, but they are working harder on these efforts than most other organizations in the world.

The talent landscape is changing and as a leader responsible for attracting and retaining the best talent, it's your job to adapt the organization accordingly. George Corona is the president and CEO of Kelly Services, a workforce management and staffing services company with around 8,000 employees. George believes that while talent is crucial now, it will make or break companies in the future:

Those that are going to succeed will succeed because they have the very best talent and the very best people. Understanding how to identify that talent, how to recruit that talent and how to motivate that talent, I think is going to be much more important in the future that it is even right now.

Implications for Leaders

- ◆ Invest in reskilling and upskilling programs.
- ◆ Strive to develop diverse teams and question what you are doing to make those diverse teams feel like they belong.
- ◆ Create programs that allow older workers to remain a part of your organization; for example, have them stay on as a coach or mentor.
- ◆ Help employees understand how their careers and jobs are changing and what skills they can learn to stay relevant and valuable members of the company.
- ◆ Create talent profiles and work to identify the potential jobs and opportunities that your company will have in the future. Look beyond today's talent.
- ◆ Tie diversity and inclusion and training and upskilling efforts to salary and incentive programs.

8
Morality, Ethics, and Transparency

On January 2, 2012, Forbes published a story with the title "Why Best Buy Is Going out of Business...Gradually" (Downes, 2012). Online this article has almost 4 million views. But Forbes clearly underestimated Best Buy's new CEO.

Hubert Joly is the executive chairman and former CEO (he retired in 2019) of Best Buy, a consumer electronics retailer with over 125,000 employees around the world. He joined the company in 2012 when it was struggling and many thought that Best Buy would just be another one of those retailers that would disappear. Several years later not only has Best Buy survived but it's actually thriving with higher revenues, an increased stock price (over 271% during the past five years at the time of writing this), and an aggressive growth plan for the future. Other retailers like Radio Shack and Circuit City failed where Best Buy was able to succeed. Among the several things that Hubert and his team did was invest back into the employees with new training and development programs and increased wages. Hubert helped make other people more successful so that they in turn could help the company be more successful. Not only that, but he did this while the company was struggling, something that took tremendous courage. Where other leaders would cut wages and training programs during tough times, Hubert increased them.

When I spoke with Hubert I felt like I was speaking with some-one who is part business leader, part philosopher, and part monk. Although our discussion was on the future of leadership, he weaved in stories from history, religion, business, and his own life. Perhaps more importantly, I felt like I was speaking with someone who had a strong moral and ethical true north. It's no surprise that Best Buy was ranked among the world's most ethical companies by the Ethisphere Institute. In Hubert's own words:

> If you believe your role as a leader is to be the smartest person in the room and to make sure that everybody knows how smart you are, you're wrong. If you believe that your role as a leader is to create an environment in which others can be successful, then you're on the right track. You need to be a values-driven leader. Integrity in this world of transparency is more important than ever. It's not just about complying with the rules. It's about doing the right thing.

Ethics versus Morals

Generally speaking, ethics refer to right and wrong, but in the con-text of an external source such as policies or codes of conduct for the organization. Ethics usually apply to everyone. Morals on the other hand are internal guiding principles that are far more subjective and apply specifically to you. In the context of leadership, your morals will impact the ethics of the organization. Take the collapse of Enron, one of the greatest cases of corporate fraud and deception in the modern business world. Clearly what the leaders of Enron did was not ethical; it violated numerous rules and codes of conduct. But if these leaders had their own strong moral compasses that pointed them in the right direction, they wouldn't have steered the organiza-tion and all the stakeholders down a path of treachery and unethi-cal behavior.

Wolf-Henning Scheider (whom we met earlier in the book), the CEO of ZF Friedrichshafen, offers great guidance on this:

> Future leaders must practice constant reflection and transparency, not just by themselves but with their teams. When I hold meetings, anyone is allowed to question a practice, a policy, or a behavior in our company and they are also allowed to question me as a leader. There should be no place for leaders to hide in their organizations.

According to the Association for Talent Development, organizations that have a strong ethical foundation do better financially, have higher employee retention, and see more customer referrals and higher customer satisfaction numbers (Smith, 2017). These numbers should not be surprising. Ethical organizations are made by ethical and moral leaders. Further research by Bentley University found that 86% of millennials, which are going to make up over 75% of the workforce by 2030, consider it a top priority to be a part of an organization that conducts itself in an ethical and responsible way (Bentley, 2018). Unfortunately, according to a study by Deloitte, less than half of millennials actually believe that businesses behave ethically and less than half believe that business leaders are working toward improving society as a whole (Deloitte 2019). As a leader, if you don't make this a focus, you will miss out on being able to attract the majority of the world's talent. Another study, published by the *Harvard Business Review*, found that based on a study of 195 leaders in 15 countries and spanning over 30 global organizations, having "high ethical and moral standards" was ranked as the top leadership competency (Giles, 2016).

The Impact of an Ethical Leader

Being an ethical leader also has a significant impact on the decision-making of the rest of the organization. The 2018 Global Benchmark on Workplace Ethics report found that across 18 countries in corporate cultures that were identified as "weak" when it comes to ethics, employees were far less likely to seek guidance when they were unsure of what ethical action they should take. The flipside of this is also true. In organizations with a strong culture of ethics, over 70% of employees stated that they seek guidance when uncertain (Ethics, 2018). This has profound implications because it means that if you want your employees to be ethical, it has to start with the leaders. Mark Feldman is the CEO of GSN, which is home to GSN Games and also the Game Show Network. He does this by leading by example.

"The question I ask myself every day is 'Does every person in this organization see that I model in my behavior what I expect of them?' Put another way: 'I hope there's not a person in this organization who thinks there's anything I would ask them to do or has been affected by anything that I don't ask of myself or expect of myself.'"

Today, employees, customers, and all stakeholders want to be a part of an ethical organization that has strong moral leaders, and this trend is only going to increase. A Cone Communications Millennial Employee Engagement Study found that 75% of millennials would take a pay cut to work for a company that is socially responsible and 64% won't take a job if a potential employer doesn't have strong corporate responsibility practices (Dailey, 2016). For over a decade Ethisphere has been putting out the World's Most Ethical Companies list. Each year they find that publicly traded companies that appear on the list consistently outperform the markets. A study by LRN found that 94% of employees say it is "critical" or "important" that the company they work for is ethical (LRN, 2007). A study by Accenture found that a company's ethical values and authenticity influence purchase consideration for 62% of consumers. Another 74% of consumers want more transparency in how companies highlight issues like sourcing products and ensuring safe working conditions (Barton, 2018).

Bill Rogers is chairman and CEO of SunTrust Banks, Inc. (around 23,000 employees), which recently announced a merger with BB&T (37,000 employees) to form Truist Financial Corporation, the nation's sixth largest bank. According to Bill, "Leadership will be a much more public endeavor than it has been in the past. It will require increased awareness of social issues and a recognition that clients want to do business with companies that contribute to a greater social good."

While being an ethical leader is crucial, it's often your morals that will be the true guide of the decisions you make. A few years ago, Indiana signed a law into effect that allowed businesses to refuse service to gay, lesbian, and transgender people. This was ethical; in fact, it was so ethical that it became a law so everyone who followed this law could say they were doing the ethical thing. But was this moral? Marc Benioff, the CEO of Salesforce, didn't think so. As a result, he offered a relocation package to any employee who wanted to leave the state, and he said he would cancel all programs that would require any employees or customers to travel to Indiana, which would have dramatic financial implications for the state. Eventually the law was changed to prohibit this kind of discrimination. Marc wasn't the only CEO or public figure to oppose this law, but he was absolutely leading the charge. He didn't do this because of ethics; he did this because his morals guided him on right and wrong.

In an interview he said, "I'm all for a healthy mind and a healthy body, but I'm also about having a healthy planet and a healthy country and taking care of others who don't have as much. That's my spirituality." In other words, that's his moral compass.

Unfortunately, we don't have too many leaders like this. In "The State of Moral Leadership in Business" study conducted by LRN in 2018, only 17% of respondents said their leaders normally tell the truth. Sadly, only 23% of employees said that their managers are moral leaders (LRN, 2018). According to a study led by Jim Lemoine at the University of Buffalo, which did a meta-analysis of over 300 sources, "Leaders who value morality outperform their unethical peers, regardless of industry, company size or role" (Biddle, 2018). Another study conducted by researchers at the University of Sussex, the University of Greenwich, the IPA, and CIPD found that when leaders display purposeful behaviors such as showing strong morals, employees are less likely to quit, are more satisfied, and are better performers (Bailey, 2018).

The issue is that morality is subjective, which means that not everyone will agree with your morals and you likely won't agree with everyone else's. That's okay. The problem arises when your team doesn't know what your morals are and what you stand for as a leader, which is why it's so important for you to be honest and clear about these things.

Diane Hoskins is the co-CEO of Gensler, a global architecture, design, and planning firm employing more than 6,000 people around the world. I really like how she put this:

> Most successful organizations communicate clear values. That is foundational. As organizational leaders, we also need to stand for something as the people we are. Our talent and clients want to know what our firm is committed to, and they want to know what our leaders are committed to as part of their professional and personal lives.

Leaders Must Be Transparent

As a leader, if you want to build trust, you have to focus on transparency, which is simply being honest and forthright about what is happening in the company now and in the future. According to career website Glassdoor, 90% of job seekers say it's important to work for a company that embraces transparency (Glassdoor, 2018). Of course, this is not something that only employees want; customers expect it as well. A study by Label Insight found that 94% of consumers are likely to be loyal to a brand that offers complete transparency and 73% of consumers would actually be willing to pay more for a product that offers complete transparency in all attributes (Label Insight, 2016).

"You can't fake it. You've got to be transparent. You've got to be candid. You've got to be trustworthy." This is what Steve Smith, the CEO of Amsted Industries, told me. He leads a team of over 18,000 employees and the company is 100% owned by the employee stock ownership plan.

Leaders can no longer hide behind bureaucracy or hierarchy. We have all seen our fair share of scandals and lies, whether from organizations like Enron or from Volkswagen, with their emissions scandal that is still dramatically hurting the company several years after being uncovered. Everyone who interacts with your organization expects that as a leader you will create an ethical and transparent company and that your morals will be the guiding compass for making this happen.

Andree Simon is the president and CEO of FINCA Impact Finance, which employs over 10,000 people. She gave me a fantastic visual of what it feels like to become a transparent, authentic, and even vulnerable leader. In other words, what it feels like to be your true self where those around you understand who you are, what you stand for, and what you believe:

For a long time, I thought that leaders had to look and behave a certain way and that they had to behave with absolute authority and never show weakness. I had the opportunity to work with this amazing coach. She made this comment to me at one point: "You know, it's kind of like you're wearing a gorilla suit a lot of the time. You're zipped up inside this hot, sweaty suit. But you're really not acting like yourself." It was a really liberating thing to hear. I took that gorilla suit off and I became true to myself in terms of what I believe in as a person and how I communicate with people, and I allowed myself to be really confident.

Implications for Leaders

- ◆ Understand your own moral compass. What is it that you stand for and believe?
- ◆ Overcommunicate the importance of doing the right things and being ethical and moral.
- ◆ Offer guidance and support to other leaders and employees who are struggling with ethics and morals.
- ◆ Be as transparent as you can in as many areas as you can.
- ◆ Take a stance. It's no longer good enough to float in neutral territory.

9
Globalization

Globalization is defined in many ways. I like to think of it as making the world a smaller place in which the language you speak, the currency you transact in, where you are located, and the culture you subscribe to are no longer barriers to doing business. The world is becoming like a big city and today every company can be a global one.

There used to be a time when the things we created, the ideas we had, the currency we used, and the culture that we subscribed to came from and stayed in one particular part of the world. Over time this expanded. Merchants and explorers traveled to different lands, bringing new cultures, ideas, currencies, and things with them. Migrants started relocating and soon our little village became connected to many villages. Fast forward to today and now our goods and services, financial markets, and technologies are intertwined with many countries globally. You may live in the United States and have a car imported from Japan, eat at a local German restaurant, buy meat imported from New Zealand, wear clothes made in Thailand, use technologies manufactured in China – you get where this is going.

People, ideas, technology, information, and pretty much anything else you can think of has become dynamic, like a never-ending flowing river or perhaps more like raging rapids. Nothing stays in its place, and with the continued advancement of technology all of these things are traveling faster, more cheaply, and more efficiently to every corner of the planet. A study done by the Association of Talent Development found that only 18% of multinational companies believe they have a strong leadership pipeline to meet future business challenges (Wellins, 2016).

Diversity and Curiosity Are Key

All of this means that leaders today, and more so in the future, are going to have to be global citizens. Understanding different cultures and ways to communicate and collaborate, how to attract and retain talent in different parts of the world, working with diverse and remote teams, and aligning a global workforce on common goals are all requirements for the future leader. Globalization means that as a leader you need to become an explorer, someone who is fascinated, curious, and interested in people who are different than you and ideas and cultures that are unfamiliar to you.

Unfortunately, leadership development programs today are not designed for this new type of future leader – something that will be addressed later in this book.

Pierre-André de Chalendar, the CEO of Saint Gobain, which employs over 180,000 people around the world, put this nicely:

The world is simultaneously becoming more global due to digital technologies and infrastructures, and more local, with a strong comeback of regional specificities where a good knowledge of local culture is a crucial condition for success. Consequently, the leaders of companies have to deal with these two opposing trends.

Implications for Leaders

◆ Experience leading in different parts of the world throughout your career.
◆ View foreign ideas, cultures, and people as opportunities to learn, rather than as things to fear.
◆ Understand the big picture of the business as opposed to just focusing on a particular segment.
◆ Pay attention to global macro trends.

10
Are We Ready for These Trends?

The previous six chapters presented the top trends that CEOs around the world identified as impacting the future of leadership. But are we actually doing anything about these trends today, and if so, how well? The survey of almost 14,000 LinkedIn members asked people if they, their managers, and their senior executives were aware of these trends and were taking actions to prepare the company to address them. Respondents were allowed to select from four responses:

No

Somewhat

Yes, definitely

Not applicable—I don't have any managers

The responses were then broken down by seniority, including individual contributors, managers, and senior executives. The results were startling, as seen in Figure 10.1. (A few responded with "not applicable," which is not included here.)

This alone shows that collectively, employees are not confident in their managers' or senior executives' ability to prepare their

Taking Action on Leadership Trends

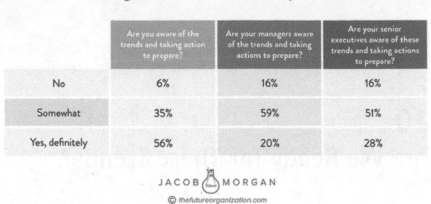

	Are you aware of the trends and taking action to prepare?	Are your managers aware of the trends and taking actions to prepare?	Are your senior executives aware of these trends and taking actions to prepare?
No	6%	16%	16%
Somewhat	35%	59%	51%
Yes, definitely	56%	20%	28%

JACOB MORGAN
© thefutureorganization.com

FIGURE 10.1 TAKING ACTION ON LEADERSHIP TRENDS.

organization for the trends shaping the future of leadership. It's also interesting to see that employees are more confident in their own actions versus those in leadership positions. How can people work for organizations when they don't have confidence in the abilities of their leaders?

The data becomes much more interesting when comparing the responses of individual contributors versus those in leadership positions, who were classified as either managers or senior executives. In Figure 10.2, you'll see that the more senior the individual, the more they believed they were taking actions to prepare.

When all the leaders (managers and senior executives) were asked if they are taking actions to prepare, 61% of them responded with "yes, definitely." However, when individual contributors were asked this same question about their leaders, only 21% responded with "yes, definitely." This means there's a massive 40% gap between how leaders view their actions toward these trends and how their employees view their actions toward these trends.

Only 20% of all employees believe that their managers are definitely aware of these trends and taking action, and only 28% of employees believe that their senior executives are definitely aware of and ready for these trends. Yet 50% of individual contributors said

Are You Taking Actions to Prepare for the Trends Shaping the Future of Leadership

	All Respondents	Individual Contribitors	Managers	Senior Executivess
No	6%	9%	4%	2%
Somewhat	35%	36%	36%	29%
Yes, definitely	56%	50%	58%	68%
Not sure	3%	4%	2%	1%

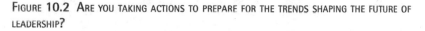

JACOB MORGAN
© thefutureorganization.com

FIGURE **10.2** ARE YOU TAKING ACTIONS TO PREPARE FOR THE TRENDS SHAPING THE FUTURE OF LEADERSHIP?

that they are taking action, 58% of managers said they are taking action, and 68% of senior executives said they are taking action (58% of those who are self-employed said they are taking action). When comparing the responses of individual contributors to those of leaders (managers and senior executives) who said "yes, definitely," there is a 41% gap between how all employees view leader's actions versus how leaders view their own actions (Figure 10.3).

Finally, let's compare the responses of managers with those of senior executives (Figure 10.4).

Even here we can see that large gaps exist between managers and senior executives. Here's what the gap looks like across the organization. For example, 20% of individual contributors don't think their managers are taking actions to prepare, whereas only 4% of managers self-identified as taking no action to prepare. This results in the 16% gap seen in the first "No" column (Figure 10.5).

When taking into account all of the survey data and the feedback from the CEOs I interviewed, the findings are concerning. But they also show that there is a rather large opportunity for leaders and organizations around the world. I learned a few things.

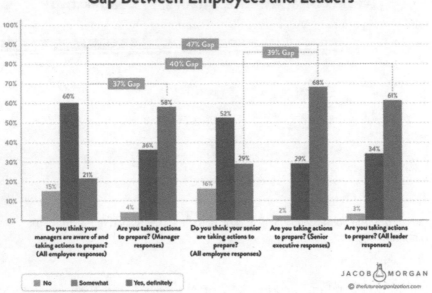

FIGURE 10.3 GAP BETWEEN EMPLOYEES AND LEADERS.

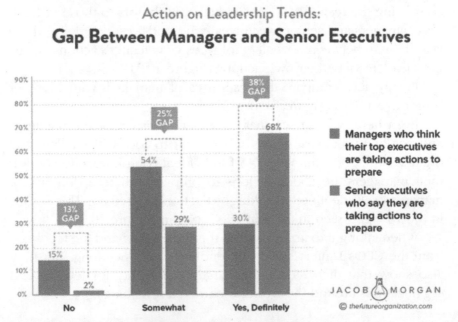

FIGURE 10.4 GAP BETWEEN MANAGERS AND SENIOR EXECUTIVES.

Gaps in Taking Action on Leadership Trends

	Gap between individual contributors and managers	Gap between individual contributors and executives	Gap between managers and senior executives	Gap between all employees and all leaders (Managers and Senior Executives)
No	16%	17%	13%	13%
Somewhat	22%	22%	25%	25%
Yes, definitely	37%	40%	38%	33%

JACOB MORGAN
© thefutureorganization.com

FIGURE 10.5 GAPS IN TAKING ACTIONS ON LEADERSHIP TRENDS.

We Need Less Talk and More Action

CEOs at over 140 organizations around the world identified these specific trends as being crucial to the future of leadership, yet it doesn't appear that their words are matching their actions, especially because the CEOs I interviewed kept telling me that they were doing something about these trends. Dare I say that many leaders around the world are simply paying lip service.

My assumption was that if a CEO identified a trend as being crucial, then surely that organization would be taking action to address it. Of course, identifying trends is not the same thing as doing something about them. CEOs and leaders around the world need to step up to make sure that they and their people are aware of these trends and are actively doing something to address them. Right now, the words are speaking louder than the actions but we need the actions to speak louder than words. This is true across the organization for mid-level managers, senior executives, and CEOs – everyone in leadership positions needs to step up. Host open discussions about these trends, allocate resources to explore them, make them a part of your regular conversations, run your own internal research projects with your employee base, and make sure the entire executive and leadership teams are doing the same.

There's an Organizational Breakdown

There is clearly a breakdown among employees at all levels in organizations as far as awareness of these trends and how they are being addressed. The majority of leaders believe that they have a handle on these trends, yet the vast minority of employees who work for these leaders actually agree (a 41% gap under "yes, definitely"). This can be due to numerous things, such as strict hierarchy in organizations with lots of bureaucracy, lack of communication and collaboration, fear on behalf of leaders forcing them to focus on their own self-preservation, or any number of other factors. The fact that the more senior the leader, the larger the gap between them and their employees shows that perhaps they are removed from the day-to-day aspects of their organizations and need to spend more time understanding what's happening on the ground floor.

The point is that leaders must do a better job of learning about and communicating about these trends, showing their teams that they are indeed aware of them and are doing something about them. As a leader, you may feel that you are quite comfortable with how things are changing, but your employees need to know that, otherwise they won't have the confidence and trust that's required for you to lead effectively. You can't lead if your employees don't believe in you, and your employees won't believe in you unless you communicate your understanding of these trends, visibly demonstrate what you are doing to prepare for them, and show that you are helping others prepare as well. Remember, employees often emulate leaders, so by being more communicative and open about what you're doing, you are also helping your employees be more successful as well. Ask employees about these trends and what they think about them. Learn what trends your employees are paying attention to and why. Come up with a shared plan for you and your team and become more aware of these trends along with action items.

Employees Are More Confident in Themselves Than in Those Around Them

Employees across all levels believe that they are more aware of these trends and are taking actions to prepare better than those around them, meaning that they have more confidence in themselves than they do in those with whom they are working. In psychology there is a concept known as illusory superiority or the above-average effect, which is a cognitive bias where individuals overestimate their own qualities and abilities. In fact, we see this in many areas. People tend to believe they are better drivers and listeners than they really and that they are more self-aware than they really are. Of course, this is one possible explanation for why people believe they are doing a better job of preparing for future trends than those around them. Another could be that we are collectively legitimately ready for the changes that are coming our way. However, my general perception from all the work I've done during my career tells me that this is not the case. I encourage organizations to create and develop resources and assessments that continuously allow employees to evaluate their preparedness for the future of leadership. These will give you a great gauge on just how prepared you and your organization are. These can be fun and engaging activities; you'll find an example of how PwC does something similar later in the book. I also included the responses from self-employed individuals, and you can see from the data that they are close to the range of managers.

The research is clear: leaders can do better, and they must do better. Your people want to know that you are thinking about the future, about their future. Your people should be confident in you to guide them and lead them. There is a tremendous opportunity here. Let this serve as your battle cry to step up. What are you going to do about it?

11
Challenges

Leaders have always been faced with challenges, and that won't change. But what are the most crucial challenges that future leaders will have to know how to overcome over the next decade and beyond? According to the over 140 CEOs I interviewed, these are the greatest challenges that leaders of the future will face:

- Short-term versus long-term thinking
- Leading diverse teams
- Adapting to technology advancements and changes
- Reskilling and upskilling employees
- Keeping up with overall pace of change
- Attracting and retaining talent
- Thinking beyond the business to focus on doing good
- Sticking with what worked in the past
- Making sure the organization stays "human"

I asked the CEOs, "When it comes to leading organizations in the next 10 years, what will be some of the greatest challenges for the leader of the future?" I then listened to the open-ended responses from the CEOs and classified them into various categories; the ones above were the most common responses. These answers were then added into the LinkedIn member survey and respondents had the opportunity to select their top three. You can see how the priority of the challenges differs across seniority levels. Admittedly, however, since the CEO responses were open-ended, they may have simply forgotten to mention a specific challenge or perhaps they assumed that these were already future challenges. Still, I included their responses for comparison. Figure 11.1 shows the top three responses for individual contributors (ICs), managers, senior executives, and CEOs. Figure 11.2 gives the full list of challenges and how each group prioritized them.

The ICs, managers, and senior executives were almost perfectly aligned on the top-three challenges for future leaders, and in fact for all of the challenges discussed above. However, when comparing the CEO priorities, the alignment is not even close. For starters, reskilling and upskilling employees was a high priority across the board but the CEOs hardly mentioned this as a challenge during our interviews (around 40% versus 11%). Attracting and retaining talent was another challenge that was actually number one for all groups but didn't even make it into the top three for CEOs. Making sure the organization stays human was almost dead last for CEOs, whereas it was in the middle of the pack for all other groups. Again, this discrepancy could have occurred for a variety of reasons, since the CEOs had open-ended responses while the other groups had to pick from those that CEOs identified.

All of these challenges fall under two categories, which I call "futurize" and "humanize" (Figure 11.3). The futurize challenges are shifting from short-term to long-term thinking, adapting to technology advancements and changes, keeping up with the overall pace of change, and moving away from what worked in the past. The humanize challenges are leading diverse teams, reskilling and upskilling, attracting and retaining talent, focusing on doing good, and making the organization human.

Futurize

To futurize means exactly what it sounds like: to bring our organizations into the future. This applies to all aspects of the business, ranging from technology to leadership and everything in between. Leaders can't expect to drive forward if they are constantly stuck looking in the rearview mirror.

Top 3 Challenges for Future Leaders

Individual Contributors	Managers	Senior Executives	CEOs
Attracting and retaining talent	Attracting and retaining talent	Attracting and retaining talent	Keeping up with overall pace of change
Adapting to technology advancements and changes	Adapting to technology advancements and changes	Adapting to technology advancements and changes	Leading diverse teams
Reskilling and upskilling employees	Reskilling and upskilling employees	Keeping up with overall pace of change	Adapting to technology advancements and changes

JACOB MORGAN
© thefutureorganization.com

FIGURE 11.1 TOP-THREE CHALLENGES FOR FUTURE LEADERS.

Top Challenges for Future Leaders

	Individual Contributors	Managers	Senior Executives	CEOs
Short-term vs. long-term thinking	27%	26%	29%	10%
Leading diverse teams	31%	38%	36%	38%
Adapting to technology advancements and changes	42%	45%	45%	25%
Reskilling and upskilling employees	40%	40%	39%	10%
Keeping up with overall pace of change	35%	36%	41%	55%
Attracting and retaining talent	47%	46%	46%	16%
Thinking beyond the business to focus on doing good	22%	20%	20%	10%
Sticking with what worked in the past	7%	5%	5%	4%
Making sure the organization stays "human"	32%	29%	27%	10%

JACOB MORGAN
© thefutureorganization.com

FIGURE 11.2 TOP CHALLENGES FOR FUTURE LEADERS.

Challenges for Future Leaders

JACOB MORGAN
© thefutureorganization.com

FIGURE 11.3 "FUTURIZE" AND "HUMANIZE" CHALLENGES.

SHORT-TERM TO LONG-TERM THINKING

We have all been conditioned to look at the short-term. We expect quarterly results from our organizations; if we work out for a few months, we expect to be athletes; if we build our personal brands for a short time, we expect to be famous; and if we study something quickly, we assume we've become subject matter experts. We live and work in a world of instant gratification, which I believe has caused us to neglect a crucial element of success: patience. As Paul Polman from Unilever has stated, "Too many CEOs play the quarterly game and manage their businesses accordingly. But many of the world's challenges cannot be addressed with a quarterly mindset."

A study published by the *Harvard Business Review* actually found that a company's short-termism is negatively correlated with innovativeness (Knott, 2017).

As a future leader, you must be able to shift your perspective from one that is purely focused on the short-term to one that is focused on the long-term success of the organization and the people who work there.

PAST VERSUS FUTURE

As leaders, we are often tempted to take something that has worked in the past and apply it to present-day situations, only to find that the same result is no longer attainable. Just because something worked in the past doesn't mean it will work in the present, or for that matter, the future. For many decades in the world of chess, grandmasters played certain opening moves because they were generally accepted to be the best. But as the years went on and we gained access to computers and better theoretical knowledge of the game, these moves evolved. Today, if a grandmaster played their game based on opening knowledge from a few decades ago, they would get obliterated. The same is true in the world of business.

I love how Barbara Humpton from Siemens talks about this: "How willing am I to kick over my sand castle and start building something new? As change happens all around us, are we agile enough to recognize when it's time to move on? I think that's going to be the toughest thing for leaders."

Future leaders must learn from the past, but they must also adapt and devise new approaches for the future if they wish to succeed. Take this piece of advice from Nigel Travis, the former CEO of Papa John's Pizza and Dunkin' Brands:

During my career, one of the greatest lessons I learned was the importance of anticipation. I would always look forward but plan backwards. Meaning I would always look toward a new horizon, but I would look toward that new horizon early on. I was constantly put into positions where I couldn't use past approaches or methods, so I had to create new ones. One of the things that makes a great leader is their ability to learn from the old but to create the new.

KEEPING UP AND ADAPTING TO TECHNOLOGY

One of the greatest challenges that leaders of the future will face, even more so than now, is trying to keep up with the pace of change and adapting to technological advancements that are coming their way. Just when you feel like you are grasping what's going on around you, the landscape will shift and you will be placed in what appears to be a foreign environment. How do you keep up? After all, it's not as if there is a blueprint for what to do because inherent in "keeping up" is the idea that the future is uncertain, and that's the hard part.

Michael Neidorff is the CEO of Centene, a healthcare company with around 50,000 employees globally that is headquartered in St. Louis. He's been the CEO for over 20 years and has been doing a stellar job. He states, "The challenge of uncertainty is the greatest challenge anyone can face, but embracing innovation and technological change is key to continuing to evolve in today's environment. Instead of seeing this as an obstacle, view it as a window to the future."

For starters, leaders must embrace the idea that change isn't something you fight or rebel against. It's a certainty that exists in an uncertain world. Many people are scared of change, which is a natural reaction since we don't know what's going to be on the other side. But if you view change not as something that has a starting point and an end point but as something that is ongoing and continuous, then you will realize that there is far less to fear. Change how you think about change.

Jim Whitehurst is the president and CEO of Red Hat, an open source software company with around 13,000 employees globally that was just acquired by IBM for $34 billion. He put this idea nicely: "The world is becoming less certain, so the role of organizational leaders is to foster their teams' capacities to thrive in a world without clarity. The trick is embracing uncertainty, not taming it."

The chess grandmaster can't possibly learn every single possible move in a game of chess; as I mentioned earlier, it's a virtually limitless game. So how do they train and improve? I've played chess for most of my life and recently started taking lessons with a grandmaster. One of the things that top players pay attention to most is patterns. They may be playing against an opponent and recognize similar positions or structures that immediately trigger their "spidey sense." Leaders must be adept at understanding patterns.

Leaders must also practice "Powers of Ten." When I interviewed the CEO of IDEO, Tim Brown (who recently stepped down after 19 years), he told me about a short film that came out in the 1970s called *Powers of Ten*. (It's available for free on YouTube and is about 9 minutes long.) It starts off by showing a couple having a picnic on the grass, then it zooms out 10 times to reveal the larger park, then 10 times again to show that they are near a body of water, some buildings, boats, and streets where cars are driving. The scene continues to zoom out until viewers are 100 million light years from the couple on the grass. Then the view begins to zoom back in until we get to 0.000001 angstroms, far beyond the cellular level to the atomic level.

Leaders need to think in powers of ten, meaning they need to be able to look at the very big picture but also be able to understand the details of what that picture means and even how it was put together. In terms of technology, for example, a leader must understand the potential implications of that technology on the company, the industry, or even the world, yet also be able to understand how that particular technology might impact a single employee or task inside of the organization. Leaders must zoom out and also be able to zoom in.

Doing so will allow you to put things into perspective so you don't find yourself chasing the next shiny toy that comes your way. Being able to practice powers of ten will help you understand where your time and resources should go.

Humanize

Every company in the world can exist without technology, but no company in the world can exist without people. CEOs around the world recognize that people are and will continue to be for the fore-seeable future the most valuable asset of any organization. The humanize challenge comes down to several things: leading diverse teams, reskilling and upskilling employees, attracting and retaining top talent, focusing on doing good, and making the organization human.

Antonio Huertas is the CEO of MAPFRE, a global insurance company headquartered in Spain with around 40,000 employees around the world. He's a big believer in making organizations human. As he told me during our interview:

The way forward is being authentic, spending time with your stakeholders just as you are, leading your teams, just as you are, and even being on social media just as you are and the way you really behave. You can't expect others to be authentic and transparent if you as a leader are not prepared to be these things yourself. In this hyper-connected world, we have to lean toward humanism, putting people at the center of things.

LEADING DIVERSE TEAMS

At some point in our careers we have all been a part of a team where everyone looks the same, believes in the same things, has similar backgrounds, and does the same kind of work. Many of you reading this book might be a part of that kind of a team as we speak. I've seen many of these teams first hand. Often when I get brought in to speak with executives at global organizations, I immediately notice that I'm in a room filled with older white guys in suits. The funny thing is that after these events, people quietly come up to me and make fun of the fact that their teams are so homogeneous. It's time to stop making fun of our teams and start changing them.

A diverse team isn't just composed of people who don't look alike. Diverse teams can mean that people are from different generations, backgrounds, cultures, religions, sexual orientations, physical locations, and so on. Leading a homogeneous team is easy; it's a cop-out where you typically end up with a bunch of yes-men or -women. The challenge here is twofold: having the courage as a leader to make sure that diverse teams are actually created, and then adapting your mindsets and skillsets to be able to effectively lead these diverse teams.

In his book *Team of Teams: New Rules of Engagement for a Complex World,* General Stanley McChrystal talks about some of the challenges he ran into during the Iraq War. He was the leader of a diverse group of teams, including the Navy SEALs, Army Special Forces, and others. Although all of these teams were individually skillful, it was challenging for them to collaborate and bring their abilities together. As a result, McChrystal did things such as diversify the teams (McChrystal, 2015). A commando, for example, would spend a few months working in an analyst unit and an analyst would spend a few months working with commandos. As a result of creating these diverse teams, the silos crumbled and the greater team became more powerful than the individual parts.

George Oliver is the CEO of Johnson Controls, a multinational conglomerate with over 120,000 employees around the world. According to George, "What translates into success is having a diverse team that is proven to be more innovative than one that looks the same and is built on the past. What we are building at Johnson Controls is a diverse culture that is based on teamwork, team incentives, and ultimately everyone being focused on the same goal of winning with teams being recognized for their success."

ATTRACTING AND RETAINING TOP TALENT

For the foreseeable future, the greatest asset that any organization in the world has is its people. People are the ones who design products and services, build relationships with customers, imagine and create the future, and lead others. It's the people who will determine the future success of your organization.

This has always been a challenge for business leaders around the world, but with each passing year it becomes harder for organizations to attract and retain the very best talent. Organizations are more actively investing in things like employee experience to create more desirable places to work, skillsets are evolving, many leaders are having a hard time even filling existing roles, and employees have a more powerful voice than ever before to share what they care about, what they value, and what they expect to see in organizations. It's no longer about people trying to convince organizations why they should work for them; now it's about the organizations convincing people why they should work for them. This is a complete reversal in the world of talent.

A recent McKinsey Global Institute study estimates that employers in Europe and North America will require 16 million to 18 million more college-educated workers in 2020 than are going to be available. Companies are going to have a hard enough time filling one in ten roles, let alone be able to fill those roles with top talent (Keller, 2017).

Barri Rafferty is the CEO of Ketchum, a global communications consultancy with more than 2,000 employees. She had this to say about talent:

If you want to attract and keep top talent, then you need to make sure to invest in their experience. Employees have more power and this will only continue to increase. We have to build organizations with our people, not for them. Leaders must understand that they and their organizations are nothing without the people who work there.

RESKILLING AND UPSKILLING EMPLOYEES

New technologies are emerging on a regular basis and the overall pace at which technology is advancing is staggering. These new technologies enable new ways of working, never before seen business models, and novel challenges and opportunities. The challenge for future leaders here is not only to make sure new employees have the right skills in place to adapt but to also make sure that existing employees can pivot to fill new roles. We have always assumed that the things we have learned in our educational institutions and our organizations would last us for most of our careers. Most organizations have no idea what jobs, careers, skills, or mindsets they are going to need from a future workforce, so how can they train and hire for them?

How will you respond as a leader when a large percentage of your workforce is legitimately worried about being displaced by technology? A true test of leadership is the ability to continually invest in your team. We distinctively invest in front-line teammates to give them opportunities for growth beyond the standard career ladder. Professional development additionally requires an investment in personal self awareness and mindfulness. Encouraging teammates holistically drives the motivation and resilience when new technologies emerge.

This came from Kent Thiry, the CEO and executive chairman of the board of directors at DaVita Inc., a healthcare company with almost 80,000 employees.

I wish more leaders embraced this kind of mentality, that reskilling and upskilling your workforce isn't just something to do because it makes business sense, but because it shows just what kind of a leader you are and that you're willing to look after your people.

Amazon, for example, recently announced something called "Upskilling 2025," where they are investing more than $700 million to train 100,000 employees (a third of their workforce) for higher-skilled jobs through 2025. The training programs will be made available to employees across the organization. This means employees will also have greater internal mobility in the company if they decide to pursue another role. For example, a worker in manufacturing would be able to learn the skills necessary to transition into something more technical like machine learning. These programs include things like Associate2Tech, Amazon Technical Academy, and Machine Learning University. It's no wonder Amazon is focusing on this; as of this writing, the company has over 20,000 vacant positions they are struggling to fill. Amazon is also looking beyond their organization by offering certifications that can be used at other companies (Matsakis, 2019).

Organizations like Accenture, AT&T, JPMorgan Chase & Co., and others have also developed longer-term reskilling plans where they are investing hundreds of millions of dollars in the future of work.

Doing Good

As individuals, we care about being a part of an organization or transacting with an organization that cares about more than just making money. We want to be a part of organizations that focus on creating a positive impact on society, the community, and the world at large. It's a bit sad to see that this is even identified as a top challenge but with our constant obsession with quarterly profits and making money, the human stuff tends to get pushed to the side. It's a challenge because not only do leaders need to make this shift, but they also need to guide and teach others to make this shift as well, including all of their stakeholders.

Lynn Jurich is the CEO of Sunrun, the United States' leading home solar and energy services company, with more than 4,000 employees across the nation. Lynn is very passionate about this:

There has to be a broader awareness for leaders about how you're operating in other spheres, in addition to just the capital markets. Leaders must understand how their organizations operate within our political system, our social system, with disadvantaged communities, and the like. Leaders of all institutions need to ask themselves how they are contributing to the greater good and how they are impacting people.

Future leaders must be able to demonstrate and articulate how the work the organization is doing is helping to make the world a better place. It won't be enough to just showcase great financial returns and performance.

Smile Brands is a dental service organization in the United States with over 5,000 team members. Not only does the company have almost a perfect five-star rating on Glassdoor but their CEO, Steve Bilt, has a 98% employee approval rating as well, a combination that almost no other organization has. The company culture has been built around a simple three-word mission: Smiles for Everyone®. While this may sound like marketing-speak, at Smile Brands, this is a powerful mantra that guides interactions with patients, providers, employees, suppliers, and even community partners. After a change in ownership in 2013, the two founders of the company, Steve Bilt and Brad Schmidt, left. The new owners attempted to put their stamp on the organization and they did this by changing the mission and posting their new version in all practice locations. The new mission, "to give providers and their dental teams the freedom to put patients first so they can become the most preferred dental office in their community," was full of business speak and failed to connect with the hearts and minds of the employees. Not only did it lack the simplicity of the former mission, but more importantly, there was a big disconnect between management actions and their new stated mission. In 2016, when Bilt and Schmidt returned, long-time employees pleaded to bring back "Smiles for Everyone" – and that's still their current mission. According to Bilt, "Our business is and always will be about people, that starts with our people and our culture. When we get that right, it naturally extends to the patient and our broader communities. Ultimately, connecting with our people and our purpose is the 'how' behind our 'why' of delivering Smiles for Everyone."

MAKING THE ORGANIZATION HUMAN

Think about what most organizations do when they have a bad quarter: they immediately cut the humans as if they are expendable cogs. In fact the word "cog" is a synonym for "employee" and this is exactly how we have been treating them for decades.

Making the organization more human means that as leaders we view those who work with and for us as more than just employees. We view them as individuals who have families and friends, fears and points of stress, hopes and dreams, hearts and minds, goals and aspirations, and above all as human beings just like you. In a technology-driven world we often lose sight of our humanness, but remember, you're the lighthouse always guiding your people to the future and to safety, not toward the rocks.

Mike McDerment is the CEO of FreshBooks, a 300-person company that provides accounting software for self-employed professionals. I'm very fond of this quote from Mike: "Even with the pace of technological innovation, here's the one thing that doesn't change: people are still looking for a human experience. We all are." At FreshBooks, to keep the organization more human, employees can volunteer to be set up on blind dates. These aren't romantic dates, though; they're professional dates with people from different teams who would rarely get the opportunity to interact with one another. They can go grab coffee or lunch. The whole point is for employees to get know each other as humans as opposed to just workers. Leaders can better get to know their people, stay on top of what is happening on the ground floor and across the organization, and learn from and share ideas across departments and seniority levels. It's fun, and human.

At Barry-Wehmiller, a 12,000-person manufacturing company, they measure turnover and retention, just like any other company would. However, they don't refer to this as headcount; instead, they call it heart-count to remind themselves that the people who work there are humans and not expendable and replaceable cogs. Think of every employee in your organization as a heart and soul instead of just a head or a pair of hands.

Bobby Chacko is the CEO and president of Ocean Spray, an agricultural cooperative with over 2,000 employees. He understands the importance of seeing employees this way: "As organizations get more complex and as leaders start to leverage more technology, they oftentimes miss the human element. Instead, leaders must constantly be thinking about how to use technology to connect to the human side of work and to never lose that, regardless of how much technology they start bringing in."

We Aren't Ready for These Challenges

One of the questions that the LinkedIn survey asked was how ready the respondents were to face these challenges. This question was also broken down by seniority level (Figure 11.4). The data

We Aren't Ready for Challenges Facing Future Leaders

	How prepared are your managers to face these challenges? (Individual Contributors)	How prepared are you to face these challenges? (Managers)	Gap between individual contributors and managers	How prepared are your senior executives to face these challenges? (Individual Contributors)	How prepared are you to face these challenges? (Senior Executives)	Gap between individual contributors and senior executives	How prepared are your senior executives to face these challenges? (Managers)	Gap between managers and senior executives
Not well at all	23%	4%	19%	23%	3%	20%	21%	18%
Somewhat well	40%	33%	13%	39%	28%	11%	40%	12%
Reasonably well	28%	47%	19%	27%	47%	20%	30%	17%
Very well	8%	15%	7%	9%	22%	13%	8%	12%

JACOB MORGAN
© thefutureorganization.com

FIGURE 11.4 LACK OF READINESS FOR CHALLENGES FACING FUTURE LEADERS.

clearly shows that across the board there is not much confidence that managers and senior executives are ready to tackle these challenges.

Of the individual contributors, 63% said their managers are either somewhat ready or not ready at all to face future leadership challenges, which is in stark contrast to 62% of managers who self-reported to be in either the "reasonably well" or "very well" categories. These numbers were quite consistent with senior executives as well. Individual contributors put 62% of their senior executives in these bottom two categories; meanwhile 69% of senior executives put themselves in the top two categories. Managers also put 61% of senior executives in the bottom two categories for preparedness for these challenges.

Looking at the data we can see the massive opportunity that leaders and organizations around the world can seize, assuming that they actually take action.

These are the top challenges that leaders of the future must be able to overcome. In fact, we are already seeing these challenges today, but not at the scale they will be in ten years from now.

What does this mean for how you as a future leader can adapt to the trends described earlier, and what can you do to overcome the challenges outlined above? You start by arming yourself with a new and upgraded arsenal of mindsets and skills that I call "The Notable Nine."

Enter the Notable Nine

From all of the research done for this book, four mindsets, along with five skills, kept coming up as being essential for the future leader to possess: the Notable Nine (Figure 11.5). The four mindsets are those of the explorer, chef, servant, and global citizen. These are covered in detail in Part 3. The five skills are those of the coach, futurist, technology teenager, the translator, and Yoda. These are covered in detail in Part 4.

FIGURE 11.5 THE NOTABLE NINE: MINDSETS AND SKILLS.

Mastering and using the Notable Nine, along with making sure that others around you are doing the same, will make you a great future-ready leader, future-proof your career, and increase your value tenfold for any organization.

PART 3

THE FOUR MINDSETS OF THE NOTABLE NINE

12
The Explorer

Before we explore the specifics of each of the four mindset types, I need to explain what I mean by mindsets. A mindset refers to how you think, which in turn influences and shapes how you act.

Take, for example, a leader who believes in having a strict hierarchy where it's his or her responsibility to tell everyone what to do, where they make all of the decisions, and believe that they should never be questioned because of their status inside of the company. This type of leader will be much more close-minded to outside perspectives and ideas, won't practice any kind of empathy or self-awareness, and will end up creating a toxic culture. Then consider another leader who believes in serving those around them, someone who believes in questioning assumptions and challenging the status quo, who understands that work and life are blurring together. This type of leader will build a much more human team based on trust and psychological safety where employees are valued and treated fairly.

What you as a leader believe will influence the type of organization you are a part of and help create. This is a tough thing to change because many of us were taught a style and approach to leadership that no longer works or is relevant. With mindsets, you can't fake it, meaning that you can't secretly believe in command and control yet put up a facade of openness and transparency; your people will know and you will fail as a leader.

4 Mindsets for the Future Leader

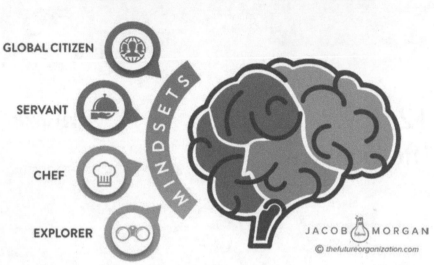

GLOBAL CITIZEN

SERVANT

CHEF

EXPLORER

MINDSETS

JACOB MORGAN

© thefutureorganization.com

FIGURE 12.1 FOUR MINDSETS FOR THE FUTURE LEADER.

During my interviews, CEOs identified just over a dozen mindsets that are essential for leaders of the future. Several of these mindsets were related and intertwined with another, so I grouped them together (see Figure 12.1). For example, curiosity and learning were two separate mindsets but one cannot exist without the other so they became the mindset of the explorer. The mindsets outlined in this section were defined by CEOs around the world as being most crucial for future leaders through 2030 and beyond. As a current or future leader, you must understand and practice all of them. From this day forward, this is how you must think as a leader.

An Overview of the Explorer

History is riddled with stories of explorers who have discovered new lands, people, things, and ideas. Explorers are seekers who traverse the unknown but not all explorers are also leaders, Sir Ernest Henry Shackleton was both, yet most people don't know about him. He was born in Ireland but lived in Britain. In 1914 he was a part of an expedition to explore the Antarctic, with the goal of crossing it from sea to sea, spanning 1,800 total miles. They never completed their quest, but what followed was one of the greatest lessons in leadership ever told.

To find a crew, Shackleton took out an ad in a newspaper, which was rather blunt yet honest: "Men wanted for hazardous journey. Small wages, bitter cold, long months of complete darkness, constant danger, safe return doubtful. Honour and recognition in case of success." Imagine if your company was just as brutally honest about what it was like to work there. Would people still apply? For most organizations the job descriptions wouldn't sound that dissimilar to Shackleton's except in the case of success most employees don't get the honor and recognition!

A few dozen men applied and the journey began. It didn't take long for disaster to strike. While they were navigating through the Weddell Sea near the Antarctic coastline, their ship, *Endurance,* became trapped in the ice for ten months. Ultimately the ship was crushed by the ice and sank and still hasn't been recovered to this day. Before the ship submerged, the crew gathered all of the supplies, along with three lifeboats, and made an ice floe their home for the next five months. They didn't know how long they would be able to survive.

Eventually the ice started to thin and melt before cracking, forcing the crew into their lifeboats. Shackleton decided to head to Elephant Island, a five-day journey battling high winds and waves. By the time they arrived it had been over a year since they set foot on solid land. Elephant Island was uninhabited and uninhabitable and Shackleton knew that if they stayed there they would all surely perish. He took the least damaged boat and set out with a crew of five to South Georgia Island 800 miles away to get help. Traveling by the direction of the sun, which appeared only a few days through the overcast skies and storms, they finally made it sixteen days later. But the journey didn't end there. Upon reaching the island they still needed to make contact with a whaling station on the other end of the island. Shackleton and two crew members were to make the trek to the whaling station while the rest of the men stayed with the lifeboat. They took screws from the lifeboat and inserted them into the bottom of their shoes to get traction in the snow and began walking for almost two days straight across glaciers and snow fields.

Exhausted, hungry, and frail, they finally made contact with the whaling station. They were then able to rescue the few men who stayed behind with the lifeboat but it took three attempts and three months to rescue the almost two dozen men who remained on Elephant Island. All 28 members of the crew survived. Several years later Shackleton began another expedition to Antarctica but just as it began, he died of a heart attack at age 47. He was buried on South Georgia Island.

What makes this story so amazing isn't just the fact that everyone survived; it's how they survived. Even when they were on the ice floe, Shackleton tried to entertain the crew so they wouldn't think about their precarious situation. He encouraged his men to tell stories and toast their loved ones. They even played hockey together and had singalongs. His constant message was that strength lies in unity. In the eyes of his men his spirits never wavered, as evidenced by the recovered journals of his crew, which documented his optimism, strength, respect, and admiration that he had for those he traveled with. He put the needs of everyone else before his own.

Lionel Greenstreet, the first officer of that crew, described the one they called the "boss": "Shackleton's first thought was for the men under him. He didn't care if he went without a shirt on his back so long as the men he was leading had sufficient clothing" (Dartmouth, n.d.).

When I was reading through the many stories written about Shackleton, I kept wondering how many corporate leaders today would behave in the same fashion had they been put in Shackleton's shoes. We all know the answer: not many. Leaders today focus on profits, but just imagine what it would be like to lead when your focus isn't on money but on the very lives of the people you work with, including your own.

The story and history of Sir Ernest Henry Shackleton is a fascinating one, and there are many books and several films about him. He wasn't just a great explorer but also a great leader, which is why he embodies the true mindset of the explorer that leaders of the future must possess. This means you are curious, a perpetual learner, have a growth mindset, are open minded, and are agile and nimble.

CURIOSITY

When Michael Dell was asked to name a single attribute that CEOs will need to succeed in the future, his response was "curiosity." This is also echoed by none other than Walt Disney, who famously said, "Around here, however, we don't look backwards for very long. We keep moving forward, opening up new doors and doing new things, because we're curious ... and curiosity keeps leading us down new paths." Even the great Albert Einstein admitted, "I have no special talent. I am only passionately curious."

As children we all grow up with a certain sense of curiosity and wonder, of wanting to understand how things work and what our limits are. But as we go through our education system and then get hired by corporations around the world, our ability to express curiosity decreases. In schools we are taught always to have the right answers to pass the test, and in business we are incentivized and told to do our jobs, make money, avoid failure, and be efficient. But curiosity goes against these principles; inherent in being curious is taking chances, being wrong, and challenging the status quo. As Pablo Picasso once said, "All children are artists. The problem is how to remain an artist once he grows up."

What is rather apparent in the corporate world is that employees, even if curious, aren't able to express or pursue that curiosity. Children have no issues vocalizing and showing their curiosity and they certainly have no problem challenging authority and questioning the status quo. In most organizations, however, someone who does this is viewed as a problem employee. This is why many employees still ask questions but they do so in their own minds; we all have ideas we want to explore, things we want to try, and improvements we'd like to suggest, but unfortunately we keep these things to ourselves. There's a big difference between being curious and being able to act upon and express that curiosity.

As the world continues to change, our organizations must adapt, and it's the curious leaders who are going to be at the helm of these organizations. This is the mindset that will force the pursuit of new ideas, products, services, and methods of doing things.

Bradley Jacobs is the CEO of XPO Logistics, which has over 100,000 employees globally. He previously founded United Rentals, the largest equipment rental company in northern California, and during his career he has led over 500 acquisitions and has been ranked among the world's best CEOs by places like Barron's and Glassdoor. Bradley is fueled by curiosity; he told me, "Curiosity is like the fountain of youth when it comes to effective leadership."

More seasoned leaders also typically believe that they've been in the game long enough and as a result can afford to coast along, doing things the same way they always have. SOS International is the world's largest medical and travel security services firm, with over 11,000 employees. At the helm of this organization is Arnaud Vaissié, who co-founded the company almost 40 years ago. He's been a leader for decades, longer than almost any other CEO I had the opportunity to interview. It's easy to assume that he has seen and done it all. As Arnaud told me, "Because of the fact that I have been in leadership for so long, I need to maintain an edge on curiosity and not be blasé. Because at some point you say, I've seen it all,' and frankly with the changes going on, nobody has seen it all."

I like the following definition of curiosity put forward in a research paper (Kashdan et al., 2017): "Curiosity can be commonly defined as the recognition, pursuit, and desire to explore novel, uncertain, complex, and ambiguous events." Essentially it asks, "what if?" "why?" and "how?"

Mark Smucker is the president and CEO of the J.M. Smucker Company, which employs over 7,000 people. Mark told me, "I think organizations are hungrier now than they ever were for understanding why, why we're changing, why we're doing 'this,' why our business is challenged. What can we do differently? But the why is very important."

Over the past few years Dr. Todd Kashdan has been leading a team to study curiosity. He joined with Merck KGaA to create the "State of Curiosity Report," published in 2016 and again in 2018; the 2018 version was based on data collected from over 3,000 survey respondents (Kashdan, 2018). The research found that the highly curious individuals with the greatest potential to innovate inside of organizations possess four distinct characteristics:

Joyous Exploration

This is where we gain great pleasure from recognizing and seeking out new knowledge and information and get joy from learning and growing. According to Todd, this is where most people stop when it comes to curiosity; they assume curiosity is just about tinkering and exploring new things the same way children do.

Deprivation Sensitivity

This occurs when individuals recognize that there is a gap between what they know and what they want to know and then try to close that gap. For example, after I identified that curiosity was one of the top mindsets for the future of leadership, I needed to learn as much as I could about this topic to close my knowledge gap. I read books, examined studies, and spoke with experts like Todd. This can be a hectic and stressful experience, kind of like writing this book! Todd pointed out that this can also be an area where leaders mess up because this doesn't look like our traditional notion of curiosity (joyous exploration).

Openness to People's Ideas

Cultivating curiosity requires being open to diverse perspectives and ideas from others and also intentionally seeking out new ways of doing things. Leaders need to be okay with saying "I don't know" and valuing the perspectives and ideas of other people, as opposed to just assuming that because they are leaders they are inherently smarter, make better decisions, and are more valuable to the organization. Almost 20% of the CEOs I interviewed specifically called out being "open minded" as crucial for future leaders.

Candido Botelho Bracher is the CEO of Itau Unibanco, the largest financial conglomerate in the southern hemisphere, with revenues over $42 billion, assets over $400 billion, and an employee base of over 100,000 people globally. During our interview, he greatly stressed this idea of being open minded as essential for future and current leaders:

> As business transformations become much more frequent and necessary, the leader of the future must always be open to questioning ideas and assumptions from those who report

to him or her or from third parties. Under these circumstances, the leader cannot be expected to always have all of
the knowledge, information, and answers. Increasingly leaders will have to rely on their people with varied backgrounds
and perspectives to make the best decisions. This means that
in order to have a successful company, leaders must be open
minded to ideas that are not their own.

STRESS TOLERANCE

This last characteristic is not necessarily one we think about when it
comes to curiosity. After all, curiosity should just be fun, relaxing,
autonomous, and exploratory, right? It should all just be joyous
exploration. Actually, as I mentioned above and as Todd and his
team identified, curiosity can be stressful because you are exploring
something new, unfamiliar, and uncertain. As a leader, not only do
you need to know how to manage this, but you also need to help
your team understand how to cope with it as well.

We Need More Curiosity

Looking at these four characteristics, it's quite easy to see why we
don't have more curiosity in the workplace. Most of us have no time
to seek out new knowledge at work and are barely keeping our heads
above water with our current workloads to begin with. According to
LinkedIn's "2018 Workplace Learning Report," which surveyed 4,000
employees around the world, 94% of workers would stay at their company longer if it invested in their career development, yet the number-
one reason why employees say that they feel held back at work is
because they just don't have the time to learn the skills they need to
stay relevant and successful in their jobs (LinkedIn, 2018).

Any kind of vulnerability is typically frowned upon, and the tools
and learning programs that many organizations have at their disposal
are outdated by several decades, which means employees won't

bother using them. Schools and organizations teach us to focus on being right, bringing in the most amount of money, staying efficient as possible, and minimizing risk. Also, teams often comprise individuals who look the same, act the same, believe the same things, work in the same geographic location, and even work on similar projects, which means there is lack of cognitive diversity.

Elena Donio is the CEO of Axiom, a legal services provider with over 2,000 employees globally. According to Elena: "It's really important to be inquisitive, to be listening, to be hearing, and profiling for ideas in all places of the company, to be able to be vulnerable and know that the best answers very often don't come from the top officers, but rather come from a syndicate of individuals who are closest to the client, closest to the problems and opportunities that we're seeing in the field, and to really be active in creating and enforcing and rewarding that kind of dialogue."

Melissa Smith is the CEO of Wex Inc., which employs around 4,000 people around the world. When we spoke about this, she said, "I love diversity of thought; it creates competitive advantages for companies because they will innately be wired in different ways, based on bringing in different types of leadership."

Part of the reason curiosity appears to suffer inside our organizations is because of our obsession with focusing on the short-term and our comfort with the familiar. The hierarchy itself is one of the most resilient structures ever created and is designed to push away anything new and unfamiliar, which means change of any kind is hard to achieve. Curiosity is almost seen as a problem in most organizations because it disrupts the machine. Leaders need to see the new and unfamiliar not as threats but as opportunities. In the *Star Trek: The Next Generation* series, Captain Jean-Luc Picard provides voiceover as the show begins:

> Space: the final frontier. These are the voyages of the Starship *Enterprise*. Its continuing mission: to explore strange new worlds. To seek out new life and new civilizations. To boldly go where no one has gone before!

If most leaders today were to create their own voiceover, it would probably sound something like this:

Space, it's a new frontier, but why bother? These are the voyages of the Starship *Enterprise*. Its continuing mission: to make sure we maintain the status quo. To keep our heads down and to avoid change. To go to the same places we have already been!

Sounds like a great show, right?

As I mentioned earlier, the types of filters you have in place for leadership will reflect the types of people who become leaders. Those who focus purely on short-term results will find that their teams will struggle with curiosity, whereas those who focus on longer time horizons will see the opposite impact. Recall the story of Hubert Joly and Best Buy; his turnaround efforts took several years to manifest. Had Hubert focused only on quarter-to-quarter financials, Best Buy would likely no longer be in existence.

When curiosity isn't supported inside the organization, employees at all levels shut this muscle down and eventually you get cogs. How, in this type of environment, can any sliver of curiosity possibly be cultivated? It can't.

3M employs 100,000 people around the world and they are involved in creating products and services for a variety of industries, including manufacturing, healthcare, consumer goods, and even worker safety. They have a unique culture where employees can spend 15% of their time to pursue ideas that they are genuinely excited about and interested in. Of course, employees still need to make sure they are able to deliver on their existing responsibilities, but they are given that time to be curious. As a result, 3M has seen many innovations spawn from employees' curiosity, including multi-layer optical film, Cubitron abrasives (used on tools like sanding discs for automotive repair and manufacturing), Post-it Notes, and hybrid air purifiers. But this 15% time doesn't have to be used for making a product or creating a service; it can also be used for something like trying to improve a process or creating an employee special interest group. Intuit has something similar in place where employees can spend 10% of their time pursuing things they are interested in.

Not all organizations take on this approach of allocating a specific amount of time for experimentation. Others simply give employees space or they create programs that employees can opt into where they receive time and resources to explore their ideas. Microsoft has the Garage, where employees are encouraged and supported to hack and make things. At Capital One, employees across all levels are encouraged to suggest new ideas, ask questions, and challenge the status quo, regardless of their title or function in the company. They focus on the merits of ideas, which trumps any hierarchy.

Bain, a management consulting firm, has an externship program where employees are able to work at different companies and nonprofits around the world for six months at a time. By doing so, employees are constantly exposed to new ideas, cultures, and perspectives. This helps foster curiosity.

Pretend for a moment that your role is "chief curiosity officer" at your company. What sort of programs or ideas would you put into place to help create and encourage this mindset? Why aren't they in place currently?

I had the privilege of speaking with Francesco Starace, the CEO of Enel, an Italian energy company that employs almost 70,000 people. Enel is Europe's largest utility company by market capitalization and has over 73 million global customers. Francesco is one of the many CEOs who stressed the importance of curiosity for leadership. "They have to have an inbred curiosity that keeps them hooked and connected with what changes or happens around themselves, not to lose touch."

"Not to lose touch." I love that Francesco said that, because losing touch is exactly what happens when we stop being curious: we get disconnected from our teams, our customers, our organizations, and from those around us.

Employees and leaders who are a part of an organization that is already thriving may be more hesitant to show curiosity. After all, clearly something is working, otherwise the company wouldn't be doing well, right? There is a tendency to challenge the status quo and to exhibit curiosity only when things are not going well. The worse the company is doing, the more curious we might become. This is typical in innovation circles. Organizations usually make innovation a priority when things aren't doing well and they need to think of something new to get out of their slump. Usually the CEO will hold some kind of an all-hands meeting and say, "We've had a few tough quarters, so we really need some new ideas to help us improve." It's far easier to explore new ideas and approaches to something when things are going well, as opposed to trying to force curiosity when the ship is sinking.

Even successful organizations need curious leaders and employees. Pixar Animation Studios has been an enormously successful company, with a track record of hit movies like *Inside Out, Toy Story, Cars, Finding Nemo, Monsters, Inc.,* and many others. New employees who join the company are often hesitant to question the already successful ways that the company does things. To combat this Ed Catmull, cofounder and president, makes sure to bring up all the times when Pixar made bad choices. Ed encourages new employees to be curious and to challenge the way things are done from day one.

When it comes to leaders, Ed is absolutely correct when he says that leaders aren't supposed to prevent risk; instead they are supposed to build the capability to recover when failures inevitably occur. Shellye Archambeau is the former CEO of MetricStream, a computer software company with over 1,500 employees. She's also a board director at Verizon and Nordstrom. When I asked her about this, she said, "Those who learn and are able to take the best risks will drive the best performance. With all these things changing around you, unless you're a risk taker you are just not going to be able to capitalize on the opportunities that exist out there."

According to the research that Todd and his team have been working on, the three most important curiosity enhancers are autonomy (independence to accomplish tasks); responsibility (direct accountability over projects); and freedom (receiving the time necessary to explore new ideas). Do you and your employees have these things?

A recent study of 3,000 employees conducted by Francesca Gino at Harvard Business School found that "only about 24% reported feeling curious in their jobs on a regular basis, and about 70% said they face barriers to asking more questions at work" (Gino, 2018). The study also found that when curiosity is triggered, we make fewer decision-making errors, innovation increases, group conflict is reduced, and more open communication occurs, which leads to better team performance. According to Francesca, "Cultivating curiosity at all levels helps leaders and their employees adapt to uncertain market conditions and external pressures. When our curiosity is triggered, we think more deeply and rationally about decisions and come up with more-creative solutions. In addition, curiosity allows leaders to gain more respect from their followers and inspires employees to develop more-trusting and more-collaborative relationships with colleagues."

Francesca also discovered two common barriers to curiosity, especially when it comes to leadership. The first is that leaders believe that encouraging employees to be curious will make it harder to manage the company since employees will be allowed to explore their own areas of interest. Leaders also believe that curiosity would lead to disagreements, and the ability to make and execute decisions will slow down, thus costing the company money. The second barrier to curiosity is the quest for efficiency at the cost of exploration. This means that we become obsessed with delivering on our current projects and don't actually spend time asking questions or challenging conventional ways of working or thinking. Notice that the barriers to curiosity come down to money. When leaders prioritize money above all else, that is what they and their people will chase at the cost of everything and anything else.

In the 1990s Reed Hastings rented *Apollo 13,* starring Tom Hanks, on videocassette. It was a terrific film about the seventh manned mission intended to land on the moon; of course, that never happened. Unfortunately (or perhaps in this case very fortunately!) Reed misplaced the cassette and ended up with a $40 late fee. I too remember renting VHS cassettes in the 1980s and was always confused how a rental fee could be more than the cost to buy the cassette! My parents were never thrilled when they had to pay for my mistake.

As Reed was driving home, annoyed that he would have to tell his wife about his large late fee, a thought popped into his head. What if a video rental business was run like a health club? At a health club you pay a single monthly fee and then you go as often as you like, so why couldn't something similar exist for video rentals? Thus, Netflix was created. Today, Netflix is revolutionizing the entertainment industry and they are constantly asking themselves "what if?" "why?" and "how?" It's no surprise that curiosity is now one of Netflix's nine company values. Today Netflix has over 7,000 employees and is valued at over $152 billion.

Curious leaders are the ones who will challenge the status quo and change the world.

Super Perpetual Learning

Marissa Mayer, the former CEO of Yahoo! is on the board of Walmart. When we met she was recounting a story of an employee meeting between the global CEO of Walmart and the head of Walmart in the USA. During the meeting someone raised a hand and asked, "How do you spend your time together?" The two CEOs looked at each other and responded that they spend about three-quarters of their time together learning.

Explorers like Sir Ernest Henry Shackleton are perpetual learners. Any member of his crew could come and talk to him at any time, a type of "open door" policy that is often talked about in today's business world. Shackleton also put together a diverse team of individuals, including a biologist, artist, photographer, physicist, and meteorologist. These people came from different parts of the world, including the United States, Scotland, Britain, Germany, Australia, and India. He also encouraged members of his crew to cross-train beyond their respective fields and to learn about the different aspects of the ship and of the expedition. Shackleton himself spent time with whalers in Antarctica to learn about the Weddell Sea before setting off on the expedition. Even when he was younger he was a voracious reader, which ultimately sparked his passion for adventure. At age 16 he left school and since his family didn't have much money, he couldn't join the naval or the mercantile cadetships. Instead he apprenticed as a seaman on a sailing vessel, where he traveled the world, built relationships, and learned how to live, communicate, and collaborate with people from all walks of life. Eventually he traveled up the ranks until he was finally qualified to command his own ship (PBS, 2002).

Where you are today professionally as either a leader or an individual contributor is not where you will be in the future. Where your organization is today is also not where it will be in the future. As a leader, when you learn, so do the employees who work with you.

For decades, we have assumed that everything we needed to know to be successful professionally and personally would be taught to us either by our educational institutions or by organizations that employ and train us. That assumption was correct for a while, but it's already proven to be an outdated way of thinking and in the coming years it will be completely eradicated. By the time most people graduate from a four-year university, most of what they have learned is now obsolete.

Jo Ann Jenkins is the CEO of AARP, the world's largest nonprofit organization dedicated to empowering those who are fifty and older. The organization has over 38 million members and 2,300 employees. Jo Ann believes that learning is an invaluable asset:

Future leaders must instill a learning culture in their organizations. Organizations that are not continually learning and adapting will lose their competitive edge and ultimately won't survive. We've seen this over and over, and we'll see it happen more often and faster in the future. Moreover, organizations that do not develop a learning culture will not be able to hire and retain the kinds of talent they need to succeed. Those people will just go somewhere else. For future leaders, this type of perpetual learning is as essential as air and water.

Super perpetual learning has a few components to it. The first is quite obvious, it's learning new things on an ongoing basis. However, learning new things is also just a part of life. You know and have experienced things this year that you didn't know and experience the year before or the year before that. But perpetual learning isn't just about sitting idly by and letting new things come to you; it's about actively seeking out new things, people, and ideas, this is the crucial difference. The second component of perpetual learning is applying what you have learned on a regular basis and in new situations and scenarios, in the context of this book, a work environment. The last component of perpetual learning is understanding the results or the feedback of applying the things you have learned.

Learning typically happens in a few ways. The first is formal learning, which is basically what you are taught in a structured way, such as in an educational institution. The second is nonformal learning, which is more self-directed in nature but can still have some structure to it. For example, the PwC Digital Fitness app would be part of nonformal learning, as is listening to a podcast or TED talk with the goal of learning something new. The third is experiential or informal learning, which is what you might learn a bit more naturally. Think about how kids learn how to play tag. There is no structured curriculum or certification for tag but children learn by doing and experiencing. In the workplace this might be having a conversation with a co-worker or getting some insights via your company collaboration platform. This type of learning can also be intentional.

Formal learning is something that we as individuals typically do not control, which means that for leaders of the future the informal and experiential learning components are going to be essential. This also means that you need to have more accountability and responsibility over your own learning. Research things on your own time, watch TED talks to learn a new concept or idea, check out a podcast to hear insights from other business leaders, and make time to grab a coffee with co-workers. In his book *Informal Learning,* Jay Cross writes, "Workers learn more in the coffee room than in the classroom. They discover how to do their jobs through informal learning: talking to others, trial and error, and simply working with people in the know. Formal learning is the source of only 10 to 20 percent of what employees learn at work" (Cross, 2011).

One of the reasons why I started my podcast, *The Future of Work with Jacob Morgan,* is to learn. I get the opportunity to interview the world's top business leaders, authors, and futurists on a regular basis and ask them things that I'm genuinely curious about. To date I've interviewed over 300 leaders on my show and I don't plan on stopping any time soon. Leaders need to put themselves in positions of learning, which means not staying in a cubicle or your beautiful corner office.

The second component of being a super perpetual learner is applying what you learn. After all, it's great to learn something but in the business environment what you learn isn't that useful unless you can actually apply it. This can take many forms. Perhaps you watched a video or took some courses in your spare time on workflow auto-mation. Are you able to apply this in an environment where you have to keep taking information and copying and pasting it into different forms or documents? If you've been reading up on empathy or self-awareness, are you actually applying those concepts when dealing with customers or during tense situations with employees?

The final component of being a super perpetual learner is being aware of the feedback that you get and then reapplying what you learned from that feedback. Are those around you noticing any changes based on how you are applying the new things you learned and are you getting any feedback on it? Are you noticing any changes around you? Perhaps employees are more trusting of you as a leader and are more engaged in their jobs now that you have been practicing empathy and self-awareness. Maybe a co-worker praised you on your ability to defuse a difficult customer situation. Pay attention to these things and adjust as needed.

Organizations around the world are making super perpetual learn-ing a more explicit part of their culture and way of doing things. AT&T has over 270,000 employees around the world and recently made a startling discovery about its workforce. Half of the people who worked there did not have the necessary skills in a variety of areas that the company required and 100,000 of their workers were in jobs that required them to work with hardware that would likely not exist in the next ten years. This prompted the company to launch a massive initia-tive known as Future Ready, with a billion-dollar price tag. At the core of this effort is partnering with institutions like Coursera and Udacity to give employees easy online access to a variety of courses and programs that they can use to upskill themselves. These are often referred to as micro-degrees because they are highly specialized and focused and don't require the financial and time commitment of a four-year university. In fact, many of these programs can be completed in just a few days or weeks. The most fascinating part of the program is a platform they created called Career Intelligence.

If you've ever invested in the stock market, the platform you use allows you to see things like projections, trends, performance, and other relevant data you might need to make proper financial decisions. That's what AT&T designed Career Intelligence to be, but for skills and jobs. It's an online portal where employees have insights into the jobs that are available within the company, the skills that the particular job requires, the salary range, and whether the area is projected to grow or shrink in the coming years. Imagine if all employees had access to this kind of skills and jobs roadmap that aligns employees with the future direction of the company.

To date employees have completed over 3 million online upskilling courses and earned over 200,000 certifications.

The CEO of AT&T also went in front of his employees and basically told them that if they aren't willing to be perpetual learners, then they should leave the company. This means that while the company will provide the necessary tools, resources, and support for employees to be perpetual learners, sometimes employees might have to spend their own time and resources to learn something. This is the new world we live in, where we as individuals have to take more accountability and responsibility to learn the things that will make us successful in work and in life.

At the WD-40 company, which produces lubricants and cleaners, all employees are required to take the "Maniac Pledge":

I am responsible for taking action, asking questions, getting answers, and making decisions. I won't wait for someone to tell me. If I need to know, I'm responsible for asking. I have no right to be offended that I didn't "get this sooner." If I'm doing something others should know about, I'm responsible for telling them.

This puts the accountability of learning in the hands of everyone who works there. You will hear directly from their CEO Garry Ridge later in the book.

According to a study done by Udemy, 42% of millennials in the United States say that learning and development is the most important benefit when deciding where to work, second only to health insurance (Udemy, 2018). Another study done by HR and staffing firm Robert Half revealed that in the UK less than half of organizations run training and development programs to help build employees' skills and support career development (Robert Half, 2018).

As a future leader you must accept that when it comes to learning new things, your job is never done. Edwin Paxton Hood, an author from the 1800s, knew this many years ago:

Our whole life is an Education—we are "ever-learning," every moment of time, everywhere, under all circumstances something is being added to the stock of our previous attainments. Mind is always at work when once its operations commence. All men are learners, whatever their occupation, in the palace, in the cottage, in the park, and in the field. These are the laws stamped upon Humanity.

A Family of Super Perpetual Learners

When I think of being a super perpetual learner I think of my family.

I come from a family of immigrants. My parents (and surrounding family), who didn't know each other at the time despite living near each other, both fled from the Republic of Georgia in the late 1970s. They fled from the communist regime and from persecution for being Jewish. At the time my mom lived in a small two-room apartment with five family members. My maternal grandfather, Alex, was a music teacher and was a part of the Georgian Chamber Orchestra and was first cello in the Georgian Opera House. It was impossible to survive on the salary of one job so he had three. My maternal grandmother, Genya, taught Russian and history.

My dad also lived in a small apartment with his parents and his brother and sister. My paternal grandmother was a straight-A student and a very bright woman who gave up a potential career to raise her kids. I never met her. My paternal grandfather was a salesperson in a clothing store. I only met him once when he came to visit Los Angeles to make sure his son (my dad) was able to build a good life for himself and his family; he passed away shortly after his visit.

A few years ago I visited the Republic of Georgia, where I actually proposed to my wife. I was shocked and saddened to see where and how they had lived. I remember the stairs leading up to the apartment were not sturdy, the floor was rubble, and without question these were third-world living conditions—a far cry from the new middle-class life they worked tirelessly to create for themselves in Los Angeles, where they have a pool and much more that would seem a distant dream from the run-down streets of Tbilisi where they spent much of their lives.

When my mom and her family fled Georgia, they were allowed to take only $200 per person and had to leave behind their passports and all other documents like birth certificates, IDs, and diplomas. They snuck out a small family heirloom, a diamond, in the handle of a knife. My dad fled Georgia alone and left the rest of his family behind, clearly realizing that he might never see them again. In fact, he never saw his mother or brother again and saw his dad only once when his father made that visit to Los Angeles. His sister eventually moved to Los Angeles.

From Georgia they ended up in Vienna for a few weeks, before heading to Italy, where they spent 10 months. Italy was where my parents actually met. To make money my family sold camera equipment, linens, and Russian dolls at a flea market. After Italy my dad came to New Jersey and my mom's side of the family went to Australia. My mom enrolled in a university and my grandparents tried desperately to find work. My grandparents, Alex and Genya, held a variety of jobs. They both worked as cleaners in a chocolate factory and Alex also worked as a taxi driver, and musician (he played the cello for most of his life). My grandmother later worked as a waitress and a salesperson in a deli. Eventually she became a Russian and history teacher to politicians and military leaders in Australia.

Meanwhile, my dad caught the "American Dream" bug and wanted to move to the United States, so he came here first to get settled while my mom waited in Australia for word via letter for over two years (I didn't exist yet). Although his dream was to live in Los Angeles, my dad ended up in New Jersey, and started looking for jobs as a trained engineer. His big problem was that he didn't speak the language, nor did he know anything about American culture or society.

In New Jersey he lived in a low-income neighborhood but purposefully chose one where there were no Russian speakers so that he would be thrown out of his comfort zone and forced to learn and survive. For months he watched the Johnny Carson and Merv Griffin shows with an English-to-Russian translation dictionary so that he could understand and practice the words. Being an engineer, he would try to read some technical books, again with the aid of the dictionary. He spent over eight hours a day practicing while staring into a mirror so that he could work on his mouth movements for pronunciation. After all, it's not enough to simply know the words; you also need to be able to say them correctly and without a heavy Russian accent. He also spent time learning about the celebrities on TV so that he could understand more about American culture and society. He made sure to devote time each day to work on his handwriting since computers were still not mainstream. He worked hard to assimilate into American life and culture, as did my mom, who studied philosophy at Melbourne University and learned English by memorizing and singing popular American songs. Her little sister— my Aunt Irena—had to start first grade without speaking a word of English as well. She was bullied until she could finally start to communicate with the English-speaking kids.

This was all before the internet and all the wonderful tools and resources we have at our disposal now. My dad is an old-school super perpetual learner. He told me a story of how he saved up money to fly to Los Angeles for an interview; upon getting to the company, the secretary told him that the manager who was supposed to interview him was on vacation in Lake Tahoe. My dad had several experiences where he was given the runaround. Finally he went for an interview at another organization and with his broken

English he answered the questions as best as he could. After the interview the guy sitting across from him said, "Thanks for your time, we'll get back to you." At this point my dad had enough of being pushed around and told to wait, and he said something along the lines of, "No, tell me now. You've interviewed me and talked to me, you know if you're going to hire me or not." The interviewer paused for a minute and then stretched out his hand and said, "Congratulations, you have the job." It turns out the guy was the president and owner of the company and he liked my dad's honesty, determination, and desire to be a part of the company. At the time my dad's last name was Mamisashvili, but no one could pronounce it when they wanted to page him on the PA system. So my dad decided he wanted an American-sounding name that started with the letter M, and thus our family name changed to Morgan.

Even today my mom and dad are constantly pushing themselves to learn. Their personal values include living a life of continuous improvement, growth, and learning. They both inspire me when I think of being a super perpetual learner. My dad still has that dictionary that he keeps at work to remind himself to keep learning new things and growing, and occasionally he uses it to look up a new English word. My mom is constantly reading new books, going to seminars, and traveling all over the world, eager to chase new experiences and knowledge. She actually went back to school a few years ago to become a marriage and family therapist after spending the majority of her career as a computer programmer. She was miserable and decided it was time for a change. They never stopped being hungry for more, and I am the same.

Growth Mindset

When was the last time you failed at something? It could have been a test, a project, a competition of some sort, or perhaps just something personal. After you failed, did you feel that you could improve or did you get discouraged and decide that you can't progress?

Carol S. Dweck, a professor at Stanford University, has been studying the power of mindset for decades. In her best-selling book

Mindset: The New Psychology of Success, she shared her findings; it's worth a read. In studying how students approach failure, she noticed that some are able to rebound and excel where others are not. What separated these two groups was their mindset. According to Carol, we possess two types of mindsets: fixed and growth (Dweck, 2016). Those with a fixed mindset believe that things like creativity, intelligence, or personality are the way they are and that there is nothing they can do about it. These individuals also try to avoid challenges; they give up easily when faced with obstacles; they often view effort as a fruitless exercise; they don't believe in constructive negative feedback; and they are threatened by the success of others (Mindset Works, n.d.).

On the other hand, those with a growth mindset believe that things like creativity, intelligence, and personality can be developed and there is always room for growth and improvement. These individuals embrace challenges, overcome obstacles they are faced with, believe in effort as a path toward mastery, see constructive negative feedback as something to learn from, and are inspired by the success of others and try to learn from them. Satya Nadella from Microsoft actually built the company culture around this very mindset.

Those with a fixed mindset are constantly looking for approval, but those with a growth mindset are constantly looking to learn and grow. Reading the descriptions above, what kind of mindset do you think you possess: growth or fixed? Well it turns out that you're both – we all are. The type of mindset can change depending on the environment or the situation we are confronted with. Carol uses an example of someone who might frequently be in a growth mindset, but upon meeting someone who is more successful or better at something than they are, their mindset shifts toward being fixed. The point is to identify what triggers your mindset to shift and what actually happens to you. Maybe you get anxious or nervous, your body language might shift, or perhaps your tone changes; in my case, I find myself getting angry or frustrated. Once you identify your triggers and your responses, then you can figure out how to keep your mindset from moving from growth to fixed and also how to shift your mindset from fixed to growth.

Graybar is a Fortune 500 company that specializes in supply chain management services. They have almost 10,000 employees and are led by CEO Kathy Mazzarelli, who has been at the company longer than I've been alive. She's one of only two dozen female CEOs who represent the Fortune 500. Kathy started out as a customer service and sales representative and has worked in sales, marketing, customer service, human resources, corporate accounts, strategic planning, operations, and product management, among other areas. She knows that business inside and out and one of the reasons why she became CEO is because she's a super perpetual learner. In her own words, "leaders must possess a growth mindset in which they are constantly learning, innovating and exploring new ideas. They must learn to ask different questions and analyze issues critically, rather than relying on past experience and long-held assumptions to make decisions."

Explorers are masters of this. Shackleton viewed his obstacles not as failures but as things he had to overcome, challenges he had to conquer. If he had only a fixed mindset, then surely he and the rest of his crew would have died during their expedition. You must believe that you always have the potential to grow, to learn, and to improve. If you believe this and show this, then so will those around you.

Adaptability and Agility

On the back of every shampoo bottle you can find very clear instructions: wash, rinse, and repeat. This was the approach that leaders have always been encouraged to use. What they learned in schools and in their MBA programs would be applied at one company and then recycled in every other team or at every other company they joined. It was a leadership template. However, as CEOs around the world have identified, the pace of change is one of the strongest trends shaping the future of leadership and work. This means that leaders can no longer follow this approach. What worked in the past won't work in the future.

Meet Gary Goldberg, the CEO of Newmont Mining, who leads a team of over 13,000 employees. He's one of the many CEOs who stressed the importance of adaptability: "Future leaders must be adaptable in order to understand trends that increasingly impact how people choose to invest their time. This includes everything from robotics to climate change."

Ernest Shackleton had to be nimble and agile in order to save the lives of his entire crew. His goal had to shift from exploring the Antarctic to saving the lives of his men. Most leaders have a very hard time changing course over short time horizons. In Shackleton's case, new obstacles were thrown his way on a daily basis, whether it was losing his ship and living on an ice floe, finding ways to keep up the morale of his men, or coming up with how to give his shoes traction so that he could hike in the snow to reach the whaling station. Leaders can plan, read, and analyze as much as they want, but if you are constantly set in your ways and aren't able to adapt to the changes happening around you, then you won't be able to lead successfully.

John Pettigrew is the CEO of National Grid, a British multinational electricity and gas utility company with almost 23,000 employees globally. He summarized this concept nicely in our interview: "Change and disruption are becoming commonplace. Leaders will therefore need to be able to do things quickly and will need to pivot regularly, meaning they will need to be agile."

There is, however, a difference between simply being able to cope with change versus actually being able to adapt to it and thrive in the face of it. Coping just means you are keeping your head above water, but you must do more than that. In order to be adaptable and nimble you must have humility and vulnerability, knowing that you are not the smartest person in the room, that you will need to ask for help and admit you don't know how to do something, and being able to surround yourself with people who are smarter than you.

Sylvia Metayer is the CEO of Worldwide Corporate Services at Sodexo, a facilities management and food services company. As a whole, the company has 460,000 employees globally and Sylvia is responsible for over 174,000 thousand of them. When we spoke she drew a great analogy between yoga (something she does a lot of) and being agile. Anyone who has tried yoga knows that you can't do all of the positions on day one. It takes time and practice before you can put your body in the various required yoga poses. The same concept applies to leaders; you need to be willing to work on getting outside your comfort zone, adapting your skills and mindsets to the new world of work. It takes time and practice but you will get there.

How Leaders Can Develop The Mindset of the Explorer

Sir Ernest Henry Shackleton once said, "The only true failure would be not to explore at all."

Throughout history, explorers have risked their lives and have traveled to the farthest corners of the earth and beyond, for a variety of reasons. These included everything from the spread of religion to the search for goods, claims to new land, or fame and wealth. But the truth is that exploration is part of human nature, our constant quest and obsession with asking questions and seeking answers; we have done so since our existence and will continue to do so. Organizations who try to stifle this are literally going against one of our core human qualities.

You already have that explorer mindset in you somewhere, but some do a better job of letting it free whereas others try to keep it hidden and subdued. Not only is it your responsibility to be an explorer yourself, but you must also help create a company of explorers. Mark Smucker from the J.M. Smucker Company does this by sharing at least one article with his company each week about what's going on outside of their four walls that could impact them. According to Mark, this keeps the organization in tune with any external forces that might impact the business. It's a simple act but one that Mark says is crucial.

As a leader, one of the most impactful things you can do is ask questions and challenge the status quo. It's likely that your organization has certain customer or employee policies, procedures, and ways of doing things that have been around for decades, long before you ever joined the organization. But if, as the world's top business leaders have identified, the pace of change is one of the greatest trends shaping leadership and work, then it's time to revisit how work gets done and how we lead.

If you ask questions and challenge convention, then so will your team members.

This comes from Peter Simpson, the CEO of Anglian Water, a utility company in the UK with almost 5,000 employees:

As a leader, you must be comfortable with creating innovative cultures. This means being open to and actually encouraging people at every level and every part of the business to ask questions and challenge you as a leader with new ideas and ways of thinking. Asking questions and challenging a leader and the status quo used to be viewed as a problem; today this needs to be celebrated.

Curiosity specifically also requires time and space. If you are constantly feeling suffocated with tasks, projects, and meetings, then you won't be able to ask the questions that will help drive change. We are obsessed with constantly telling people how busy we are and we pride ourselves on getting so many emails each day that we can never get to what is now known as "inbox zero." When someone is this busy, they are viewed as being important, but instead we should view them as lacking time management skills and being a control freak who can't let others make decisions. What if, instead of obsessing over how busy we are, we obsessed over how we can give ourselves more time to be curious.

Give yourself time each day to be without technology and without meetings just to think and ask questions. There's no set time allotment for this but if you can do an hour a day that's great; if not, go for 30 minutes. As a leader you also want to make sure your team has this same opportunity. Inherent in this is the importance of being able to say no. Steve Jobs famously said, "People think focus means saying yes to the thing you've got to focus on. But that's not what it means at all. It means saying no to the hundred other good ideas that there are. You have to pick carefully. I'm actually as proud of the things we haven't done as the things I have done. Innovation is saying no to 1,000 things." It's easy to say yes to everything, but most of us do so at the expense of saying no to ourselves; this is a terrible way to live and lead.

For many years I would say yes to everything and everyone. Want to "pick my brain"? Sure! Have a few questions you want to ask? Absolutely, send them over! Want to just have a chat to say hello? Of course, I'd love to. Want me to come to your event just to meet someone and get "exposure"? Sounds great!

After saying yes all the time I realized that at the end of the day, not only would I feel exhausted but I wouldn't actually have gotten anything done. As soon as I stopped saying yes to everyone and everything else and started saying yes to myself, my business grew.

As Todd Kashdan found with his research, curiosity can also be stressful, and when that happens leaders may misconstrue curiosity for something negative. With the rapid pace of change we are all experiencing, being able to understand when you are stressed and having mechanisms to cope with that stress is also helpful. It can be something like meditation, exercising, playing chess, or listening to music, but make sure you have tools at your disposal to help you. This is also why many organizations invest in various health and well-being programs.

Shift your focus on to the longer time horizon. Shackleton and his crew spent over a year without stepping foot on land, yet today's business leaders are obsessed with quarterly profits. You can't be an explorer if you're constantly tied to the dock. A pure focus on the short term stands in stark contrast with the explorer mindset that's all about experimentation, testing out ideas, growth, and adaptability. Often this won't yield any results in the short term and may in fact produce negative results. Leaders must be able to stand up to the enormous quarterly pressures they are faced with to focus on the longer-term horizon.

Explorers are also super perpetual learners, but to embrace this you must tell yourself that this is the kind of leader you are or want to be; it's a conscious decision. Once you have done that you can start by getting rid of the assumption that what you learned in school or in your organization is going to be all you need for personal and professional success. There is no more "wash, rinse, repeat." Thinking like this is a killer for leaders. Instead, you must accept that you are ultimately responsible for your own learning and development in this rapidly changing world, as are the employees you work with (although you can ultimately support them by giving them access to tools and resources). Chess is virtually a limitless game; there are more possible moves in a game of chess than there are atoms in the universe. Leadership is also a limitless game, which means that while you may never be perfect, you can always get better, and this can't happen unless you are a super perpetual learner.

The good news, though, is that you can leverage the many tools and resources at your disposal to learn new and relevant things. Your organization might provide some resources here and if it does, take full advantage of them. If not, turn to TED talks, YouTube, Udemy, Coursera, or the many free programs provided by companies like MIT, Stanford, Harvard, and many others (check out www.edx.org).

There are different ways we learn and one of the most effective ways is through relationships. Talk to your customers, partners, suppliers, employees, and when you can, your competitors. You can't learn in isolation and you also can't learn when you are surrounded only by people who think, act, and look like you.

Apply the various things you learn even if the end result doesn't yield success. You can learn from the mistake and move forward. Remember the concept of a growth versus a fixed mindset and be aware of the triggers that cause you to shift from one mindset to the other.

As Patrick Doyle, the former CEO of Domino's Pizza, told me, "The successful future leaders will be those who are willing to take risks and be bold. Future leaders must be willing to get things wrong but then have the ability to adapt and move on. It's not the mistakes and failures that matter; it's how you respond to them."

During the course of your career you will likely have to reinvent yourself a few times and perhaps you will even change careers. But regardless of what you do or where you end up, I can promise you that the mindset of the explorer will serve you well. Think of yourself as the Ernest Shackleton of leadership and embark on your journey.

13
The Chef

One person is largely responsible for bringing French cuisine to the American public: Julia Child. Not only did she bring gourmet cooking to America, but she removed the mystique and the perception of French cooking as inaccessible, strange, and even too exotic. She wanted everyone to appreciate the great food and chefs that came from France. Julia was born in 1912 in Pasadena, California, not too far away from where I grew up in Granada Hills. She attended Smith College, where she graduated in 1934 with a degree in history. While at Smith she got her first culinary experience as the chair of the refreshment committee for the senior prom and fall dance.

Julia had a short stint writing advertising copy for a furniture store in New York City but World War II soon began and she wanted to serve. Julia tried to join the Women's Army Corps but at 6'2" she was told that she was too tall, so she joined the Office of Strategic Services instead. This took her to places like Sri Lanka and Kunming, China. Her first foray into cooking came when she was asked to come up with a way to keep sharks from setting off underwater explosives, which were being used to blow up German U-boats. She experimented with different ideas and eventually came up with a repellent that, when sprinkled into the water, would ward off sharks.

While in China Julia met Paul; they married and eventually moved to Paris, where Paul had previously lived.

Julia fell in love with the cuisine in Paris. She attended the famous Le Cordon Bleu cooking school and worked with many of the Parisian master chefs. She really gained fame when she coauthored the 726-page *Mastering the Art of French Cooking,* along with Simone Beck and Louisette Bertholle. The book blew up and led to her writing various articles for popular magazines and eventually her own TV show, *The French Chef,* which aired for over a decade and helped pave the way for the many cooking shows and contests that we enjoy today. Julia also went on to create the American Institute of Wine and Food in 1981 and the Julia Child Foundation for Gastronomy and Culinary Arts in 1995. Julia was not only a lover of food but also an inspiration for many around the world who wanted to learn about food and become better cooks. Julia passed away in 2004, just two days before her 92nd birthday. Her last meal was French onion soup.

When I think of Julia, I think of a master of balance. Not only did she have to balance ingredients to make delicious dishes but she also had to balance taste with nutrition and French cooking with American expectations and culture. Her ability to balance helped make her successful. Any great chef will tell you that one of the things that makes a dish taste amazing is the balance of ingredients. Too much of one ingredient in a dish will throw off the entire flavor profile and too little of an ingredient will make the dish taste bland. Creating the perfect dish and balancing flavors and ingredients is as much an art as it is a science. Leaders of the future must have the mindset of a chef.

We Need More HumanIT

During my interviews I started to notice that CEOs were constantly referencing the balance that must exist between the human side of work and the technology side of work. In other words, leaders must be chefs who balance these two most crucial ingredients in any business. I call this HumanIT (humanity). (See Figure 13.1.)

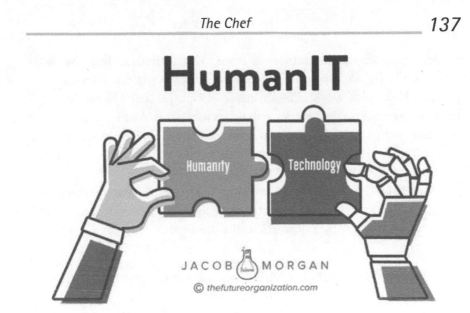

FIGURE **13.1** HUMANIT.

Nancy Brown is the CEO of the American Heart Association, which is the nation's largest and oldest voluntary health organization, with over 3,000 employees. Their mission is "To be a relentless force for a world of longer, healthier lives." Nancy told me:

> There's so much focus on technology and how it's going to change the workflow, the work product, and how we communicate with customers and employees. It's vital to not lose sight, however, that the world still goes around because of relationships between people. I think current and future leaders need to be able to work both with people and technology, which will require more collaboration and teamwork.

The humanity or human side of work is primarily about things like purpose and caring for the employees who work with or for you. It can include building relationships, making friends at work, employee experience, and psychological safety. The human side of work is where things like ideas, relationships, loyal customers, leaders, and social impact come from. The human side of work is ultimately why we work for the organizations we are a part of.

The IT side of work is much more about the technology in terms of tools, software, hardware, apps, devices, and AI and automation we can use to actually get our jobs done. The IT side of work is where things like efficiency, productivity, speed, and often cost and decision-making take place.

Kiran Mazumdar-Shaw is the chairperson, managing director, and founder of Biocon, a biotechnology company with around 10,000 employees. I really like how she talks about this:

A leader of the future will have to be astute enough to balance automation with the human touch. They have to decide what types of tasks to automate so that people can spend more time on high-value activities and also decide which businesses will continue to benefit from human judgment.

Relying purely on technology while eliminating any human components will create an organization where employees don't want to work and where customers likely won't want to transact. On the flipside, relying purely on humans without much modern technology will create an organization that is slow to move, makes poor decisions, and isn't as efficient or productive as it could be. Neither of these scenarios are optimal. Leaders are charged with finding what that balance is, which is just as much an art as it is a science. Leaders must remember that technology is simply a tool, and how that tool is applied is what matters. It's important to view technology as a partner for humans, not a replacement for them. This is purely a choice. If, as a leader, you view technology as something that is designed to replace humans and eliminate them from your organization, then that is exactly the type of organization you will create. However, if you view technology as a human partner, then that is ultimately what will happen. Technology doesn't control you – you control it.

As a leader you must embrace technology while balancing being purpose-driven and truly caring about those around you and the people you are lucky enough to serve. Think like a chef: your teams and organization are the dish, and you want it to look and taste amazing, which means you need to get that balance of ingredients just right.

Embracing Technology

"Leaders who understand how to use technology and all the things that come with it, like data and analytics, are going to have a real advantage in the future. This is already true today but will be an absolute requirement in the coming years. To be a future leader you must embrace technology, not run from it." This is what Mike Capone told me; he's the CEO of Qlik, a business intelligence and data visualization company with over 2,000 employees globally.

The CEOs I interviewed for this book made it abundantly clear that fearing technology or being skeptical and hesitant about it will get you nowhere. What I quoted from Mike above is what dozens of other CEOs told me. However, leaders are often tempted to rely too much on technology to cut costs, improve productivity, and increase efficiency, but at the expense of making their organization less human. Interestingly enough, we don't really hear about leaders who are tempted to make their organizations more human at the expense of technology. In fact, we can and should use technology to make our organization even more human.

This is an important point to stress because many organizations use technology simply for the sake of having it. For example, have you ever dialed a 1-800 number and interacted with a "smart customer service agent"? When I get those on the phone I start mashing buttons relentlessly until the bot gets confused and says, "I'm sorry, I didn't understand you. Let me transfer you to a customer service representative who can help you." Why not just give me the human to begin with? Or how about those chatbots that now every company seems to be using. Has anyone ever found a chatbot helpful? Nope! Technology shouldn't be used to put an additional layer between people; it should be used as a way to remove a layer to get people closer together.

Jim Loree is the CEO of Stanley Black & Decker, a manufacturer of industrial tools and household hardware that has been around since 1843. Today they have around 60,000 employees. Jim is a big believer in making organizations more human: "The leader's job will be to humanize everything. Humans in the end require the human touch to be inspired. They can't be inspired by interacting with robots and artificial intelligence."

As a leader you must understand the abilities and limits of both humans and technology. The future is not about technology versus humans; it's about technology working with humans against a problem. However, this only works if you understand what humans and technology can and cannot do. We are already starting to see the integration of more technology in many aspects of our jobs and lives, whether that's robots on the manufacturing floor, smart assistants in our homes and offices, or bots that can automate routine aspects of work. This will only increase dramatically over the next decade, and understandably it can cause fear, tension, and even resentment. Balance between keeping the organization human and using technology to help those humans while making the organization more efficient and productive is what is required from leaders.

Ace Hardware Corporation is the world's largest retailer-owned hardware cooperative with over 100,000 associates around the world and it's consistently ranked as one of the top companies for customer experience. CEO John Venhuizen told me, "When a human being interacts with another human being, in an emotionally connected way, it stirs something in them. It engenders loyalty."

Most businesses in the world, whether dealing with customers or with employees, still fundamentally operate on basic human interaction and engagement. The difference is that now, with technology, we can focus even more on the human aspects of work while letting technology handle the more mundane aspects of our jobs.

A recent article titled "Collaborative Intelligence: Humans and AI Are Joining Forces" points out that in their research of 1,500 organizations, the ones that achieved the most significant performance improvements were those where humans and technology worked together (Wilson, 2018). Think of how you might build a team today. Ideally you would put people together who complement one another's strengths. The same is true when working with technology. For example, humans will excel at things like creativity, making human connections, and leadership, but technology will dominate in areas like data analysis, speed, and decision-making. As the authors point out, these are both necessary and required to have.

The consumer goods company Unilever has over 160,000 employees around the world and they have recently implemented technology in the form of AI to help with hiring. In any given year the company recruits over 30,000 people and processes almost 2 million job applications. This used to be done manually and, as you can imagine, required intensive time and resources. Now, when a prospective employee applies to work at Unilever, they are asked to play a series of games on their phone or desktop. These games actually collect a lot of data about the people playing them, such as their logic, risk profiles, rational reasoning, and the like. Then all of this data is used to see if they are a good match for the job they applied for. According to Leena Nair, the chief HR officer at Unilever, this has saved over 70,000 hours for employees. The second stage of the interview process involves a 30-minute video interview, but here too technology is used not only for natural language processing to understand what the prospective candidate is saying but also to look at body language. Again, all of this data is used to determine who might be a good fit. Humans ultimately make the decision on whether a candidate is a good fit for the role.

Once employees start at the company, they are given access to Unabot, a chatbot that acts like a digital co-worker. You can ask Unabot about parking availability, find out the timing of shuttle buses, get information about benefits, or even learn when the next salary review is going to take place. Some have argued that this is relying too much on technology, which is certainly a fair criticism. There's a delicate balance here, but the ultimate goal is always to use technology to help people and to allow the organization to be more human. If technology isn't doing that, then reconsider how it is being used.

There are certainly other areas where technology is clearly benefiting humans. Unilever also launched something called FLEX Experiences, which is an AI-powered platform that allows employees to find relevant open career opportunities across the organization in real-time. These suggested opportunities are based on an employee's profile, such as their strengths, skills, and experiences, and also takes into account their career aspirations and goals. This is something organizations used to do manually and not very well. Now, thanks to technology, Unilever is putting the power of career growth and development directly into the hands of employees.

David Meek is the CEO of IPSEN, a pharmaceutical company with over 6,000 employees. He does a great job of putting this into context:

People keep saying, "Oh, technology, technology." Well, I've never had lunch with technology or built relationships with technology, have you? I've had lunch and built relationships with people. You can have great assets and great technology but if you don't have great people, then you aren't going to maximize those things. It's the human and emotional intelligence component that is crucial today and will be more so in the future. I'll take an emotionally intelligent person over a piece of software any time. ... Combine the two and unleash breakthrough results!

By all means, embrace technology, but remember never to put technology ahead of the hearts, minds, and souls of the people who work with you and for your organization.

Purpose-Driven and Caring

Although CEOs specifically identified being purpose-driven as a core attribute for future leaders, during my many interviews I realized that they weren't just talking about purpose from the perspective of connecting the work that employees do to outcomes; they were also talking about the meaning that employees get. As I mentioned earlier, most of us tend to put the words "purpose" and "meaning" together, so I think it's important to make that clarification here.

Paul Polman shared this with me during our interview: "I have always passionately believed that the single most important attribute of a leader is to be driven by a deeper sense of purpose. You have to connect with the people and world around you, commit to a cause bigger than your own self-interest and, crucially, put yourself to the service of others." Paul is the former CEO of Unilever (he stepped down in 2019) and has been an avid proponent of purpose and meaning in the workplace for much of his career. In fact, he was one of the pioneers of championing this in the corporate world.

In the 1970s famed economist and Nobel Memorial Prize winner Milton Friedman said, "There is one and only one social responsibility of business – to use its resources and engage in activities designed to increase its profits so long as it stays within the rules of the game." In fact, he wrote a now-famous article for the *New York Times Magazine* called, "The Social Responsibility of Business is to Increase Its Profits" (Friedman, 1970). This has been the primary doctrine for leaders around the world for decades. Fortunately, not everyone agreed with Milton Friedman. In 1979 then – Quaker Oats president Kenneth Mason refuted this notion by saying, "Making a profit is no more the purpose of a corporation than getting enough to eat is the purpose of life. Getting enough to eat is a requirement of life; life's purpose, one would hope, is somewhat broader and more challenging. Likewise with business and profit."

While purpose and meaning were among the top trends shaping the future of leadership, being purpose-driven and caring is also a mindset that leaders of the future must possess. But being purpose-driven and caring isn't at odds with creating a successful organization; the two actually complement each other.

James Downing, MD, is the CEO of St. Jude Children's Research Hospital, which has around 5,000 employees. The organization focuses on the research and treatment of pediatric cancer and other life-threatening childhood diseases worldwide. I recently had the opportunity to speak with their leadership team and tour their facilities to see the amazing work they do. Dr. Downing told me, "You're not there to advance your career, you're not there to get accolades to be a great leader. Your job is to take care of the workforce, to attribute and to make sure that you are providing people with the environment that allows them to contribute maximally."

A purpose-driven and caring leader believes that the organization should be profitable as a way to contribute to society, whereas many leaders today look for ways that society can help make the organization more profitable. It's a complete reversal in thinking. Hamdi Ulukaya is the CEO and founder of Chobani, the top-selling Greek yogurt brand in America and operator of the largest yogurt facility in the world. In his recent TED talk he said, "Today's business book says: business exists to maximize profit for the shareholders. I think that's the dumbest idea I've ever heard in my life. In reality, business should take care of their employees first" (Ulukaya, 2019). Recently he announced that he would be giving shares of the company to all of the over 2,000 employees who work there. Some people called it a PR stunt but Hamdi was very clear that this was simply a gift to the people who helped create and build his company and he wanted to say thank you by taking care of them. There's no doubt Hamdi could have used the many shares he gave away to keep more money for himself and the company, but he didn't. He took care of his people before worrying about increasing profits. That's what being a purpose-driven and caring leader is all about. It's why people work for Chobani and why the company has had such success. Hamdi isn't a purpose-driven and caring leader to make more money, but because he is purpose-driven and caring it allows the business to grow – there's a big difference.

Mandy Ginsberg is the CEO of Match Group, which employs over 1,400 people and owns several popular dating websites, including Tinder, Match.com, OkCupid, and others. During our discussion Mandy expressed this very idea:

My philosophy is that you have to love and respect the people you work with to be a great leader. You have to want to see people really succeed in order to lead them. I think that people in an organization need to know that someone is looking out for them and their career, in order to build loyalty. For me, it's about finding the people who are great, and building a real working relationship with them so you know how to keep them motivated and inspired, and they, in turn, continue to deliver phenomenal results for you.

"Love and respect" – how often do you hear a leader utter this phrase about those they work with? How many times have you said or thought this about those you work with?

How Leaders Can Develop The Mindset of the Chef

At the very base of this mindset is the understanding that your job as a leader isn't just about making the business more money. You need to look beyond the organization to see how the work you are doing is impacting society, local communities, and the world. Again, from my interview with Paul Polman:

The world is arguably more chaotic and unpredictable than at any time in recent memory. Gross inequality has left billions behind without access to basic human needs, such as work, education, healthcare, and sanitation. Ideological differences are straining national cohesion, which has fueled mass migration and the refugee crisis. The fourth industrial revolution, defined by rapid technological advancements, is fundamentally transforming industries and the world of work. And, most alarmingly, we are facing a climate emergency that threatens the future of humanity. This combination of volatility and change has understandably bred huge insecurity and disillusionment and led to a world where trust – particularly in political leaders and governments – is extremely low. These are enormous challenges for future leaders, who must find a way to reconnect with citizens and restore confidence in a reformed economic and social system that is more inclusive, equitable, and sustainable.

This means that you need to care, really care. But this is the tough part; how do you get people to care? I wish I knew the answer, and that I could make all of the leaders in the world start caring more about the human side of work.

Simply telling people to care doesn't mean that they will. From what I have observed in purpose-driven and caring leaders, they have a few things in common (see Figure 13.2). First, most of their time is not spent in their office. They are constantly out talking to customers, communities, and employees, and when I say employees I don't just mean other executives; I mean everyone, including the ground-floor employees. Second, these leaders practice a great deal of empathy and self-awareness (both of which we will explore later in this book). Third, these leaders have a cause or a reason for being that they fight for, something that they care deeply about. It could be climate change, refugees, diversity and equality, underprivileged children, or any number of other causes. Leaders must fight for something beyond the business. Fourth, these leaders see their employees

FIGURE **13.2** TRAITS OF PURPOSE–DRIVEN AND CARING LEADERS.

as human beings, a theme I have mentioned several times in this book. Employees are not just numbers on a spreadsheet, they are not cogs, they are not job descriptions – they are people, just like you. Finally, leaders realize that being purpose-driven and caring is a choice that only they can make.

Viktor E. Frankl, the author of the profound book *Man's Search for Meaning*, wrote, "between stimulus and response there is a space. In that space is our power to choose our response. In our response lies our growth and our freedom" (Frankl, 1984). Leaders are responsible and accountable for the choices they make; it's up to you to make the right one.

How do chefs balance the ingredients that go into a dish? They typically do two things. The first is to taste frequently. If you watch a chef cook, you will notice that they are constantly tasting whatever it is they're making to see if it's too bland, spicy, sweet, or if it needs a little something. Chefs also pay attention to what others say about their dish. What's the feedback that customers provide? Do they finish the dish when they order it? Does it get talked about a lot? Is it a best-seller? All of these things matter.

As a leader you must understand that people always come first, no exceptions. Technology always comes second – again, no exceptions.

The same techniques that chefs use can also be applied to leadership. First, taste often. This means that you are constantly paying attention to what is happening in your organization and are always looking for ways that you can augment your human workforce with technology (not replace them!). If you see employees are struggling in an area where they are constantly having to do routine soul-sucking work, then perhaps you can add a bit more of the technology ingredient into the mix. Professional services firm are a great example. At Deloitte they use technology to help with things like processing tax returns or providing risk assessments. When an organization typically sells a business unit, it used to take dozens of employees over 6 months to review legal documents looking for a change of control. Today, it takes a team of around 6–8 employees less than 30 days to do the same work. They also use technology to go through millions of lines of accounts payable and receivable data during mergers and acquisitions, something that used to take over four months and now takes less than a week. Accenture similarly automated over 17,000 jobs in accounting and finance without losing a single employee. The work these employees did revolved around number crunching, something that technology can clearly do better, faster, and more accurately than a human. These 17,000 employees were upskilled to focus on the strategic aspects of their jobs, such as helping clients understand what the numbers mean and providing advice and guidance on what actions to take.

If you see that one area is overly focused on technology and is missing some of the human components, then you can add that ingredient. Elon Musk, CEO of Tesla, recently shared that he relied too much on technology and automation in his manufacturing facilities, which led to what he said was a "crazy, complex network of conveyor belts." Quality control also went down dramatically and customers started receiving cars with damaged parts. As a result, their entire approach to manufacturing was scrapped and re-created with a much stronger emphasis on humans who are aided by technology.

As a leader, you can only taste the dishes if you are in the kitchen with the rest of the team. You can't sit in an office far removed from everyone else and then comment on how a dish looks or tastes. You need to be right there with an apron on and spoon in hand.

The second piece of this is paying attention to feedback that you get from those around you. This could be customers, employees, partners, and the like. For example, in Elon's case he clearly saw that his customers were not happy with the cars they were receiving so he made a change. In fact, Elon frequently makes changes based on what his customers and employees tell him. Recently he rolled out "Dog Mode," a customer suggestion that keeps unattended pets in vehicles comfortable while also displaying a message on the car dashboard that says the owner will be back soon and also shows the temperature in the car; this way, people who pass by the car won't be worried about the pets inside.

Simply listening or collecting data will only get you so far, though. As a leader, what you do with the feedback you get is just as important as getting the feedback. What good is information if you don't do anything with it? If you want to practice the mindset of the chef, then make sure that those around you are going to hold you accountable.

Fully embrace technology and the potential it can have on your organization and leave fear at the door. However, when doing so, focus on the strengths of your teams and look at how technology may be able to supplement and further enhance those strengths. Try to understand how technology might help your employees or customers and make them feel more valued. Technology has tremendous potential to create better experiences for employees and for customers.

Now, get cooking!

14
The Servant

The word "servant" dates back to the thirteenth century and comes from the Anglo-French word *servir,* which means to serve or to be useful. I find it fascinating that throughout history servants have been considered lower-class individuals typically without a higher set of skills and abilities. These individuals worked for those who were wealthier, more connected, and perceived to be smarter and better than they were. Ironically enough, centuries after the word was even introduced, it's the servant mindset that is among the most valuable for leaders to possess; it's why we keep hearing about this concept of servant leadership.

Being a leader doesn't mean that you get to sit at the top of the pyramid and tell everyone else what to do. It means that you stand at the bottom of the pyramid and help prop up everyone else. This is in stark contrast to what the business world is used to. Doug DeVos, the president of Amway, which employs around 20,000 people, put this rather simply and poignantly: "Leadership is serving those around you in a way that helps them be the best they can be and therefore achieves the results for your organization or team."

Service orientation for a leader manifests in four crucial ways: service to your leaders, service to your team, service to your customers, and service to yourself. Most of the time when we hear about service orientation or being a servant leader it's in the context of how leaders can serve their employees; while this is important, it's just a small part of the bigger picture. There's also not much discussion about serving the leaders themselves, which is another piece that is frequently missed. Service orientation is a two-way street and in your organization ideally everyone will be serving everyone else regardless of rank, title, or function. When all four of these components come together, then a true service orientation mindset is developed not just for leaders but for the entire organization. It's about being human.

Service to Your Leaders

In this particular context I'm referring to serving people for whom you work, if any. Most employees in an organization work for or with a leader, even if they are leaders themselves. Serving your leaders means helping make sure you have a good relationship with them and that you are there to support them and, when possible, make their lives easier. For example, if your leader is about to step into a meeting and you have some useful information they need to know about, tell them. If your leader is stressed out and overwhelmed with projects and you have extra resources, offer to help. One of the best ways you can help serve your leaders is by finding solutions to problems. If you notice that something isn't working, don't just point it out; come up with a solution to solve the problem.

A recent study published in the *Washington Post* found that people who think of their immediate supervisor as more of a partner as opposed to a typical boss are significantly happier both in their day-to-day lives and with their lives overall (Ingraham, 2018). Having a good relationship with your leader is not only important for your career but also for your own well-being. Swedish researchers from the Stress Research Institute in Stockholm studied 3,100 men during a ten-year period. The men who reported having leaders they didn't respect were 60% more likely to suffer a heart attack or another life-threatening cardiac condition (Nyberg, 2008).

Leaders are human just like you. They get burned out, stressed out, upset, frustrated, and happy just like everyone else.

Service to Your Team

Whenever an athlete like LeBron James, Roger Federer, or Serena Williams gets interviewed, they say same the same thing: "I couldn't have done it without my team." They typically give credit to their team when they win and they also shield their team from criticism or consequences when the team loses (or when they lose).

As I mentioned earlier in this book, this starts with embracing a simple belief that as a leader, your job is to show up to work each day to help make other people more successful than you. If you believe this, then the actions that you take will reflect this belief. However, the opposite is also true: if you believe that as a leader it's up to everyone else to serve you, then that is what your actions will reflect.

SMG is a customer feedback management firm that recently conducted a survey of over 40,000 associates in restaurant and retail and asked what they value most about their leadership team. One of the top responses was someone who is supportive and helps out.

 A core responsibility of a leader is to create other leaders. In the most recent Global Leadership Forecast published by EY and DDI, "developing 'next gen' leaders" was ranked as the number-one challenge by 1,000 CEOs around the world. Luciano Snel is the president of Icatu Seguros S/A, one of Brazil's largest insurance companies, which serves over 6 million people. Luciano told me that the very purpose of a leader is to create other leaders. Serving your team can manifest in many ways, such as coaching and mentoring employees, working side by side with them to complete a project, recognizing and rewarding their hard work, or any number of other ways, including those that are a bit more subtle.

Garry Ridge is the CEO of WD-40 company, which is headquartered in sunny San Diego and employs around 500 people globally. Garry has a rather unique leadership practice that is both easy to implement and impactful. Every morning at 4 a.m., regardless of where Garry is in the world, he sends a message to his entire company via email. He starts off his email with "For today from . . ." and this could be from San Diego, Sydney, Kuala Lumpur, or wherever else he is traveling to. In these daily emails Garry sends an inspirational quote based on something he has seen or felt through the organization, in the community, or something he wants to send just because. By doing this, he is able to feel connected to his "tribe," who in turn always knows where Garry is, and it also lets the tribe know that they can always reach out to Garry. As he told me, "It puts me in their presence every day so that it opens that line of communication." Employees also frequently come up to Garry to talk to him either about the quotes he sends out or about something else entirely, but they use the quote as a lead-in. In other words, it helps make employees feel more comfortable that they can come to Garry with anything.

Here are some examples of the quotes that Garry sends:

"My to-do list for today: Count my blessings, let go of what I can't control, practice kindness, listen to my heart, be productive yet calm, just breathe."

"Insights from the Dalai Lama: constant fear, constant anger, and hatred actually eat our immune system. A calm mind, compassionate mind increases positive body elements."

"You're never too important to be nice to people."

Garry is not your typical leader. In speaking with him, I genuinely got the impression that he would do anything for his team, and that's a rare quality.

As a leader, serving your team also goes beyond simply work-related issues. Alexander Wynaendts is the CEO of Aegon, a financial services organization with 30,000 employees globally. I met with Alexander in person in The Hague, Netherlands, for an event I was speaking at and he told me a moving story. One day he was walking around his office and noticed that one of the employees was crying. Alexander found out that her husband had just learned he had terminal cancer and had a 1 in 20 chance of survival. Alexander hugged her and told her that he knew of a specialist whom her husband should go see, someone most people don't have access to but Alexander did. After several treatments, her husband was cured. I loved this story because it really shows that serving your team doesn't just stop when your team leaves the office. As a leader, you are in constant service to your team both as employees and as individuals because of the blurring of work and life.

Perhaps one of the most effective and easiest ways that leaders can serve their teams is by recognizing them for the work they do. This is something we all need and deserve. David Novak is the former CEO of Yum! Brands. When he was CEO the company had around 1.5 million team members around the world, including franchisees. I'll never forget the story David shared with me when we spoke about a moment that had the biggest impact on his career. Years ago David was running operations at Pepsi-Cola. He was new in the role and wanted to learn as much as he could. He was conducting a roundtable discussion in St. Louis with about 12 merchandisers. David asked, "Who's really good at merchandising?" and everybody started raving about this guy named Bob, saying things like "Bob is the best there is" and "He taught me more in one day than I learned in my first three years here" and "You should see how Bob handles customers." David looked toward Bob and saw that he was crying. This really took David by surprise so he asked Bob what was wrong. Bob explained, "I've been at the company for 47 years and I'm retiring in two weeks. I never knew people felt this way about me." This hit David in the gut like a ton of bricks and since then he made a conscientious decision that he would do everything in his power to make sure he recognizes his people. He didn't want to have any "Bobs" working for him, ever.

David went on a recognition crusade and he had a lot of fun along the way. When he was president of KFC, he would give employees rubber chickens. He numbered each one and wrote what the person did to get it and how it was driving results. Then he would take a picture with the employee and their chicken, frame it, and send it to them, and tell the employee, "You can do what you want with it, but I'm going to put your picture in my office because you're the one who is making things happen. It's what you do that makes our business great." David would also give them $100 because, as he told me, "You can't eat a floppy chicken."

When he became president of Pizza Hut he used the same approach with Green Bay Packer Cheeseheads. Then again, when he became the CEO of Yum! Brands, he gave away wind-up teeth and (you guessed it) wrote on them, numbered them, and took pictures with employees. This practice spread across the entire company and the various brands. The president of Taco Bell started doing this with sauce packets and other leaders would use things like boxing gloves for a "knockout performance." Everyone started coming up with their own recognition awards and the best part was that this worked everywhere around the world – China, India, the United States, UK, you name it and people responded to it. David never mandated this program but everybody started doing it, to the point where if you were a leader at the company, your recognition award was like your company calling card or symbol.

It's amazing that something as simple as a rubber chicken, cheese hat, or wind-up teeth could have such an amazing impact on people, and it all started with Bob. How many "Bobs" do you think are working for you or in your company at this very minute? What can you do to recognize your people?

In my previous book, *The Employee Experience Advantage,* I wrote about a concept called Moments That Matter, which are basically moments during the course of someone's life that matter to them. Leaders must understand these moments and there's no greater moment that matters that's wasted than an employee's first day at work.

Imagine you are just starting a job. The night before, you pick out your outfit and set your alarm a few minutes earlier than usual, excited for that first day. Then that day comes, the alarm clock goes off, and you spring out of bed, put on your best outfit, have your coffee and breakfast, and make your way out the door as your spouse or significant other says, "Good luck on your first day. I'm sure it will be amazing!" You show up at work but you can't find a parking spot so you're forced to park far away and sprint into the office. By the time you arrive you're few minutes late and sweating profusely. Someone greets you in the lobby to go through a security check before escorting you to your cube. You arrive at your desk and find a folded-down laptop with a Post-it Note that says "Welcome." You open the computer, only to find that you can't log into anything because nothing was set up for you yet. After spending hours with the IT department, it's time for lunch. You sit by yourself and eat your salad, attend a few meetings, and then the day is done and it's time to hike back to your car. When you get home your spouse asks, "How was your first day?" and your response is

"I'm not sure I made a good choice. Nobody acknowledged me or even knew I was there!" This is what a first day looks like for many employees around the world. This is not a hard thing to fix and it makes a huge impact.

Carrie Birkhofe, the CEO of Bay Federal Credit Union, which employs 220 people, told me that she's a believer in serving her team from day one – actually, from hour one!

I meet employees the first hour on the first day they start at the Credit Union. New employees are welcomed as a group and when new hires start together, I'm there. I greet them, I welcome them, and I answer any questions they may have. All new employees, regardless of their position, are seen, heard, respected, and listened to by the leader and they know that I'm there to serve them, not the other way around.

Think about what you can do from day one to let your team know that you are there to serve them.

Service to Your Customers

It should come as no surprise that serving your customers and creating an amazing experience for them is a part of being service oriented. We live in a commoditized world where customers have many choices for products and services that look like yours, cost the same as yours, and do the same things as yours. In that kind of environment, it's the organizations who serve their customers and create better experiences for them that are going to stand out. Nowadays people don't just buy products, they buy experiences, and this trend is only increasing. In fact, 89% of consumers have switched to doing business with a competitor following a poor customer experience.

According to a study put out by Walker, a management consulting firm, by 2020 customer experience is projected to overtake price and product as the key brand differentiator (Walker, 2013).

Funnily enough, I'm married to one of the world's leading experts on customer experience, Blake Morgan. Her new book, *The Customer of the Future,* outlines ten guiding principles that leaders must follow to serve the customer, as outlined below.

REALIZE THE POWER OF THE CUSTOMER EXPERIENCE MINDSET

Attitude is everything. The leaders who provide elevated customer experiences are completely aligned on their focus and mindset across the company. Blake was originally going to write a book about technology, but after we took a trip to Amazon HQ in Seattle, she realized it was simply the mindset that made all the difference. All the leaders we met with talked about being customer obsessed even though they weren't all in customer experience roles.

BUILD A CUSTOMER-CENTRIC CULTURE

The customer will eventually feel the culture of the employees. Companies need to focus on the culture first before they think about the external experience of the customer. Culture is often the missing link for companies who struggle with customer experience.

DEVELOP CUSTOMER-FOCUSED LEADERSHIP

Great leaders are not born, they are developed. CEOs come and go. It is up to the company to create ongoing development and training programs for leaders (which is what this book is about!).

DESIGN THE ZERO-FRICTION CUSTOMER EXPERIENCE

In some areas of customers' lives they are getting zero-friction seamless customer experiences. Examples include Amazon, Netflix, Apple, and Spotify. But in other areas customers are required to provide too much effort. Zero friction should be the goal.

CREATE CUSTOMER EXPERIENCE-FOCUSED MARKETING

In the C-suite, the CMO is often the one tasked with driving customer experience. Marketing is the group within the company that has its finger on the pulse of the customer. Marketing now has more influence than ever as customers increase the number of channels they want to engage on. It's an opportunity for marketing to serve.

Leverage Customer Experience Technology to Make Customers' and Employees' Lives Easier and Better

Technology isn't everything but increasingly it shapes our most beloved customer experiences. A great technology strategy can be a huge uplift in both the employee and the customer experience, and both are important.

Undergo a Digital Transformation

Leaders must solve traditional and new business challenges by utilizing technology. Digital transformation requires a long-term investment, but Blake's research shows big companies that undergo a digital transformation have better long-term stock price performance (Morgan, 2019).

Focus on Personalization for the Customer Experience of the Future

In the future, the companies that leverage data to personalize the individual experience are the ones that will win customers. These are companies that anticipate future needs and create tailored experiences for the individual.

Embrace Customer Experience Analytics

Companies today have access to a treasure trove of data. This data can be used to create better experiences and increase sales. Analytics are the future of the modern customer experience.

Define Your Code of Ethics and Data Privacy in Customer Experience

We are at an inflection point with data; 92% of customers are not comfortable with their data being auto-collected because they don't believe the data is safe (Lara, 2018). With AI and machine learning gaining steam, companies will need to figure out their stance on data privacy and ethics. The earlier you do this, the better.

Carnival Cruise Line employs almost 40,000 people and they have received prestigious honors in their industry, including "Best Value for Money" and "Best Service" in Cruise Critic's annual Editor's Picks Awards. Serving customers is embedded in their DNA, their CEO Arnold Donald told me: "Our core thing is to exceed the expectations.

If we do that, we're in business. If we don't do that, it doesn't matter what else we do, because we're a hospitality business."

Service to Yourself

When is the last time you practiced a bit of self-care? For example, do you do things like taking a bit of down-time, going on vacation, or even something simple like a morning meditation or exercise?

Often positions of leadership require more time, more effort, and more resources on behalf of the leader. This leads to burnout because more is constantly demanded of them. According to the Mayo Clinic, "Job burnout is a special type of work-related stress—a state of physical or emotional exhaustion that also involves a sense of reduced accomplishment and loss of personal identity" (Mayo Clinic, n.d.). Being burned out isn't an official medical diagnosis but we have all experienced it and have seen its effect on co-workers.

But for leaders, not making time for self-care can be rather detrimental to themselves and to the organization. A few years ago, Harvard Medical School did a study and found that 96% of senior leaders feel somewhat burned out, and a third describe it as extreme. Unfortunately, many leaders also believe that because they are in positions of leadership, they constantly have to perform at 110%, they can't ask for help or say no, and they can't admit weakness or vulnerability of any kind (Kwoh, 2013). They just have to "power through it." Fortunately, we're not robots, we're humans, and believe it or not, it's okay to act like a human, even at work. We aren't just leaders or employees who are a part of an organization; we are also sons, daughters, fathers, mothers, grandparents, and friends. All of us are these things before we are leaders or employees and sometimes we forget that.

As a result of not practicing self-care, leaders may make poor business decisions, snap at employees or customers, and experience physiological and psychological symptoms such as depression, weight gain, and insomnia. Of course, these things are not exclusive to leaders; I believe we all need to practice self-care.

IBM recognizes that leaders' well-being has an impact on their effectiveness. In fact, they think of their leaders like high-performance athletes. No top athlete has ever gotten to their level of success by not taking care of themselves. Of course they work hard, but they need to have the tools and resources at their disposal always to be on top of their game. At IBM they have found things like early morning exercise and yoga sessions to be effective tools for leaders and they have incorporated these things into their management leadership programs.

It's no wonder that so many organizations around the world are investing in health and wellness programs for their employees. But of course, it's also up to the employees to take advantage of these things themselves.

During the safety briefing on any airline, you are always told that during an emergency you should put the oxygen mask on yourself before you try to help others. The same is true for leadership. Today and more so in the future, it's going to become even more crucial for leaders to be able to serve themselves. Basically, take care of your own well-being so that you can be an effective leader for others. As a leader, if you are constantly burned out, stressed, and overworked, you will not be able to practice many of the skills and mindsets outlined in this book, and as a result you won't be an effective leader.

Richard Branson, the founder of Virgin Group, credits his success with staying active and taking care of himself. Being active forces him to apply himself both mentally and physically. He actually starts off every day with some form of exercise. According to Branson, "I seriously doubt that I would have been as successful in my career (and happy in my personal life) if I hadn't always placed importance on my health and fitness" (Branson, 2017).

You can take care of yourself in many different ways. Personally, I use my hobbies and passions such as chess and exercising as a way to take care of myself and focus on nonwork activities. My wife and I also focus on eating nutritious and healthy foods and exercising regularly. I check email and social media once a day, at 4 p.m. *only,* and I've disabled all notifications to my phone. I don't have a TV in my bedroom, I try to get at least seven hours of sleep each night, and my wife and I make time for date nights. Since we both travel extensively for work, we also invest in getting regular massages.

Several executives I talked to told me that they carry flip phones instead of smart phones during off hours. Only a few people have the number to that phone, such as family members and some senior executives. That way when these executives are not at work, they know they don't need to worry, and if there's an emergency, the flip phone will ring.

Whatever you need to do to take care of yourself, do it.

For leaders, embracing and practicing the servant mindset isn't just about creating a better organization; it's about creating a better society and a better world for all of us to be a part of. Serve your leaders, serve your teams, serve your customers, and don't forget to serve yourself. Bob Chapman is the CEO of Barry-Wehmiller, the company we met earlier that uses a heart-count instead of a head-count. He put this beautifully:

We imagine a society where people think of others first and where people feel cared for. When they feel cared for, they care for others. Our model of leadership, whether it's in healthcare, education, the military, business, or government, fosters environments where people feel valued and when they feel valued they go home and treat their spouses well, their children well, and those children witness a mother and father who feel valued and treat each other well. By creating better jobs through more caring working environments, we can create a better world.

Humility and Vulnerability

You can't serve without having humility and vulnerability. If you believe that you are a great leader who never makes mistakes, who always makes the best decisions, and who should never be questioned or challenged, then the servant mindset will be a very difficult concept to understand and practice. Simply put, you have to get over yourself.

A research paper titled "Do Humble CEOs Matter? An Examination of CEO Humility and Firm Outcomes" defines three themes that are crucial for defining and understanding humility. The first is the willingness to obtain accurate self-knowledge, something I also talk about in this book under "emotional intelligence." The second is keeping an open mind and being willing to constantly learn and improve; again, this was discussed in this book. Finally, the appreciation of the others' strengths and their contributions is essential (Ou et al., 2015). Simply put, humility means that you are humble and don't have an overinflated opinion of yourself; you don't view yourself as superior to others. I asked Ajay, the CEO of Mastercard, what one moment in his career had the most impact on his approach to leadership. Here's what he told me:

> My father was among the first graduates of the military academy in independent India. He served 35-plus years in the Indian Army and retired as a three-star general. He was strict about certain things: timing, keeping your word, and caring about people. At one point, we lived in a huge house with a big compound in Hyderabad, and every day on the way out, he would talk to the army guard at the gate with the same interest in his eyes that I saw him talking to a visiting general from a different country, or his boss or somebody else who was a colleague of his. And I think that's the single most important lesson I got from him. Yes, it's important to be on time. Yes, it's important to care about stuff. But it's really important to connect to people at every level, because that's where you'll get the tips and information and knowledge from – and the ability to be a better person.

For decades we have taught and practiced this concept that leaders who sit at the top of the corporate pyramid are the ones who are the most important. Not too long ago, leaders were so obsessed with this that they would actually count how many tiles were on their ceiling to see how big their offices were and would concern themselves with what their desks were made out of since the higher the quality of the wood, the more important you were. This was the era of the "celebrity leader," and it's over. In his book *Good to Great,* Jim Collins talks about the research he did on nearly 1,500 companies over a 30-year period (Collins, 2001). He wanted to find out what separates the truly great companies from all the rest. It turns out that one of the qualities that leaders of the great organizations possess is humility. In the CEO study mentioned above, the authors found that executives with humility "build integrative top management teams, promote pay equity among their top management teams, and establish ambidextrous and profitable firms."

When you believe that you are the smartest or the best person in the room, you treat everyone else and their ideas as inferior to yours. This is no way to lead now or in the future.

Jan Rinnert is the chairman of the board of management at Heraeus Holding GmbH, a family-owned German company with a focus on precious and special metals, medical technology, quartz glass, sensors, and specialty light sources. They have over 13,000 employees around the world. During our discussion he told me:

> It's not this alpha type of leader that we need in the future. We need a humble person who is able to unleash the potential of people. I very much believe in the idea of modesty, staying humble and approachable. In fact, I spend a lot of time with employees at all levels of the organization, which is something I found to be very helpful. It teaches me a lot, especially when I talk with younger employees. My advice for current and future leaders is to spend as much time outside of the ivory tower as you can with employees at all levels, not just other executives. It will make you a better leader.

The actual definition of "vulnerable" is "capable of or susceptible to being wounded or hurt," or "open to moral attack, criticism, temptation, etc." Sounds a bit scary, right? Who wants to be susceptible to being wounded or hurt? Nobody does, especially in the corporate world, and so this idea of being vulnerable is never taught or encouraged; in fact, the exact opposite is emphasized. However, being vulnerable isn't about making yourself susceptible to being hurt; it's about being open and honest with how you feel. Imagine for a minute that you are a knight getting ready for battle. You put on your heavy and virtually impenetrable armor, grab your sword and shield, and then walk out onto the battlefield, ready to slay whoever stands in your way. It sounds like an episode of *Game of Thrones,* but this is exactly how most people approach just showing up to work, especially leaders. What would it be like to show up to work without your armor, sword, and shield and without the mentality of having to crush everyone you see?

Not too long ago I was brought into a large manufacturing company to meet with their executive team. After I gave a talk, one of the executives came up to me and shared a story of vulnerability. When this leader first started working at the company, he was the typical stoic leader. He didn't show emotion at work, acted like he knew the answers to everything, and never revealed anything personal to those he worked with. Shortly into his tenure, one of his mentors who had known him for several years said to him, "What are you doing?" The leader was confused and said, "What do you mean?" The mentor said, "I know who you are as a person. I know about your love for basketball, that you have two great kids and a wonderful wife, and that you care deeply about animals. I know what you're scared of, what you don't like doing, and what your strengths are, and what stresses you out." The leader was still confused, "So?" The mentor replied, "How come I know these things about you and nobody else does?" It turns out that this leader had gotten a reputation that people just didn't want to be around him or work with him because he didn't seem human.

Finally, the leader understood. He had two personalities, one for work and one for outside of work. At work he was the stereotypical manager whom people didn't really want to be around. At home he was a loving husband and father, a sports fanatic, animal lover, and generally a fun guy whom people enjoyed being around. He decided to just be himself. The changes were dramatic. Employees across all levels would approach him and share ideas and feedback, team members became more engaged and productive, and he also felt better about himself. Going to work shouldn't feel like a *Game of Thrones* episode; drop the weaponry and be human. With all the emphasis given to technology at work, we forget that being human is one of the most important things we can do!

You can still lead an organization and treat other people with respect, hear their ideas and perspectives, ask for feedback and suggestions, and admit that you can't do something. You can still laugh, cry, and express emotion. This doesn't make you weak; this makes you a strong human leader.

How Leaders Can Develop The Mindset of the Servant

This mindset continues to be difficult for many leaders to embrace. In a recent conversation with Horst Schulze, the founder and former CEO of Ritz-Carlton, he told me about a visit to one of his hotels. During a team meeting, he was encouraging all of the employees to speak up, to ask questions, and to challenge ways of doing things. After the meeting one of the hotel managers approached Horst, quite upset, saying that he is the manager and employees should be doing what he told them to do instead of asking questions and speaking up. The manager was so upset that he quit.

Remember that truly embracing the mindset of the servant means you serve your leaders (if you have them), your team, your customers, and yourself. You don't get to pick and choose. For example, you can't just serve yourself and say you are practicing the mindset of the servant.

You must also consider if you have different personalities for work and life and how you can combine the two so there is just a single human version of you. It's not an easy thing to do but it is what's required for the future leader. Several CEOs I interviewed actually said that it's important not to take yourself too seriously as a leader and to have more fun, something I completely agree with. Many of us forget how to have fun at work. Life is short, so if you aren't enjoying yourself at some level, then why bother doing the work or being a part of the organization?

You can start with small acts of service across each of these four mindsets and gradually build up to doing more. Talk to a customer on the phone and help them solve a problem, take your team out for lunch and let them know how much you appreciate their hard work, grab a cup of coffee for your leader on a busy day, and use your weekends to spend time with your family and friends, doing things you enjoy. Being a servant is all about action, so to embrace this mindset you must "do" or "serve."

Ask yourself these questions on a regular basis and you will find that they will change your behavior:

What did I do to help my leader today?

What did I do to make the lives of my customers easier and better?

What did I do to help make employees more successful than me?

What did I do to make sure that I am taking care of myself and allowing myself to be the best leader that I can be?

Did I have fun at work today?

If you aren't able to come up with an answer, it's likely that you are focused on getting other people to serve you instead of trying to serve others. Above all, the simplest way you can start being a servant is simply by serving.

15
The Global Citizen

Ilham Kadri is the CEO of Solvay, a materials and specialty chemical company with about 24,500 employees globally. Ilham was raised in Morocco by her illiterate grandmother, who was also her first role model. As a child she was told that girls in Morocco have two exits in their life. The first is from their parents' home to their husband's home and the second exit is to the grave. Ilham's grandmother encouraged her to find a third exit, which she did in the form of education, majoring in mathematics and physics. She received her master's degree in 1991 and her PhD in 1997.

Ilham has negotiated large contracts in Japan and Latin America, managed projects in the Middle East and Africa, overseen expansions of projects in Kenya, Ghana, and Nigeria, led marketing projects in Belgium, helped open a new office in North Carolina, studied in Canada and France, and the list goes on. She's lived in more than 15 locations around the world.

She learned the importance of patience when working in Japan, that a verbal commitment is just as important as a written one in Saudi Arabia, the importance of going slow to go fast in Africa, that nothing is impossible in China, what entrepreneurship is in the United States, and the importance of balancing a healthy life in Europe.

During our interview Ilham shared a great story of how she earned the nickname "Water Lady" while leading the water business for Dow in EMEA (Europe, the Middle East, and Africa). She negotiated a large deal between Saudi Arabia and the United States to build the region's first reverse osmosis plant. With her knowledge and experience of both cultures, she bridged both worlds and their different speeds and culture. The result was a successful deal for everyone.

Ilham is the type of person you can drop anywhere in the world and she will be able to lead. She learned to be open to the ideas of others, to surround herself with people who are not like her, and to respect and understand different cultures and ways of doing things. This has been crucial to her growth and her success. As Ilham told me:

Being a global citizen is not automatically about living in different countries or traveling all the time. It's about having a global mindset. You have to be open to other people and ideas and to respect the diversity of cultures, religions, ethnicities, races, thoughts, and orientations. This is essential for the future leader. Leaders must be curious connectors and understand the perspectives of those who are not like them, use those perspectives, and adapt to different ways of doing things. Listening to this diversity as well as including it, appreciating the richness of humanity, makes me more balanced, more grounded, and more impactful. People still buy, sell, and work with people, so being a global citizen means you understand people, all people.

The Benefits of a Global Citizen Mindset

Leaders who embody the mindset of a global citizen are able to think globally, lead a team of diverse and distributed employees, spread ideas and messages across the globe, and find and attract the best talent regardless of where they might be. In today's connected and rapidly changing world, it's almost impossible to think locally, regionally, or even nationally. Instead you must think globally.

Organizations no longer need to open entire offices in new locations to be able to enter a market. Instead, small and nimble teams can work out of their homes or co-working facilities in order for the company to be able to claim they have a "presence" in a certain part of the world. Not only do leaders need to consider how to enter new markets, but they must also understand how to spread ideas and messages and how to find the best talent, regardless of where in the world they might be.

"You can't be a leader of a world-sized organization without having a world-sized mindset." That's what Glenn Fogel told me; he is the CEO of Bookings Holdings, the company behind OpenTable, Bookings.com, Priceline.com, and several others. They employ around 25,000 people around the world.

As I discussed earlier, this means thinking about culture just as much as it means thinking about distance. This, of course, is crucial for CEOs and other senior executives, but it's also important for leaders at any level if they want to continue to grow and excel in their careers. To use another chess analogy, thinking globally means being able to see the entire chessboard instead of the one section where you think the action is happening. It also means being able to play against opponents with different styles and approaches to the game.

It doesn't matter how small or large your company is. I work with a team of ten people, most of whom I've never met. They live in various cities in the United States and in places like Serbia, Macedonia, and the Philippines. Through technology, we are all able to work together to achieve the goals of the business. As a new or existing leader, you have to work with, communicate, collaborate, and lead individuals who don't think like you, look like you, act like you, or believe in the same things that you believe. This sounds a bit scary to many leaders, but you're not one of those leaders, are you? For you, this sounds like an opportunity.

L'Oréal is an entire company filled with global citizens. After doing some internal research, they found that leaders with multicultural backgrounds excelled in five specific areas: recognizing new product opportunities, preventing losses in translation, integrating outside perspectives and ideas, mediating with leadership, and aiding in communication between subsidiaries and headquarters. After discovering this in the 1990s, L'Oréal started specifically recruiting individuals with mixed cultural backgrounds into leadership roles. They credit this with being able to transform L'Oréal from a French company to a truly global one that sells products all over the world.

In fact, half of its global sales comes from new markets outside of North America and Western Europe. Today they are present in 150 countries, have 34 international brands, and employ almost 100,000 people. By having a team of global citizens, they more effectively understand the needs of their employees, their customers, and the markets in which they serve (Deloitte, 2015).

According to Jean-Paul Agon, chairman and CEO of L'Oréal, "A diversified workforce in every function and on all levels strengthens our creativity and our understanding of consumers and it enables us to develop and market products that are relevant" (L'Oréal Group, n.d.).

Not having a global citizen mindset can also be quite costly. A number of years ago, the leaders at Disney decided to open a theme park in Paris called Euro Disney. The leaders assumed that everything that worked in the wildly successful American theme parks would also work in Europe. Unfortunately, this wasn't the case. For starters, the currency used in Paris is the euro, which means that the name of the park was literally "Dollar Disney." Paris is also a culinary hotspot, so guests to the park found it rather insulting to have to use plastic cutlery in the restaurants. Euro Disney also banned alcohol in a part of the world where having wine with lunch is a common practice. In the first two months of the park opening, 10% of the total staff simply quit because leaders assumed that the same approach to teamwork that worked in the United States would work in Paris. It didn't. Several worker strikes also made things difficult for the company and the leaders who ran it. The entire operation almost went bust, but Euro Disney borrowed $175 million in two years of operation, simply to stay alive. The list of mistakes made with Euro Disney extends far beyond what is described here. The park has since been renamed Disneyland Paris and has recovered. Disneyland in 2018 announced a further investment of $2 billion euro to expand and enhance it (Global Mindset, n.d.).

Decades ago, global leaders like Jack Welch, the former CEO of GE, didn't need to be global citizens. Instead, these leaders were able to create successful organizations with more limited perspectives and approaches. Even Jack Welch said, "The Jack Welch of the future cannot be like me. I spent my entire career in the United States. The next head of [General Electric] will be somebody who spent time in Bombay, in Hong Kong, in Buenos Aires" (Decarufel, 2018).

For the first time since 2015, in the 16th annual Forbes Global 2000 list, which includes publicly traded companies from 60 countries, China, and the United States split the top 10. China is home to 291 companies on the Global 2000 list while the United States has 560. South Korea, Japan, and the UK were also among the five countries with the most companies on the list (Forbes, 2019). We all live and work in a new globally connected and dynamic world, which means we need leaders who truly embrace the global citizen mindset. Every leader must be a global citizen.

Jeff Green is the CEO of the Trade Desk, a technology advertising company with around 1,000 people globally. He summed up having a global mindset quite well:

> You have to have the skill to navigate differences, as well as to celebrate them, so that we can respect cultures from around the world and respect different perspectives. As you bring people from around the world together to share in a common vision, leaders of the future will have to navigate that so much more frequently than they do today. The era of isolationism, if you will, is coming to a close, because we're just proving again and again that it doesn't work. If you don't respect the fact that our economy is a global economy, and not just respect but embrace the fact that our economy is a global economy, then it becomes almost impossible to be successful. In the future, there is no such thing as an American company; there are only global companies that happen to be based in the United States. If you don't have the cultural sensitivity to rally resources from around the world, it becomes almost impossible to be successful at any large scale.

How Leaders Can Develop The Mindset of the Global Citizen

Just because you are a part of a global company doesn't make you a global citizen, and neither does eating at new ethnic restaurants in your neighborhood. What's required here is truly a different way of thinking and acting. Ask yourself, how would you do right now if you were plucked out of your current environment or geographic location and put into another one, especially one that is foreign to you? Would you be lost, confused, and ultimately struggle, or would you be able to adapt and ultimately succeed?

Some of the skills and mindsets in this book will inherently help you become a global citizen. For example, thinking like an explorer and practicing emotional intelligence are both powerful contributors. However, there are also other things you can do. If your situation allows for it, one of the best things you can do is to learn to lead from different perspectives, and the best way to do this is by experiencing those perspectives. This means traveling to, living in, and/or seeing different parts of the world and, perhaps more importantly, immersing yourself in those places. After all, simply locking yourself in a hotel room won't do much good. This also means leading teams from different departments if you can. If you've been a leader in a technology company, would you be able to lead a team in healthcare? If you've led a manufacturing team, would you be able to lead a consumer packaged-goods team? To use a cliché, I encourage you to "mix it up." This requires courage because you might already be successful in your niche and pivoting away from that can be a bit intimidating, but it's what great leaders do. Embrace the uncomfortable to grow.

In 2009 William W. Maddux from INSEAD and Adam D. Galinsky from Northwestern University published a very interesting study, "Cultural Borders and Mental Barriers: The Relationship Between Living Abroad and Creativity." As the title suggests, they wanted to find out if living abroad had an impact on an individual's creativity. They ran five experiments and found this: "The relationship between living abroad and creativity was consistent across a number of creativity measures (including those measuring insight, association, and generation), as well as with masters of business administration and undergraduate samples, both in the United States and Europe, demonstrating the robustness of this phenomenon" (Maddux, 2009).

I don't want to make it sound as if you need to live out of a suitcase and travel hundreds of thousands of miles each year in order to be a leader; you don't. Korn Ferry did a study of 271 executives and found that in addition to expatriate assignments, just two cross-cultural experiences helped these leaders develop strategic thinking, multinational business operations experience, and experience building relationships with culturally diverse people. In fact, this study found that living in another country isn't even a requirement for developing multinational operations experiences, but occasionally traveling to new places and regularly working with people around the world is. Perhaps the most interesting finding from this study is that leaders who were exposed to cultures most unlike their own developed superior thinking capabilities. The study uses the example of an American leader being exposed to China as opposed to the United Kingdom (Korn Ferry, 2014). The emphasis here isn't on quantity; it's on quality.

When you see, live in, and visit different parts of the world, you gain access to new insights, ideas, experiences, cultures, perspectives, and ways of doing things, both personally and professionally. I've had the privilege to travel to over 50 countries for work and pleasure and have experienced and learned a great deal from these various adventures. Whether it was being followed by the secret police in Tibet, having a conversation with a taxi driver in Uganda about American pop culture, dealing with office politics during a presentation in Sao Paulo, being hustled for $100 on the streets of Berlin, trying to order food off a non-English menu in Chengdu, or trying to remember how many cheek kisses you're supposed to give in Italy or Peru, all of the experiences both good and bad, personal or professional, allow me to see the world in a new way. If your organization allows for these opportunities, take advantage of them, especially if you are a younger leader.

You should also actively seek out others who are different than you. I stress the word "actively" here because I'm not just talking about being okay as a part of a diverse team, I'm talking about asking for it and demanding it. You can't possibly cultivate a global citizen mindset if you are surrounded by older white men wearing suits (especially if you're an older white guy in a suit!); it's just not going to happen. Actively seek to be a part of and to create teams of individuals with physical and cognitive diversity, people who come from different backgrounds and cultures, who have a mix of skills and perspectives, religions, sexual orientations, and people who are not just going to agree with everything you say. This same concept applies to your broader network and can even extend to whom you surround yourself with outside of work. Do you have enough diversity around you? It takes courage to do this, and you and I both know that you have it.

16

How Well Are We Practicing These Mindsets Today?

The explorer, the chef, the servant, and the global citizen: from the perspectives of over 140 CEOs around the world, these are the four most essential mindsets that leaders of the future must have in order to be successful over the next decade and beyond. Success, by the way, doesn't just mean making more money; it also means having a positive impact and making the world a better place. It means being the lighthouse that guides others.

How many of these mindsets do you practice well on a regular basis? If you can master them and teach others to do the same, then you will be on your way to future-proofing yourself and truly becoming a great leader. But how well are we collectively practicing these mindsets in the corporate world today?

To answer this, we turn to the survey of almost 14,000 LinkedIn members around the world who self-identified as being employed full-time. Let's start very high level (Figure 16.1). Keep in mind that these numbers are totals, meaning that each column counts the responses of everyone who took the survey.

Most employees across all levels think they are doing a pretty good job of practicing these mindsets, with 69% scoring in the top two categories. Not bad. But when asked about their managers and

How well are companies practicing the mindsets for the future leader?

	How well do you think you are practicing these mindsets?	How well do you think your managers are practicing these mindsets?	How well do you think your senior executives are practicing these mindsets?
Not well at all	3%	19%	20%
Somewhat well	27%	38%	38%
Reasonably well	51%	31%	29%
Very well	18%	6%	9%

JACOB MORGAN
© thefutureorganization.com

FIGURE 16.1 HOW WELL ARE COMPANIES PRACTICING THE MINDSETS FOR THE FUTURE LEADER?

senior executives, 57% of managers and 58% of senior executives were ranked in the bottom two categories. Perhaps the scariest number is that only 6% of managers and 9% of senior executives were ranked as practicing these four mindsets "very well."

I wanted to compare these responses across three layers of organizations: individual contributors (ICs), managers, and senior executives. (See Figure 16.2; note that responses with "not sure" or "not applicable" were left out.) The idea here is to see if there are any gaps between seniority levels and, if so, how big those gaps are.

This is where some interesting things really start to appear. Individual contributors put 60% of their managers and 61% of their senior executives in the bottom two categories of "not well at all" and "somewhat well" for practicing these mindsets. Managers put 59% of their senior executives in that same grouping. These are shockingly high numbers. Only 8% of ICs said managers are practicing these mindsets "very well," and the number was slightly higher for senior executives at 9%. Even managers said that only 8% of senior executives are practicing these mindsets "very well." You can see just how large these gaps are across the board in the corresponding columns in the chart.

The data collected on these mindsets reveals a few things.

Practicing the Mindsets for the Future Leader:
Individual Contributors vs Managers vs Senior Executives

	How well are your managers practicing these mindsets? (Individual Contributors)	How well are you practicing these mindsets? (Managers)	Gap between individual contributors and managers	How well are your senior executives practicing these mindsets? (Individual Contributors)	How well are you practicing these mindsets? (Senior Executives)	Gap between individual contributors and senior executives	How well are your senior executives practicing these mindsets? (Manager)	Gap between managers and senior executives
Not well at all	22%	2%	20%	23%	2%	21%	19%	17%
Somewhat well	38%	28%	10%	38%	24%	14%	40%	16%
Reasonably well	31%	52%	21%	29%	51%	22%	31%	20%
Very well	8%	17%	9%	9%	22%	13%	8%	14%

JACOB MORGAN
© thefutureorganization.com

FIGURE 16.2 PRACTICING THE MINDSETS FOR THE FUTURE LEADER: COMPARISONS.

Mind the Gaps

One of the consistent themes that emerged around the mindsets is that leaders (managers and senior executives) think they are doing a far better job of practicing them than they really are. This is not only true for the mindsets collectively but I also found this to be true when looking at each specific mindset separately. While 69% of managers would say they are practicing these mindsets "reasonably well" or "very well," individual contributors put managers at 39%. Senior executives put themselves at 73% for these same two categories while individual contributors put this number at 38% and managers have it at 39%. These gaps can be seen across all of the mindsets, seniority levels, and categories of responses. As we saw in the trends section, the perspectives of managers and senior executives is nowhere near aligned with the perspectives of those who work for them or with them.

Although the scores across the board for leaders were quite poor, for managers and senior executives, the mindset they struggle with the most is the Servant. The mindsets for which managers had the highest score was the Explorer and the Global Citizen; both had 40% in the top two categories. The mindset in which senior executives scored the highest by far was the Global Citizen, with ICs and managers putting their senior executives at 41% and 44%, respectively, for the top two categories.

However, for a future leader, embracing the mindsets outlined in this section is just a part of the equation. It's also crucial for everyone around you to know that you are embracing and practicing these mindsets as well. The research shows that there is clearly a lack of alignment, communication, collaboration, and even perception around what these mindsets are and what it means to practice them. Leaders must understand that perception is reality.

Remember, the lighthouse helps all ships navigate to their destination safely. Today, these ships are crashing into the rocks and are sailing around aimlessly. We need brighter lights.

The Seniority Curse

Another consistent theme seen across the mindsets is not just that there is a disconnect among managers and senior executives but that the more senior you are, the more disconnected you are from the rest of the organization. Senior executives typically think they are practicing these mindsets far more effectively than perceived by those who work for and with them. This is the typical ivory tower problem that has plagued leaders for many decades. In business we often joke that leaders "don't get it" and that they are a bit aloof and disconnected from the rest of the workforce, but data that supports this has been relatively sparse, until now. This data clearly shows the disconnect between the most crucial mindsets that leaders of the future must possess. This is one of the reasons why we are seeing such a big shift to openness, authenticity, transparency, purpose and meaning, caring, and the like. It's because by focusing on these things, we create more human organizations where leaders are more in touch with those around them at all levels.

Isabelle Kocher is the CEO of ENGIE, a global low-carbon energy and services company, with over 160,000 employees around the world. She said this rather eloquently:

> It is crucial for a leader not to be a prisoner in an ivory tower. Leaders must be aware of the challenges facing their organization and be in touch with what their employees and customers care about and value. You cannot lead alone from the top; you must lead from the bottom with your people. The ivory tower will not fall by itself; as a leader, you must tear it down.

We must replace the ivory tower with the arena, where we are all "in it" together.

On April 23, 1910, Theodore Roosevelt gave one of the most famous speeches in history, which became known as "The Man in the Arena." In the speech he said:

> It is not the critic who counts; not the man who points out how the strong man stumbles, or where the doer of deeds could have done them better. The credit belongs to the man who is actually in the arena, whose face is marred by dust

and sweat and blood; who strives valiantly; who errs, who comes short again and again, because there is no effort without error and shortcoming; but who does actually strive to do the deeds; who knows great enthusiasms, the great devotions; who spends himself in a worthy cause; who at the best knows in the end the triumph of high achievement, and who at the worst, if he fails, at least fails while daring greatly, so that his place shall never be with those cold and timid souls who neither know victory nor defeat.

As a future leader you must constantly ask yourself if you're in the arena with the rest of your team. If not, you'd better jump in, and quickly.

Around the World

Which countries are doing the best and the worst job of practicing these collective mindsets? I looked at the top two categories of "reasonably well" and "very well," along with the bottom two categories of "somewhat well" and "not well at all." In Figures 16.3 and 16.4, you can see the responses across countries to the three questions of "How well do you think you are practicing these mindsets?" "How well do you think your managers are practicing these mindsets?" and "How well do you think your senior executives are practicing these mindsets?"

Respondents collectively think they are doing a pretty good job of practicing these mindsets, with Brazil far surpassing every other surveyed country. However, when we start to break things down a bit by managers and senior executives, we can see how drastically the numbers change. Around the world, only 36% of managers are practicing these mindsets either "reasonably well" or "very well." This number is slightly higher for senior executives around the world at 38%, but mainly because of the high scores in Brazil. Without Brazil, these numbers are closer to 30%.

Collectively, people in Brazil and DACH (Austria, Germany, Switzerland) believe they are doing the best job of practicing these mindsets, with the other countries trailing behind. Managers in these

**How well are you, your managers, and
senior executives practicing these mindsets?**

("reasonably well" and "very well")

	US	UK	DACH	India	Brazil	China	UAE	Australia
You	69	69	70	64	78	48	68	67
Managers	36	35	40	35	48	27	38	32
Senior Executives	35	32	37	43	49	39	37	31

JACOB MORGAN
© thefutureorganization.com

FIGURE 16.3 PRACTICING THE MINDSETS FOR THE FUTURE LEADER: COMPARISONS BY COUNTRY.

How well are you, your managers, and senior executives practicing these mindsets?

("somewhat well" and "not well at all")

	US	UK	DACH	India	Brazil	China	UAE	Australia
You	29	29	28	35	20	47	32	32
Managers	58	58	54	63	47	68	60	64
Senior Executives	60	60	57	54	46	57	60	64

JACOB MORGAN
© thefutureorganization.com

FIGURE 16.4 PRACTICING THE MINDSETS FOR THE FUTURE LEADER: FURTHER COMPARISONS BY COUNTRY.

parts of the world also received higher scores, with China being far behind the other countries. When it comes to senior executives, Brazil and India are at the top of the pack and Australia and the UK are the laggards. It's interesting that most people typically turn to the United States when it comes to looking at things like leadership, innovation, and workplace practices, yet the United States didn't score at the top for any of the demographics.

Figure 16.4 shows a similar chart, but instead of looking at the top two categories it looks at the bottom two categories.

Not surprisingly, China had the greatest percentage of people who scored in the bottom two categories, with India, the UAE, and Australia trailing them. Looking at managers, Brazil and DACH had the smallest percentage of managers score in the bottom two categories, whereas China and Australia had the most. For senior executives, Brazil and India had the smallest percentage in the bottom two categories. Again though, if we look at the United States and even some parts of Europe, those areas of the world didn't score as well as most would assume.

Around the world, 57% of all managers scored in the bottom two categories and 58% of senior executives scored in the bottom two categories.

Take a moment and think about what these numbers mean: that the vast majority of employees around the world show up to work each day for and with leaders whom they believe are *not* explorers, chefs, servants, or global citizens. How can we be led by individuals who don't practice curiosity, humility, and vulnerability, being service oriented, perpetual learning, embracing technology, thinking globally, agility and nimbleness, being purpose-driven and caring, having a growth mindset, open-mindedness, and embracing diversity? What kind of an environment does this create for the billions of employees around the world who work for these types of leaders? We should be furious, disappointed, and quite honestly embarrassed that this is the type of world we work in. But most of all, we should be determined and hopeful that we can change. These mindsets are not just "nice to have," they are crucial for your success as a leader and at scale for the grander success of your organization. We have created a workforce of zombies, but thankfully there's a cure – that is, if you as a leader are willing to administer it.

PART 4

THE FIVE SKILLS OF THE NOTABLE NINE

17
The Futurist

Mindsets are about how leaders of the future need to think, but in this section on skills we're going to specifically look at the things the leaders of the future need to know how to do. Again, these were identified from the over 140 CEOs I interviewed as being most crucial for leaders in the coming ten years (see Figure 17.1).

Hari Seldon is a mathematics professor at Streeling University on the planet Trantor and is known for developing psychohistory, a science that combines the disciplines of mathematics, history, and sociology to probabilistically predict the future of the galactic empire (it only works at a massive scale, not for a single person or small groups). This was the premise for one of my favorite science fiction series, called *Foundation,* written by Isaac Asimov. Through the series readers get taken on a journey of how psychohistory is used to influence world events, and it's a fascinating read. Hari is the ultimate example of a futurist, even though he's a fictional character.

When most people think of a futurist, they think of someone who predicts the future, like Hari, but nothing could be further from the truth. In the business context we frequently hear of this desire to "look around corners." Instead, futurists help make sure that individuals and organizations are not surprised by what the future might bring. This was ranked by CEOs as the number-one skill that leaders of the future must have. But how is this done?

5 Skills for the Future Leader

FIGURE 17.1 FIVE SKILLS FOR THE FUTURE LEADER.

There are more possible moves in a game of chess than there are atoms in the universe. It's a game of virtually unlimited combinations and possibilities and no two games are ever identical unless done on purpose. In a game of chess, the first dozen or so moves are referred to as the "opening." In this stage of the game, top grandmasters look at various potential first moves that they and their opponent can make. Obviously, they can't predict exactly what move their opponent will play, but with strong opening preparation they will have an idea of what their opponent *might* play and as a result they are rarely surprised. Of course, every now and then a novelty makes its way onto the board that takes the grandmaster "out of book" (meaning out of their preparation). When this happens the grandmaster relies on his or her knowledge of the game, previous experience, pattern recognition, and intuition. Thinking like a futurist is about looking at different possibilities and scenarios, as opposed to picking one and sticking with it. In a sense you're actually looking around many corners so that when your path takes you down one of them, you will know what to expect. The pace of change is one of the most profound trends and challenges shaping the future of leadership. With things changing so quickly, leaders must be able to respond to and ideally anticipate change and have plans in place. This is especially crucial to do not when your business is struggling but particularly when it's thriving and you and your team might get complacent.

Alfredo Perez is the CEO of Alicorp, a Peruvian food production company with 10,000 employees. I was fortunate to meet with Alfredo and his team in Peru, where they brought me in to give a talk. He told me:

> The fact is that adapting to change is not enough; we need to lead change and create the future. Adapting is keeping your head above water, but leading and creating is sailing on top of it. As leaders, we need to balance pragmatism and speed with careful consideration for the implications of our decisions for our companies and our people in contexts that are always new. Leaders who think of adapting are already behind; leaders who think of creating are the ones who will succeed.

Futurists use a framework to help them think about and visualize these possibilities known as "the cone of possibilities" (see Figure 17.2). Imagine that you are peering through the narrow end of a cone. This represents the closest time horizon, which might be a few days, weeks, or maybe even a year. The shorter the time horizon, the more predictable things usually are, which also means the fewer scenarios or possibilities you need to be considering. As you peer farther out into the cone, the time horizon expands and the cone gets wider, meaning that the number of scenarios and possibilities you need to consider starts increasing. There are several types of possibilities you need to consider. The first is a set of possible but not likely scenarios, the second is possibilities likely to happen, and the third is what you want to happen.

These different possibilities can be rather subjective and depend on several factors, including your ability to identify patterns, how "plugged in" and aware you are of relevant trends, and spending time scanning for signals that might give you a clue into what the future might bring. For leaders this means that you have to be more

Cone of Possibilities
Think Like a Futurist

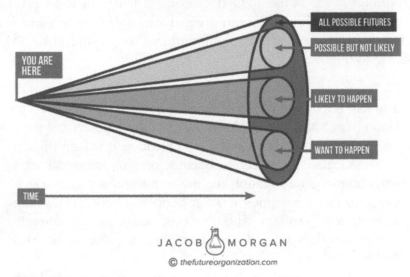

FIGURE **17.2** CONE OF POSSIBILITIES.

connected than ever to your network, which includes customers, employees, and even your competitors. When I studied foresight at the University of Houston, this was one of the most useful and powerful frameworks that we were taught and I use it regularly. Of course, there is far more than can be written about the tools and models that futurists use and one can even obtain a master's degree in foresight. But this "cone of possibilities" is perhaps the most useful and practical tool you can start to implement to think like a futurist.

How a Futurist Thinks

Let's walk through a rather practical example around AI and jobs. If you were to look at the narrow part of the cone, then it's rather clear that tomorrow, next week, next month, and even through the end of the year, things will look relatively similar to the way they are now. You won't wake up one day to find that all of the workers at your company have been replaced by bots or that the jobs apocalypse has finally arrived. But let's say that you are looking farther out into the future, perhaps five years or ten. Now, all of a sudden, the picture changes.

What might be a possible but not likely scenario here? With the continued advancement and investment in technology, I'd argue that the status quo is a possible but not a likely scenario. In other words, things won't be exactly as they are now. What is a likely scenario? One might be that in five years we see technology remove many routine jobs and displace workers in some industries, but that this displacement won't be as dramatic as many believe. Instead, many new jobs will be created and the overall impact on jobs will balance out. What is a scenario you want to see happen? Personally, I'd love to see routine and mundane jobs get replaced and the workers who used to do those jobs get retrained and upskilled to focus more on human based tasks such as strategy, client advisory, and relationships.

This is a powerful technique that futurists use to help them think about, explore, and plan for the future. In fact one of the things that futurists do is host scenario planning workshops to walk through this (and other) approaches. Of course you can come up with several possibilities and scenarios in each one of these buckets and you might find that the future might be a combination of the various possibilities you anticipate.

This is a rather simplified and basic explanation of how the cone of possibilities is used, but it's still a rather helpful framework that leaders should learn to use. The point is to get you to think in terms of possibilities and scenarios instead of focusing on a single possibility and scenario, which is what most leaders today are comfortable with doing. Here's a simplistic big picture example: let's say that you believe that over the next ten years millions of jobs around the world will be displaced, including those at your organization, and that your business strategy is based on that assumption. You invest in various technology and automation programs, prepare to cut jobs, and stop focusing on anything related to employee experience such as workspace design, culture, leadership, or health and wellness initiatives. A few years go by and it appears that even though technology has become more integral to your business, the human component is what your business ultimately runs on. Your customers still want to transact with humans, perhaps AI didn't advance as fast as some predicted, and now it appears that it's the human aspect of work (not technology) that will determine your success. Unfortunately, you've spent the past several years redesigning your organization to be less human and now you're in trouble. You made the mistake of picking one corner and walking around it instead of thinking about the many corners that you might walk around.

The future leader must be comfortable and adept at thinking in terms of different possibilities and scenarios and have plans in place should one of them come to fruition. As a leader you should focus on minimizing being surprised by what the future might bring. The framework above can be applied at a large or small scale. Thankfully, this is an area where technology can be a great aid.

Michael Kasbar is the chairman and CEO of World Fuel Services, a global fuel logistics company with over 5,000 employees. Here's how he put it:

> For many years, leaders made decisions and created strategies based on instinct and intuition. This is, of course, still important today but now we have the addition of data and technology that can help us determine if we are moving in the right direction. For leaders of the future, it's not about picking a single path and sticking to it; it's about exploring many paths at the same time, seeing around many corners to understand the best way forward.

Many leaders today are also constantly asking, "What is the future of work?" I know this because it's one of the most common questions that they ask me. This question makes two dangerous assumptions that are not correct. The first is that there is a single future and the second is that the future is something that happens to us. As I explained above, there is no such thing as a single future that is guaranteed to happen, so get that way of thinking out of your head. When we talk about the future as something that is going to happen to us, it is reminiscent of someone who is about to get punched in the stomach and all they can do is brace themselves for impact. But that the future is not something that happens to us; it's something that we can help design, shape, and create. For leaders in the coming decade, part of thinking like a futurist means dispelling these two faulty assumptions and putting themselves in the driver's seat, not by asking, "What is the future of work?" but "What is the future of work that I or my organization want to see happen, and how are we going to make it happen?" In the wise words of Abraham Lincoln, "The best way that you can predict the future is to create it."

Tom Wilson is the chair, president, and CEO of the Allstate Corporation, an insurance company with over 43,000 employees and 10,000 agency owners who operate like independent contractors. According to Tom, "Leadership is about shaping the future, not just reacting to trends. Anybody can react to trends; the question is whether you can see and shape a better future. That's what leaders do."

How Leaders Can Develop The Skill of the Futurist

Interestingly, many of us practice this skill in some form in our personal lives; we just don't realize we're doing it. Think of a time you went on a first date, had a child, bought your first house, or made any number of other decisions or life choices. When going through these things you start to ask yourself questions like, "Do I see a potential future with this person beyond the first date?" "What might a life with this person look like?" "What might the property value be in this neighborhood over the next ten years if we buy here?" "What happens if it goes up or goes down a lot?" In other words, you are already thinking about different scenarios and possibilities and mapping them out in your head. But for some reason, when we show up to work, most of us shut off this skill.

The field of foresight has a lot of components to it but from a high level the best way that you can start thinking like a futurist is by asking yourself a series of questions when presented with decisions you need to make. You will find that these questions can be applied to something as large as shifting the strategic direction of the organization or to something as small as how you want to host a meeting. Here are the questions I want you to consider:

- ♦ Why might "this" happen or not happen?
- ♦ What else might happen?

- What do I want to happen and how can I make it happen?
- What factors might influence why this will or won't happen?

Start with these four questions, and if you ask them regularly when making decisions, the way you think will change.

Another practical and useful thing you can do is learn how to play a game like chess. It might sound a bit strange to learn how to play a game in order to become a better leader, but it works. Top chess grandmasters like Garry Kasparov have written books on the many ways in which chess concepts and principles can be applied to business and specifically to leadership. Learning a game like chess forces you to think in terms of scenarios and possibilities. It forces you to look for patterns, teaches you how to work with computers for preparation, and helps you think strategically and tactically.

The last piece here is to remember to use the cone of possibilities. It's actually helpful to conduct small sessions or larger workshops to walk through these types of futurist tools and frameworks. However, some leaders just do quick mental visualizations as well, just like chess grandmasters pondering their next move.

Remember, there's no such thing as a single future, and the future isn't something that happens to you; it's something you create. What kind of future do you want to build and how are you going to build it?

18
Yoda

First appearing in the 1980s film *The Empire Strikes Back,* Yoda is the little green character that billions of people around the world have come to know and love. He is also one of the most emotionally intelligent characters ever created, I suppose he should be; after all, he was apparently 900 years old and trained many Jedi during his lifetime. In the *Star Wars* films, he appears as a guide, mentor, and teacher to many of the other characters, who turn to him for his wisdom and connection with the "Force."

Some of his most famous scenes and quotes were all about emotion:

"Fear is the path to the dark side. Fear leads to anger. Anger leads to hate. Hate leads to suffering."

"Remember, a Jedi's strength flows from the Force. But beware anger, fear, and aggression. The dark side are they. Once you start down the dark path, forever will it dominate your destiny."

"Use your feelings, Obi-Wan, and find him you will."

Leaders of the future must learn to channel their internal Yoda, which means being emotionally intelligent, specifically being able to practice empathy and self-awareness.

Emotional Intelligence (Empathy and Self-Awareness)

The word "emotional" is rarely used in the same sentence as "leader," yet many of the CEOs I interviewed stated that empathy and self-awareness will be among the most crucial skills that leaders will have to possess by 2030. In a clearly technology-driven world it's the focus on human mindsets and skills that will perhaps be the most important. Ironically, though, it's often the human mindsets and skills that are prioritized and taught least of all.

EMPATHY

Empathy is about being able to understand the feelings and emotions of another person and being able to put yourself in their shoes. It's a bit like taking "yourself" out of your own body and putting it into someone else's. To use a chess analogy, it would be the equivalent of trying to understand the plans of the person you are playing against as opposed to purely focusing on your own plans.

On the corner of the whiteboard in his office, Stephen Smith, the CEO of clothing retailer L.L. Bean (with over 5,000 employees), keeps his three leadership traits written out so that he is reminded to practice them every single day. Number one on that list is empathy, followed by transparency and integrity. From Stephen:

> Historically, empathy has not been a word that's used in business very often. But to be able to put yourself in somebody else's shoes and to look at any dilemma or any problem, or anything you're trying to solve from multiple perspectives, is one of the most important things for leaders to be able to do. Of course, you also want to build a team that has multiple perspectives as well so that you can find common ground and then get to the best possible solution.

Empathy is something leaders must practice, whether it's with an employee working next to you, a virtual employee thousands of miles away, a customer, or anyone else you are interacting with in either your professional or personal life. According to the "2018 State of Workplace Empathy" report, 87% of CEOs in the United States believe that a company's financial performance is tied to empathy in the workplace

(Businessolver, 2018). In today's business world, we have done a good job of creating sympathetic organizations where employees are good at saying things like "I'm sorry you feel that way." Unfortunately there is very little here that allows for human connection. We are told "I'm sorry" all the time from customer service agents, automated phone trees, or even chatbots we might be interacting with. We hear it from retail employees, from doctors, or airline gate agents. Enough.

As a leader, empathy comes into play in many scenarios such as trying to resolve a conflict by understanding everyone's perspectives, developing products or services for customers, improving collaboration, creating psychological safety within a team, or just making better business decisions by understanding both the business and the human implications. It's easy for us to judge others, especially in the context of the work environment, and this goes for employees at all levels. For example, it's easy for us to assume that in a moment of vulnerability, if someone asks for help at work, the employee is clearly not qualified for the job. But an empathetic response to something like that might be, "I understand how you feel; I was in a similar situation when I first started working here."

The Center for Creative Leadership conducted a study on empathy in the workplace and found, based on a sample of 6,731 leaders, that empathy is positively related to job performance and that "managers who show more empathy toward direct reports are viewed as better performers in their job by their bosses" (Gentry, 2016).

Empathy is the cornerstone of creating a more human organization.

Bradley Jacobs, the CEO of XPO Logistics (whom we met earlier in the book), had a wonderful way to describe this:

Being able to look through someone else's eyes at a situation is a very valuable trait for a leader to have. Over time, future leaders must be able to empathize and be dialectical, more than we are today. By dialectical, I mean being able to overcome your biases and being flexible in your thinking, not rigid. Leaders need to be able to get out of their own heads and understand the perspectives of customers and employees. This ability is essential for future leaders.

SELF-AWARENESS

In addition to empathy, the other piece of emotional intelligence that came up frequently during my discussions with CEOs was self-awareness, which is about being mindful of your own emotions, feelings, state of mind, motives, and desires. I had the opportunity to interview Dr. Tasha Eurich on this topic. An organizational psychologist, she is the *New York Times* best-selling author of *Insight: The Surprising Truth About How Others See Us, How We See Ourselves, and Why the Answers Matter More Than We Think,* and is one of the world's leaders on the topic of self-awareness. According to Tasha, self-awareness comprises two components: internal self-awareness, which is how we see our own values, passions, thoughts, feelings, and emotions, and external self-awareness, which is understanding how we are seen by others.

In her research Dr. Eurich and her team found that 95% of people think they are self-aware, but only 10–15% of them actually are, which is a huge gap (Eurich, 2018). When I asked Tasha why self-awareness was so crucial, her response was profound:

I'll let you in on a well-kept secret: when leaders improve their self-awareness, it creates ripple effects. Personally, it makes us better, more promotable performers, better communicators, better influencers, and helps us avoid unethical behavior. Interpersonally, it strengthens our relationships at work and at home – they have better marriages and raise more mature children. There is also evidence that self-aware leaders have more engaged employees: they are willing to work harder and are far more committed to the mission. The list goes on.

But if those outcomes are not compelling enough, there's evidence that self-aware leaders actually lead more profitable companies, and companies with large numbers of self-aware employees have better financial returns.

My question is this: Why wouldn't you spend a little bit of time working on something that's going to give you a ripple effect in every area of your life? Another way to think about it: your self-awareness will set the upper limit for all of the skills that are important to be successful in business in the twenty-first century. The people who know this and work to improve really do have a unique edge.

Blue Shield of California is a health-plan provider with around 7,000 employees that serves over 4 million members. Their CEO, Paul Markovich, takes the concept of self-awareness to heart:

Every weekend, I sit down and think about what roles I want to play. If I want to be a good father, a good husband, a good servant of the community, and an effective leader at work, then these are the things I'm going to do this week. I plan my week with purpose and that's been effective for me. I have a mission statement and it has guided my choices profession-ally – where I want to work, how I want to work.

To practice the external self-awareness piece, Paul has a coach who interviews his direct reports every six months and provides feedback of those interviews to Paul. He then reviews that feedback with his senior team and tells them how he is going to address it. Paul says this is crucial in helping him understand how he shows up to work and how he is impacting the people around him.

According to Daniel Goleman, internationally renowned psychol-ogist and author of the bestselling *Emotional Intelligence: Why It Matters More than IQ*, "Emotional self-awareness is a leadership com-petency that shows up in model after model. These are the leaders attuned to their inner signals, recognizing how their feelings affect them and their job performance" (Goleman, 2004).

In a study of 72 senior executives, the American Management Association found that a high self-awareness score was the strongest predictor of overall success. According to researcher and corporate organization psychologist Dr. Becky Winkler, this is because the lead-ers who are self-aware of their weaknesses are able to hire people around them who perform better in the areas where the leaders are lacking. One fascinating aspect of the research found that harsh, hard-driving leaders who are focused on driving results at all costs don't improve the bottom line – they actually diminish it. On the other hand, self-aware leaders are able to deliver better financial performance (Winkler, 2019).

Hans Vestberg is the CEO of Verizon Communications, an American multinational telecommunications conglomerate with over 152,000 employees around the world. He summed up this concept nicely:

The first layer of skills a good leader must master are internal: managing himself or herself as an individual human being. This includes physical health, emotional balance, self-knowledge – everything that you bring along with you to each meeting, each decision, each public event. A lot of leaders are tempted to ignore or deemphasize this most basic layer but they do so at their peril.

How to be and how others perceive you to be is exactly what being a self-aware leader means.

Other Components of Emotional Intelligence

Although the CEOs I interviewed specifically identified empathy and self-awareness as the most crucial aspects of emotional intelligence, there's actually a bit more to it which leaders need to be aware of. Daniel Goleman is a psychologist, science journalist, and one of the world's leading experts on emotional intelligence. He was among the first people to propose that emotional intelligence can matter more than IQ (intelligence quotient), something he discussed in his best-selling book, aptly titled, *Emotional Intelligence.* According to Daniel emotional intelligence actually has five components:

1. Self-awareness – the ability to recognize and understand your moods and emotions, and how they affect others
2. Self-regulation – the ability to control impulses and moods, and to think before acting

3. Internal (or intrinsic) motivation – being driven to pursue goals for personal reasons, rather than for some kind of reward (the opposite is external motivation)
4. Empathy – the ability to recognize and understand others' motivations, which is essential for building and leading teams successfully
5. Social skills – the ability to manage relationships and build networks (Goleman, 2004)

According to research done by TalentSmart, 90% of top performers in organizations are also high in emotional intelligence. However, just 20% of bottom performers are high in emotional intelligence (TalentSmart, n.d.). Further research published by the Harvard Business Extension School also cited two examples that demonstrate the impact that emotional intelligence has on organizational performance. The first example is the French pharmaceutical company Sanofi, with over 110,000 employees around the world. By focusing on the emotional intelligence skills of its sales force, which included assessments and workshops, the performance of the sales professionals increased by 13%. The second example comes from Motorola, which saw the productivity of their manufacturing plant staff increase by 90% after introducing emotional intelligence training programs (Wilcox, n.d.).

Frances Hesselbein, former CEO of Girl Scouts of the USA, is the recipient of the Presidential Medal of Freedom, which is the highest award that any civilian can receive. She also has 23 honorary doctorate degrees. She turned 100 in 2015 and still continues to advise and coach many leaders around the world. I spent a few hours with Frances and she gave me many pearls of leadership wisdom, including this one, which I took to heart and believe directly applies to self-awareness:

> We spend most of our lives learning how to do, teaching people how to do, and yet we know that in the end it is the quality and the character of the leader that determines the performance and the results. So leadership is a matter of how to be, not how to do.

A *Harvard Business Review* article, "What Makes a Great Leader" (Goleman, January 2004), stated:

The most effective leaders are all alike in one crucial way: they all have a high degree of what has come to be known as emotional intelligence. It's not that IQ and technical skills are irrelevant. They do matter, but . . . they are the entry-level requirements for executive positions. My research, along with other recent studies, clearly shows that emotional intelligence is the sine qua non of leadership. Without it, a person can have the best training in the world, an incisive, analytical mind, and an endless supply of smart ideas, but he still won't make a great leader.

If that doesn't help, then consider a bit more selfish incentive: people with a high degree of emotional intelligence make on average $29,000 more per year than those with a low degree of emotional intelligence.

A Korn Ferry study on emotional intelligence mentioned earlier in this book (Korn Ferry, 2017) found that highly emotionally intelligent leaders display a few common behaviors, including:

- They listen more than they talk.
- They emphasize the *how* and *why*, instead of simply telling people what to do.
- They engage team members and recognize their contributions, rather than continually criticizing and correcting their mistakes.
- They resolve disagreements openly and deal with people's emotions during conflict.
- They understand what energizes and engages people on their teams – and create environments that foster that energy.
- They encourage team members to stay five years or more in the organization, because they feel engaged and able to do their job effectively.

In an interview she gave for Bloomberg, the former CEO of PepsiCo, Indra Nooyi, shared an epiphany she had while visiting her mom (her father passed away) in India. They organized a bit of a gathering for friends and family members, and people would show up and then go to Indra's mother and compliment her on the great job she did with Indra and on raising a global CEO. Indra realized that much of her success was a result of her parents and how they raised, influenced, and supported her. In the Bloomberg interview, she talked about how her mom would constantly remind her to dream big and even at the dinner table would ask Indra to pretend she was the prime minister of India and had to give a speech. Indra's mom would then provide feedback and critique her performance.

In the interview Indra said, "It occurred to me that I had never thanked the parents of my executives for the gift of their child to PepsiCo." When Indra returned home, she sent a letter to the parents of each of the members of her executive team, around 400 of them. She wrote what their child was doing and then said, "Thank you for the gift of your child to our company." Indra began to receive responses from many of the parents, saying how honored they were that she would send them a letter and some of the executives told Indra that it was the best thing that ever happened to their parents. As Indra stated, "You need to look at the employee and say, 'I value you as a person. I know that you have a life beyond PepsiCo, and I'm going to respect you for your entire life, not just treat you as employee number 4,567" (Rubenstein, 2016).

Keith Barr is the CEO of InterContinental Hotels Group (IHG), a global hotel company with more than 400,000 people around the world. He told me:

Leaders have to start with self-awareness. I am amazed at people who are incredibly self-aware and I'm equally amazed by people who have no self-awareness. This is critical for success, because it goes back to learning agility and change. You must always ask yourself, "How can I do that better?" "How can I do that differently?" or "What did I do well?" And you have to take perspectives from those around you. If you aren't self-aware, then you won't have answers to these questions, and you may not even ask them to begin with. And that's no way to lead, especially in the future.

How Leaders Can Develop The Skill of Yoda

When it comes to empathy, many people turn to the advice of Dr. Brené Brown, a research professor at the University of Houston and best-selling author of numerous books, including: *Daring Greatly* and *Dare to Lead*. She has studied empathy for more than two decades and has developed a great four-step approach for practicing and showing empathy, which any leader can practice:

1. Perspective taking, or putting yourself in someone else's shoes
2. Staying out of judgment and listening
3. Recognizing emotion in another person that you have maybe felt before
4. Communicating that you can recognize that emotion

It looks and sounds simple. At the heart of empathy is creating an emotional human connection with another person. But as Brené cautions, doing so often requires us to think about, recall, or reflect on things and emotions that aren't always pleasant or comfortable and it makes us vulnerable. But that's okay; it's what makes us human. As a leader, practice these four steps on a regular basis when interacting with customers, employees, or friends and family (Brown, n.d.).

Something else to keep in mind: empathy is controlled by a part of the brain called the supramarginal gyrus, and researchers found that when decisions need to be made quickly, this region doesn't function correctly. This is why it's so crucial to start with listening and taking some time to pause before responding or taking action. It's also not possible to practice empathy unless you are in either a neutral state or a similar state to the other person. If you're very excited about a new promotion and the other person is frustrated because they got a bad review, it will be hard to connect. You must mentally put yourself in the shoes of the other person and imagine a similar experience, or at least try to get yourself to a neutral emotional state.

When it comes to self-awareness Tasha Eurich discovered something disturbing, which is that there is an inverse relationship between power and self-awareness, meaning that the more senior you become in your organization, the less self-aware you tend to be. This is exactly why it's so crucial for leaders practice self-awareness. This can be done in a number of ways for both internal and external self-awareness. For the internal aspect, the biggest piece of advice that Tasha has is to move away from asking "why" to asking "what." We frequently ask ourselves why we feel a certain way or why we did something – for example, "Why do I feel so upset?" or "Why did I say that to my team member?" We ask why in an attempt to practice introspection or self-reflection but unfortunately the "why" answer is usually in our unconscious, which means we don't really know why we do some things or feel a certain way, but we make up reasons that we then use to justify our feelings, behaviors, or actions. Instead, focus on the "what." For example, what is it that makes you feel upset? What is it that made you say that to your team member? Focusing on the "what" is more effective for helping you as a leader to develop a plan so that you can start asking yourself questions like "What am I going to do in the future to make sure I don't feel this way?" or "What can I do to make sure that in the future I make better decisions?" (Eurich, January 2018).

You can also experiment with the Benjamin Franklin technique. Franklin, one of the founders of the United States, was a big believer in self-awareness. He kept a balance sheet of his strengths and weaknesses on a regular basis to determine the overall worth of his character. It's a rather simple exercise that anyone can practice. Either on your computer, phone, or a piece of paper, simply write out all of your strengths (your assets) and then write out all of your weaknesses (your liabilities). After doing this and reviewing it, you can subjectively determine what your character net worth is. Try doing this exercise on a monthly or quarterly basis and, if you are working on yourself, you should see your overall character net worth grow. We spend so much time looking at our company financials and business metrics, maybe it's time we look at our own character. If it worked for Benjamin Franklin, it can certainly work for you.

When it comes to the external self-awareness piece the best thing you can do is to get candid feedback from others. There is extra emphasis here on the word "candid!" You don't just want people to compliment you and say how you great you are. As a leader you need to create a truly open and safe environment where your team members and peers can approach you and be honest with you. Positive feedback is okay to receive, but it's the critical feedback that will ultimately help you improve. When possible seek out those whom Tasha calls the "loving critics," the people who have your best interest in mind and are willing to tell you the truth.

As Yoda often said, "May the Force be with you." Better yet, "May emotional intelligence be with you."

19
The Translator

The word "translation" comes from the Latin word *translatio,* which means "carrying across" or "bringing across." I like to think of a bridge that connects things or people together. Translators have been around for thousands of years and are responsible for much of what we know about our collective history. Between the third and first centuries BCE, Jewish scriptures were translated into Greek, which was crucial since the dispersed Jews forgot that ancestral language. During the ninth century, Alfred the Great had Eusebius's *Ecclesiastical History* and Boethius's *Consolation of Philosophy* translated into "vernacular Anglo-Saxon," which helped with the spread Christianity. In Asia, the growth and spread of Buddhism led to massive translation efforts, which also helped that religion grow. The impact extends far beyond religion to poetry, politics, music, film, and every type of medium and genre that exists. Regardless of the continent we look at or the time period we explore, translators and their translations have had a dramatic impact on our history and continue to do so.

Leaders of the future must be translators, which means that they are great listeners and communicators. Listening and communication are leadership traits that have always been around and are considered essential and always will be. But even though these are perhaps the most basic and timeless traits for great leadership, they are also the ones that we have struggled with the longest and the ones that have changed the most. The CEOs I interviewed ranked this second on their list of the most important skills for the future leader, just barely behind thinking like a futurist.

Even though listening and communication have always been crucial, their importance is going to increase tenfold over the coming years. The world we live in now is becoming increasingly connected and distributed. Social causes are becoming business imperatives and the amount of noise and distractions that all of us are dealing with is immense. Just think of all of the channels we can communicate on and listen to, and it's growing. These channels are also causing us to change our behaviors; grown men are now taking selfies with one another and using emojis to communicate!

Now imagine what this will look like in the coming decade. It's going to be more important than ever for leaders to understand their employees, customers, competitors, and society as a whole and this isn't possible without listening. Leaders are also being put in the public eye more than ever before and their shareholders and stakeholders are constantly wanting answers and insights into what the organization is doing, so being able to communicate in this type of world is also going to be crucial.

Tim Ryan, the chair and senior partner of PwC in the United States, said:

> The leader of today has a lot of people looking at him or her. This will be exponentially the case in a world that is becoming increasingly uncertain. I've seen many people hit a ceiling in their career because they couldn't get over the number of critics that they had and what those critics were saying about them. The reality is that being able to handle this is a skill that is going to become more important. You will never please everybody but you must always listen to people's views without unraveling, be able to communicate effectively, course correct as needed, and keep moving forward.

In June 2018 the Predictive Index conducted a survey that asked 5,103 respondents about their managers. The top response when looking at the top traits of terrible managers was "doesn't communicate clear expectations (58%)." A few percentage points behind that was "doesn't listen to others (50%)," along with "is a poor verbal communicator (48%)" (Predictive Index, 2018).

Listening

Many leaders confuse hearing with listening. Hearing is simply the act of sound entering your ear. In fact, while you're reading this book you might hear various sounds around you. Perhaps you're sitting in a coffeeshop and you can hear people talking; maybe you're on a plane and you can hear the sound of the engine roaring; or perhaps you're sitting at home and you can hear the birds chirping outside. Hearing is not a conscious act and it doesn't require any kind of purposeful effort.

Listening, on the other hand, is quite different. It is the purposeful and deliberate effort of understanding someone or something. In today's distracted world, listening is actually much harder than it sounds. Think of a time when you were in a conversation with someone and you knew they weren't listening to you. Maybe they were looking at you but you could tell they were mentally checked out of the conversation. Perhaps it was even more obvious, maybe someone kept checking their phone or laptop instead of listening to you. Think of how it made you feel – probably not very good, or important for that matter.

With the many new communication channels we have access to now, listening for future leaders means having many ears to many different grounds.

I'm always fascinated with how many leaders out there like to copy what leaders of other organizations are doing. I always tell these leaders, "Stop trying to freakin' be like Google!" What's the best way to figure out what your employees and customers want? How about you just ask them and then listen to what they tell you?

Most of us have been in a relationship with someone at one time or another. Imagine if you were to take all of your cues for how to behave by reading magazines or getting advice from your friends – a very silly approach. Why not just go directly to the person you're in a relationship with and get feedback straight from them? It seems that leaders today are scared to talk to their people, a fear you need to get over quickly.

Charlie Young is the CEO of Coldwell Banker, a real estate company with over 90,000 affiliated agents and brokers. Listening is a big part of how he leads.

I didn't invent it; I'm sure it's been around for 100 years and I find it to be really useful, especially when I go into new situations or change situations, and that's a keep, stop, start exercise. I sit everybody down and ask them to tell me what we should keep doing, what we should stop doing, and what we should start doing. I ask everybody, top to bottom, on the team. What's key here is listening to the feedback from your team, analyzing the data, and then determining the best course of action. But it all starts with listening.

For leaders, listening is crucial since they can be quite removed from their customers and even from their employees, especially at large global organizations. One of the consistent findings from the research I did for this book is that the more senior you are, the more removed you are from the rest of the employees at your organization. Your perceptions of how well you are thinking about future trends and practicing the skills and mindsets explored in this book are not aligned with those with whom you work. One of the best ways to close this gap is by practicing listening.

Michael Kneeland is the president and CEO of United Rentals, which has over 18,000 employees. Michael told me, "I've always gone through the world where it's a reverse pyramid. I'm so far from my customers that the most impactful thing I think that I can be doing is listening, and understanding what's happening on the front line."

It's no wonder that many people say that listening is the greatest form of respect and love that you can show someone. By truly listening to those around you, you will be able to build better relationships, make smarter decisions, and create a more engaged workforce. However, as a leader this means that you are also encouraging your employees to speak up. There's no point in being a good listener if nobody is willing to talk to you!

As Arnold Donald, the CEO of Carnival Cruises, told me, "If you want to be an effective leader, you have to understand the motivations of those you're leading. You really need to be able to listen. If you can listen well, the world will reveal itself to you, but you must be able to listen."

Communication

The actual act of communication is easy; it's simply about transferring or sharing information from one person to another (or group). We all do this many times a day. For present and future leaders, though, it's not enough to simply share information; anyone can do that.

One of the few normal jobs I had was working for a marketing agency in San Francisco around 15 years ago. It was actually the last job I ever had working for someone else. At the time the Web 2.0 Conference was all the rage and I won a pass to attend the conference for free (a ticket cost over $2,500). The event was being held locally in the Bay Area and I asked my boss if I could attend. I didn't have any client deliverables due, I offered to make up any work needed in the evenings or on the weekends, and I also made a case that since we were a marketing agency it would be great to have a presence at a marketing conference. The response was a simple, "no." No explanation, no discussion, nothing, just "no." This same boss rarely shared company direction or strategy with employees, made no attempt to get feedback or ideas from others, had no presence around team members (he just locked himself in his office all day), and made it quite apparent that we were all there to work for him. So, I quit and went to the conference anyway, and it was the best decision I ever made, which set me on my current career trajectory.

Communication is one of the greatest tools in the leader's utility belt. It's what allows you to inspire, connect with, and align those around you. Effective communication also helps make sure that strategies get executed effectively. We've all experienced the impact of a poor and a great communicator. How many times have you had a meeting with a leader or listened to a leader present something, only to find that afterwards you were stuck asking, "*Huh?*" What about getting a whitepaper-sized email from a leader that read more like a letter to a therapist instead of something for a team? Ever get those super-long texts about a project that you now need to spend 30 minutes responding to with your thumbs?

Communication is about understanding the different channels to use and how to use them and also maintaining a presence around others that they can feel. It's both verbal and nonverbal and it's always evolving, which makes it challenging. In the past we communicated mainly in person or written text; then we added in things like phone, email, texting, collaboration tools like Slack, social media platforms like Facebook and LinkedIn, videoconferencing tools, and now we're exploring augmented and virtual reality, holograms, and who knows what else in the coming years. Every new channel means that as a leader, your message needs to be received loud and clear, regardless of how it's being transmitted – emojis included!

Tsuyoshi "Nick" Nagano is the president and CEO of Tokio Marine, a multinational insurance holding company which is headquartered in Tokyo, Japan. Nick clearly articulated the importance of communication:

As a CEO I may spend 70% of my time communicating with the people in my company. This may seem like a lot, but when you consider that I manage a global workforce of 32,000, this can mean they only listen to me speak live or virtually for 20 minutes per year on average. Thus these 20 minutes really need to count, otherwise where is my impact as CEO?

A recent study of over 2,000 people looked at what aspects of communication leaders found to be the most difficult with their employees, and 69% of managers responded with "communication in general." This was the top response, which is a rather alarming and quite frankly a scary statistic. In a distant second place at 37% was "giving feedback/criticism about their performance that they might respond badly to." Then there was a three-way tie for third (20%) with demonstrating vulnerability, recognizing employee achievements, and delivering the "company line" in a genuine way (Solomon, 2016).

I really love the way Melissa Reiff talked about communication during our interview. She's the CEO of the Container Store, a retailer of storage and organization products with over 5,000 employees. "Communication *is* Leadership. They are the same thing. Practicing consistent, reliable, effective, thoughtful, predictable, compassionate, and courteous communication every single day is essential in growing and sustaining a successful business."

According to a Holmes report that surveyed over 400 corporations with 100,000-plus employees in the United States and the UK, communication barriers cost the average organization $62.4 million per year in lost productivity. However, organizations where leaders were effective communicators saw a 47% higher return to their shareholders over a five-year period (Holmes, 2011).

How Leaders Can Develop The Skill of the Translator

Sam Walton was the creator of Walmart, which is one of the world's largest employers. Every week for almost 30 years, Sam would travel to stores and distribution centers across the country with a pen and a yellow notepad. He would spend time talking to associates and getting feedback on how they could better serve their customers. Sam would also talk to customers and even the customers of his competitors. He was the modern-day pioneer of a leader who listens. Sam knew that listening was crucial to the success of his organization. Perhaps it's no coincidence that from all of Walmart's fiercest competitors, including Sears and Kmart, only Walmart thrived and still does today.

There are some basics of listening, which many of us are familiar with: things like looking someone in the eye, not interrupting, practicing good body language, and giving verbal cues to let the other person know you're listening. But being a great listener goes far beyond that, according to some recent research.

Jack Zenger and Joseph Folkman from Zenger/Folkman did some great research on listening. They looked at data from a 3,492-participant leadership development program, which was designed to get leaders to become better coaches. After collecting 360-degree assessments, they identified the top 5% who are perceived as being the most effective listeners. Their findings revealed four conclusions.

First, a good listener doesn't simply remain silent while the other person is speaking. Actually, the opposite is true. The best listeners not only ask questions but do so in a way that promotes discovery and insight. In other words, they are meant to challenge assumptions that the person speaking might have, but in a gentle and constructive way. Being a good listener doesn't just mean you ask questions; it means you ask good questions. As the research showed, the best listeners were able to create two-way dialogue.

Second, a good listener builds a person's self-esteem and makes them feel supported and that the listener has confidence in the speaker. Creating a safe environment where issues and differences can be openly discussed was another critical component of being a good listener.

Third, a good listener creates cooperative conversations where information and feedback flow smoothly. Remember the good old days of records or CDs? If those things got scratched, the song would skip, start over, or create weird sounds. But if the record or CD was kept in good condition, the song would play smoothly. As a leader your job is to make sure the record or the CD doesn't get scratched; you want to make sure the conversation flows smoothly.

Finally, a good listener makes suggestions and explores other paths or opportunities, as opposed to just the one that the speaker might suggest. Based on this research, Jack Zenger and Joseph Folkman created six levels of listening, which build on top of one another (Zenger and Folkman, 2016).

Level 1: You create a safe environment where pretty much anything can be discussed.

Level 2: You put away distractions like phones and laptops and you make appropriate eye contact with the other person.

Level 3: You try to understand the main focus of what the other person is saying. This means you can identify the key ideas, you ask questions to clarify points or issues, and you can restate these things to make sure you understand everything correctly.

Level 4: You pay attention to nonverbal cues such as body language, facial expressions, or tone of voice. In their article, Zenger and Folkman wrote that around 80% of what we communicate comes from these signals, which means you don't just listen with your ears, you also listen with your eyes.

Level 5: You understand the emotions and feelings of the other person and you acknowledge them. This is where empathy comes into play.

Level 6: You ask good questions that are designed to let the other person see a new perspective or challenge an assumption they might have. It's important that you as the listener don't take over the conversation.

As a leader you should go through these six levels and practice them as often as you can. After you have meetings and interactions with others, you can quickly scan this list to see if you have incorporated all of them. If not, ask yourself which ones you left out, why, and how you can incorporate them in the future.

 Of course, mastering listening is only half of the equation; the other half is all about communication. David Nelms is the former CEO of Discover Financial, where he led the company in various roles for 20 years before retiring in 2019. According to David:

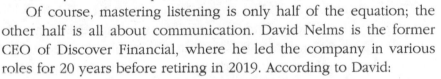

A leader who doesn't adapt to the new ways of communication will never be heard. We aren't getting and sharing information the same way we used to. Understanding the various tools we have to communicate as well as how to communicate across different channels is essential, and as the number of ways to communicate increases, this skill will only become more valuable.

When David was CEO he would constantly communicate with his teams. He hosted regular Q&A town hall meetings and annual roadshow meetings with a live video feed for all 17,000 employees. He also wrote regular blogs where employees could participate in open dialogue on a variety of topics. And it was not uncommon for David to drop in on employee huddles to talk with teams directly. He even hosted monthly customer listening sessions where he and others would listen in on service calls and then develop action plans to address any issues. Much of David's leadership style was built around constant communication, and that's what helped make him and Discover Financial so successful while he was CEO.

Adapting to new forms of communication also means that you don't forget the old ones! Amazon, for example, has a no-PowerPoint culture. Instead, team members who are presenting or sharing something are required to create a six-page document that clearly articulates their perspective, the pros and cons, shares any supporting materials, and provides a narrative. The first 30 minutes of all their meetings are spent simply reading this document together. Amazon found that this creates alignment, ensures that everyone has access to the same information and that they actually consume it, and it makes the author of the document feel good knowing that everyone is reading what they created. In other words, if you work at Amazon, your written communication skills better be top notch; you can't just be a master of emojis and texting!

Thierry Breton, the CEO of French IT company Atos Origin, with 120,000 employees, wanted to ban email entirely and replace it with internal collaboration tools. This meant that employees needed to become fluent in that way of working, communicating, and collaborating. Jack Dorsey, the CEO of Twitter and Square, has a unique policy where if two or more people meet, one of them must take notes and share those notes with all other interested employees at Square. Employees there must excel at either writing or typing summaries and key points from meetings so that even those who weren't in attendance would be able to follow along.

As a leader, ask yourself the following questions when you communicate with others:

- ◆ What are the best channels to use to get information across?
- ◆ How does the way you communicate make those around you feel?
- ◆ Are you communicating in a clear, open, passionate, and humble way? Are you being human?
- ◆ If someone communicated to you in the same way you are communicating to others, what impact would it have?

Listening and communication are timeless leadership skills. The Translator not only knows how to practice them but can also adapt to them as the methods and channels of listening and communication evolve.

20
The Coach

The "Wizard of Westwood" is considered one of the world's greatest coaches of any sport. I'm referring, of course, to John Wooden, the famous UCLA basketball coach who led his team to ten NCAA championships over 12 years, including an unheard of seven in a row. John was born on October 14, 1910, in Indiana, where his family lived on a farm with no running water or electricity.

After graduating from high school he went to Purdue University, where he studied English and played basketball with great success. He was named All-Big Ten and All-Midwestern and after graduating was actually offered a spot on the Boston Celtics professional team. He turned it down so that he could begin his teaching career and marry the love of his life, Nellie (an entirely separate but fascinating story). After his wife passed away, he continued to write her a love letter on the 21st of every month. He ended each letter by saying how much he misses her and looks forward to being with her again.

After college, John turned professional and spent some time playing with the Indianapolis Kautskys (later the Indianapolis Jets). John then spent some time in both the Navy and the Armed Forces during World War II. He also had a few coaching jobs, including Dayton High School and South Bend Central High School. Eventually he landed a job coaching at Indiana State University, where his reputation really started to grow after he won the Indiana Intercollegiate Conference title. For the 1948–49 season John was hired as the fourth basketball coach in UCLA's history and he went on to create history there. When John retired, his coaching record with UCLA was 620 wins and 147 loses.

John passed away on June 4, 2010, at the age of 99. John wasn't just a great coach; he was a great leader.

Future leaders must be great coaches. This means that you know how to motivate, engage, and inspire people, you can create other leaders, you can work across generations and cultures, and you can put together effective teams.

A recent a study looked at 1,884 leaders inside a large energy company. The leaders had their bosses, peers, direct reports, and other employees evaluate their coaching skills. They found a direct correlation between a leader's coaching effectiveness and the productivity of the team, specifically that better coaches have three times as many people who are willing to go the extra mile. Not only that, but leaders in the 90th percentile for coaching effectiveness also had employee commitment scores in the 88th percentile. The opposite was also true, though: leaders who placed near the bottom (10th percentile) had employees who were in the 15th percentile for commitment (Folkman, 2015).

"I see the leader as a coach, as a conductor, as somebody who orchestrates the efforts of many. Whoever thinks leadership is a one-man show is in for a bad surprise." This is what I heard from Luigi Gubitosi, the CEO of Telecom Italia, the Italian telecommunications company with over 60,000 employees around the world.

Many people think that coaching is only reserved for entry-level or maybe mid-level employees inside organizations. However, I was surprised how many CEOs told me that they actively work with coaches on everything from emotional intelligence to leadership advice to just general business guidance. We can all perform better with a coach. I have played chess for many years but only recently started working with a coach and immediately my performance increased. Not many great athletes or business leaders got where they are without being coached and mentored along the way.

David Baiada is the CEO of Bayada Home Health Care, which has almost 30,000 employees. He was also voted by employees as one of the top CEOs in 2019 on Glassdoor. After talking to David, I wasn't surprised to learn why. David takes the coaching skill to heart by empowering his entire workforce to coach and support one another. During our interview he told me:

Getting the right people in the right chairs and actively coaching and supporting their ability to be successful is something that I work on every day. To inspire employees to coach each other, we created a new ritual called Key Action of the Week. Every Thursday at 8:30–8:45 a.m., employees at our locations across the country gather together for a brief huddle to discuss one of the 15 key actions that make up the Bayada Way, our core values-based philosophy. It's a simple success routine, but when each employee is thinking of the same aspect of our underlying culture and sharing examples, coaching each other on that value, and living up to "what good looks like," it creates a sense of connectedness to the work and to each other, and reinforces the purpose behind what we do.

Enel, the Italian energy company we met earlier in the book, is making coaching a core part of leadership strategy. Like many organizations, they realized it's important to move away from a command-and-control approach to one that is focused on open leadership oriented toward mutual growth between the leader and those they are coaching. They launched a program in 2017 called "From Leader to Coach," involving over 1,300 managers and 7,000 HR supervisors from all over the world.

Since then they have expanded that program even further by creating certified coaches within the company. These people go through intensive programs and act as subject matter experts on coaching. Today they have over 100 of them in Italy, Spain, and Romania with several others in the pipeline. They also just launched I-coach, a series of training and development sessions that allow employees to access the Coaching approach and become better trainers themselves. These courses allow employees to get access to training materials, courses, and other coaches virtually. The big-picture idea for Enel is to train all of their employees on coaching methodologies so that regardless of the role or seniority level, they always have someone they can coach and they always have someone who can coach them. So far, 15 sessions have been carried out involving more than 500 employees. The big picture idea for Enel is to extend this to all employees regardless of their role or seniority, because it is considered a way of enhancing people's potential, helping them discover what they can become, rather than what they are.

Motivating, Inspiring, and Engaging People

Great leaders don't just tell people what to do; they make people want to actually do it. Being able to "rally the troops," so to speak, is a crucial skill for future leaders (and of course current ones). It is also perhaps the most challenging one to master. Motivating, engaging, and inspiring are related but they are definitely not the same thing. Motivating means you are able to get someone to act or behave in a certain way, typically by providing an incentive; this is often referred to as the "push." Engaging means you are able to keep the attention and efforts of someone; I like to think of this as "sustaining." Finally, we have inspiring, which means you are able to fill someone with the urge or the ability to do something, to animate them with a positive feeling. This is oftentimes referred to as the "pull." (See Figure 20.1).

Taken together, these are a powerful trifecta that as a leader means you can get people to move in a certain direction, you can keep their attention and focus to keep moving in that direction, and you can do so in a way that makes them want to do it. Separately, these are still important skills to have, but collectively, they will make you an unstoppable leadership force.

MOTIVATING

You can't motivate people unless you understand what they care about and value and not everyone will care about and value the same things. Some employees in your organization may be motivated purely by money, and that's okay. In fact, this is often typical for

3 Ways Leaders Can Unlock Human Potential

| **Push** | **Sustain** | **Pull** |
| Motivate | Engage | Inspire |

JACOB MORGAN
© thefutureorganization.com

FIGURE 20.1 THREE WAYS LEADERS CAN UNLOCK HUMAN POTENTIAL.

employees in sales, who may be more competitive and fueled by the idea of a larger bonus or paycheck. Other employees might be motivated more by praise or recognition. Instead of getting a larger bonus, these employees just want to know that you as a leader are aware of the work they put into something. This might mean acknowledging them during an all-hands meeting, taking them out for lunch, or maybe just stopping by their desk and letting them know how much you appreciate their work. Perhaps other employees are motivated more by a bit of fear, stress, and tough deadlines. Some employees really thrive under this level of pressure; they need their adrenaline going to perform at an optimal level.

There are all sorts of things that motivate people and as a leader, part of your job is to know what those things are. In fact, recent research conducted by Richard E. Clark, professor emeritus of psychology and technology at the University of Southern California, and Bror Saxberg, vice president of learning science at the Chan Zuckerberg Initiative, found that this is one of the most common traps that leaders fall into; they assume that what motivates them will motivate others, which is not the case (Clark, 2019).

Unfortunately, research done by Gallup found that only 20% of employees strongly agree that their performance is managed in a way that motivates them to do outstanding work (Wigert, 2017). Clearly, there is a lot of room for improvement here. There's no secret to this and this is isn't something AI can do for you; it's your human responsibility to get to know those you lead and serve, not just as workers but as individuals. Think of how you get to know someone on a first date or when you meet new friends. The same approach applies here.

INSPIRING

How do you fuel that burning fire in your people that truly makes them want to do something, not because of an incentive, but because of their own desire? Harvard Business School recently gathered data from 50,000 leaders and found that the ability to inspire was among the most important competencies. It's what separates the best leaders from all of the others, it's what employees want most from their leaders, and it's also what creates the highest levels of engagement. IBM recently conducted a survey of 1,700 CEOs across 64 countries. They also found that one of the most important leadership traits is the ability to inspire (Levin, 2017). When the CEO of my first company made me get him coffee, I was not inspired.

Over the years Zenger/Folkman has collected and surveyed many thousands of leaders around the world. To understand what inspiring leaders do, they looked at 1,000 leaders in their database who scored highest on the competency of "inspires and motivates to high performance." Their research revealed a few interesting insights. Inspiring leaders do a combination of both tangible and intangible things. The tangibles include things like engaging in highly collaborative behavior with others, encouraging out-of-the-box thinking, and spending time on people development. The intangibles included things such as making emotional connections with team members, being a champion of change, and being an effective communicator, all concepts and ideas discussed in this book. We've all heard the phrase "less is more," but the research done by Zenger/Folkman reveals that in order to be an inspiring leader the opposite is true: "more is more" (Zenger and Folkman, 2015).

According to research conducted by Bain & Company, which surveyed 2,000 of their own employees, 33 characteristics stood out as important for the capacity to inspire. These included several things talked about in this book, such as empathy, humility, listening, and self-awareness. But the most important attribute they found was "centeredness," which they define as a state of greater mindfulness that allows you to be fully present (Horwitch and Callahan, 2016). This helps empathizing with others, dealing with stress, and staying level-headed. It's no wonder organizations around the world are so heavily investing in mindfulness programs that allow leaders and employees of all levels to take more control over their emotions while focusing on showing that they as individuals are emotionally and physically present. According to Bain, employees who are inspired are more than twice as productive as employees who are simply "satisfied."

Pedro Parente is the chairman of the board of directors and former CEO of BRF, a food company with more than 90,000 employees globally. During our discussion he said:

If you want to get better and long-lasting results for your organization, then you must do so by being an inspiring leader. Not long ago, companies could achieve results and generate value by imposing views and standards and working through a top-down, command system. Our reality has changed dramatically and nowadays long-term results have to do with organizations that are able to change, to adapt fast enough and build cultures that are based on values. Communicating and connecting those values to diverse stakeholders of a company is one of the most important roles of a leader in any organization and I believe that can only be done through transparency, truth, and values. Telling people what to do or the best way simply does not work anymore. As leaders, we have to lead through values that make people want to be part of our organizations in their most varied roles, be it our employers, clients, or any other stakeholders. That is what I believe an inspiring leader should aim for.

The good news is that by embracing many of the other skills and mindsets outlined in this book, you will inherently become a more inspiring leader.

ENGAGING

For several decades now, leaders around the world have been investing in employee engagement programs, yet the collective scores are still abysmal. According to Gallup's most recent research, 85% of the global workforce is either not engaged or is actively disengaged at work, costing us over $7 trillion in lost productivity annually (Harter, 2017). You would think that these numbers would be improving if we are collectively spending so much time and effort on engagement, but they aren't, so what's going on? There's an adage stating that insanity is doing the same thing over and over but expecting a different result. It's not likely but certainly possible that the leaders investing in these programs are all insane.

In my previous book, *The Employee Experience Advantage,* I looked at 252 organizations around the world to figure out how the world's best are able to create a highly engaged workforce. It turns out that engagement is the outcome but the source of an engaged workforce is employee experience. We've just been focusing on and measuring the wrong thing. Employee experience is a combination of three environments that leaders can control:

◆ Technology, which is 30% of the overall employee experience, includes the tools, software, devices, hardware, and apps that employees use to get their jobs done.
◆ Physical space, which also comprises 30% of the overall experience, refers to the environments and spaces in which employees work.
◆ Culture, which is 40% of the overall employee experience, is more about how employees actually feel working for you and the organization.

Based on my research, companies that master this are more than four times more profitable, productive, and overall more successful.

(For leaders looking to learn more about this, my book is an in-depth guide to employee experience.) According to Gallup, managers account for 70% of the variance in employee engagement (Beck and Harter, 2015), and as I wrote earlier, almost all employees around the world are not engaged in their work.

Creating Future Leaders

Most people assume that leaders simply create more followers, but one of the most important things a leader can do is actually to create other leaders. I've long said that leaders need to show up to work with the belief that part of their job is to help make other people more successful than they are. This belief will then guide the actions that you take and behaviors that you exhibit. Sydney Finkelstein spent ten years and conducted over 200 interviews to find out what makes a "superboss." He spoke with leaders like football coach Bill Walsh, technology executive Larry Ellison, chef and restaurateur Alice Waters, television producer Lorne Michaels, and fashion designer Ralph Lauren. Sydney noticed something curious. When he looked at the top-ten people in any given industry, he noticed that more than half of them at some point worked for the same leader. In other words, one of the things that makes these leaders truly great is the fact that they create other leaders.

Teaching is a powerful way to accomplish this, but it extends beyond focusing on work-related themes and activities. One of the things that made coach Wooden so great was that he was focused on the process and rarely actually talked about winning. He wanted his players to build character and above all to become good human beings, which in turn would make them great basketball players. John would say, "Be more concerned with your character than your reputation, because your character is what you really are while your reputation is merely what others think you are" (Wooden, n.d.).

John developed the "Pyramid of Success," which comprised 15 blocks that included things like skill, confidence, initiative, friendship, enthusiasm, and loyalty. He taught all of his players these 15 blocks to help them achieve success.

Richard Allison is the CEO of Domino's, the pizza restaurant chain with over 400,000 franchise and corporate team members around the world. During our discussion he pinpointed a very clear change that we are seeing in business today, and one that will continue to grow. "We have to make sure that we're creating a compelling path of opportunity for people, and that we are investing in their growth and development over time. It used to be that their loyalty was assumed. Now, loyalty has to be earned. What better way to earn that loyalty than by focusing on helping create other leaders?"

Research cited earlier in this book shows that organizations around the world don't have future-ready leaders in place, nor is much being done to change that. What do you think the average age for a first-time manager is? How about the average age for someone in a leadership development program? Depending on the research, these numbers are 30 and 42, respectively. Leaders in the United States, for example, have an average age of just over 45. When I first came across these figures I thought, "You gotta be kidding me." How is it that most people don't start leadership development programs until they are middle-aged? Almost 40% of managers get leadership training between the ages of 46 through over 60. It's no wonder we have a shortage of great leaders – we simply aren't creating them. To give you an analogy, this is like trying to coach a professional tennis or basketball player in their 40s, far beyond their prime.

In 2016 Koç Group, a large industrial conglomerate in Turkey, launched a Digital Transformation Program covering more than 24 of their subsidiaries. The goal of the program is to harness the various technological developments we are seeing today to thrive in the digital future. Levent Çakıroğlu is the CEO of Koç Holdings, which has almost 100,000 employees globally, and he believes that none of this is possible without having the right present and future leaders in place. As he told me, "Our human resources lie at the heart of our long-term transformation. My biggest responsibility is to prepare the global leaders who will carry our group into the future. Accordingly, I put people in the heart of our digital transformation, rather than technology."

As a part of this, Koç Group developed a Personal Development Program (PDP) for leaders that focuses on everything from personal development and online learning, to wilderness training to test leadership limits, and coaching. Over 200 leaders have completed the program thus far.

The management consulting company Bain developed a unique approach to creating future leaders with something known as the Tiger team. Manny Maceda is the Worldwide Managing Partner (CEO) of Bain. He was offering coaching to employees but quickly realized that there were more people who could benefit from his coaching than he could ever work with directly. So Bain created a "hotline response team" to enable employees to reach out to Manny or any of the other partners for guidance, advice, and coaching. Employees can use this as often as they want, without any limits or restrictions. This ensures that not only is Manny creating other leaders, but so are the other partners inside of Bain. According to Manny:

> It is incredibly energizing because it keeps me closer to our most complicated client situations and it helps me connect with subsequent generations of partners. This spirit of apprenticeship is core to Bain's DNA, and a reason we are considered a great place to work by our teams. And I like to think it raised the bar on how we are able to have greater impact with many more of our clients at the same time.

Leaders must also think about creating other leaders beyond their organizational walls. Tom Wilson, the CEO of the Allstate Corporation, believes that businesses today and in the future have four roles in society: make profit, serve customers, create jobs, and strengthen communities. Leadership is crucial for this; in fact for Tom, working on developing the leaders of 2030 is a personal passion. Allstate does a lot with youth empowerment and helping kids volunteer through a program called WE Schools. Kids between middle school and early high school, both domestically and internationally, can volunteer for anything, such as raising money for anti-bullying, LGBTQ, the environment, making sure people have jackets during the winter, or doing bake sales. All that matters is that these kids are volunteering and doing service-based learning. Many Allstate employees also volunteer at WE Schools. The best part is that Tom and Allstate don't have a direct pipeline from this program into their company; they do it to create better leaders in society as a whole. According to Tom, that's one of the things he gets paid to do, to make sure the company and society have great leaders. Not only does Allstate help fund this program, but Tom personally helps get other funders and sponsors to help this initiative grow.

The Royal Bank of Scotland has almost 80,000 employees around the world, and creating future leaders is one of their top priorities. Ross McEwan, their CEO, told me:

We've defined the critical capabilities we believe our people and leaders need to possess to operate in the current and future world of business. We're already starting to develop leaders and colleagues against these critical people capabilities and have started recruiting against these. We've built future success profiles for leaders which we're already starting to recruit against. We've identified our future talent within the organization who already demonstrate a lot of these capabilities and we're giving them access to opportunities to influence strategy and thinking. At the same time, we're bringing in graduates, apprentices, and interns, and starting to do reverse mentoring to share skills and experience.

Not many companies that I've worked with have taken this kind of structured and thoughtful approach for their future leaders. But Ross realizes that the future of his business is all about what the company does now to make sure it has the right people in place in the future.

Working Across Generations and Cultures

Our workforce is becoming more dynamic than ever, and while this is a good thing it also creates challenges for leaders of the future who are used to homogeneous teams. I recently spoke to the leadership team of an aerospace and defense company with thousands of employees around the world. The leadership group I spoke with consisted of around 250 people. Although I was warned that their workforce is homogeneous, I didn't realize just how homogeneous it was! As I took the stage, I looked around the room and saw nothing but older white guys in suits. Not only that but the suits and collared shirts they wore were all a combination of different shades of black and blue. This is what many leadership teams look like around the world. When I see this I immediately think of an organization that hasn't yet "gotten off the train." To have a little fun with the audience, at the end of my talk I asked them, "Why are you guys all wearing suits?" They all looked at me like hundreds of deer in the headlights and collectively said, "I don't know." My hope is that over the years I will see fewer leadership teams like this.

The research for being able to work across generations and cultures is vast and extremely convincing. A recent study put together by Randstad found that 87% of workers believe a multigenerational workforce fosters innovation and problem-solving and 90% of workers prefer having colleagues of various ages and think a multigenerational workplace benefits everyone (Randstad, 2018). Another study published by Forbes found that decisions made and executed by diverse teams delivered 60% better results. The same study found that teams that include a wide range of ages and different geographic locations make better business decisions 87% of the time (Larson, 2017). The Boston Consulting Group also did some research on this and found that companies with above average diversity on their management teams had innovation revenue 19% higher than that of companies with below average leadership diversity (Lorenzo et al., 2018). Lastly, McKinsey found that in their study, organizations in the top quartile for ethnic and cultural diversity on executive teams were 33% more likely to have industry-leading profitability (McKinsey, 2018). Being able to work across generations and cultures isn't just a nice thing to be able to do; it's one of the crucial factors that will determine your success or failure as a leader.

 Sébastien Bazin is the CEO of AccorHotels, a hospitality group with almost 300,000 employees around the world. Sébastien believes this is absolutely crucial:

One mark of a future leader is the ability to work alongside people of different ages and with different backgrounds. Millennials, for example, have been changing the workplace ever since they started arriving on the scene nearly a decade ago. Craving autonomy and flexibility, millennials tend to be more confident and more adaptable when it comes to new concepts, new technologies, and so on. But their older-generational counterparts also have many things to teach these new hires: knowledge about the industry/company, interpersonal skills, and how to deal with failure. As a future leader you must be able to work with people regardless of how old they are, where they come from, what they believe, or what gender they are.

As I cited earlier in the book, McKinsey predicts that over the next decade there will be 3.5 billion people in the global workforce. Many believe that, as today, the future will also see a large shortage of skilled workers, which means leaders must expect to lead a very dynamic workforce especially as we become more global and tech-nologically connected. Most organizations today comprise employees from five and in some cases six generations. The push for more physically and cognitively diverse employees is also forcing leaders to rethink what teams look like and how they operate. This goes hand in hand with embracing the mindset of the global citizen explored earlier.

Whether we're looking at culture, generations, backgrounds, religions, or anything else, we have a tendency to focus on what makes us different instead of on what makes us similar. We have various stereotypes and biases in our heads and we need to learn to get rid of them. For example, all millennials are entitled and lazy, whereas all older workers are technologically incompetent and outdated in their workforce practices, right? You can quickly see the rabbit hole that this will send you down, and it's never-ending.

Leaders must get comfortable working with people who are different than they are in every way.

In an MIT study of MBA students and foreign nationals, the researchers found that professionals who kept in regular contact with friends they made in America after returning to their home country tended to be more innovative and entrepreneurial. They also found that cultural learning needs to be done at a deeper level instead of just at a superficial one (Relihan, 2018).

As a great coach, your job is to understand (and get others to understand) similarities and commonalities between yourself and your team but also to be able to do this among your team members. Don't fear the differences, respect them. Kent Thiry, whom we met earlier from DaVita, said:

To be an effective leader, it's important to understand teammates and relate to their hopes, fears, and preferences, regardless of their age, ethnicity, or background. We want all our teammates to think of their workplace as "a place where I belong." So leaders must demonstrate that they cultivate an environment of belonging by acknowledging that we are more alike than we are different and by celebrating each individual for who they truly are.

Creating Effective Teams

What is a team? The common understanding is that it's two or more people working together to achieve something or people who are associated together in some way. But what makes an effective team?

In an article for *Success* magazine, leadership expert John Maxwell explored why Wooden's teams won. He talked about how one of Coach Wooden's greatest strengths was selecting players and then motivating those players to achieve their full potential. Not everyone Wooden coached was an amazing player; in fact, he recruited a lot of average shooters. But, says John Maxwell, Wooden knew where on the court these players shot their best and would then design plays that enabled them to get into that spot. In other words, he would focus on their strengths and then create environments that allowed those strengths to come through (Maxwell, 2017).

Not all teams are created equal, and it's difficult to take an approach that works at one company and automatically assume it works at another company. This is what Disney did when they opened Euro Disney and it resulted in a massive employee exodus. Not too long ago, Google did an internal study called Project Aristotle, which was designed to figure out what makes some internal teams more effective than others. They found that who made up the team was not as important as how well the team actually works together. The number-one factor that determines the effectiveness of a team at Google is psychological safety, meaning that members of a team trust those around them. The other four factors are dependability, structure and clarity, meaning, and impact (Bariso, 2018). This worked for Google and it might work at your company too, but it might not.

Amazon, for example, has their famous two-pizza rule: if a team can't be fed by two large pizzas, then the team is too big. They also have a practice called the "single-threaded leader," which I learned about when visiting their headquarters in Seattle, where any big decision or project is assigned to a single leader who eats, sleeps, and breathes that decision or project and nothing else. Typically, leaders in organizations are responsible for many projects and many big decisions. At Amazon, they found that a singular focus leads to more effective teams and decision-making.

In the early 2000s, why did it take only 600 Apple engineers less than two years to develop, debug, and deploy iOS 10 while it took Microsoft over 10,000 engineers and years to develop, deploy, and then retract Vista? These teams were constructed in different ways. The team at Apple comprised all-star players and they were rewarded as a team. Microsoft at the time was using stack ranking (which they since stopped) where only 20% of every team was allowed to be in the "exceptional" category and the performance was purely based on how well you did as an individual (Vozza, 2017). Clearly, creating effective teams makes a huge difference, but it's not just about the people on the team that matters.

J. Richard Hackman, who passed away in 2013, was a professor of social and organizational psychology at Harvard University and one of the world's leaders on teams, something he began studying in the 1970s. He found that what teams need in order to succeed are "enabling conditions" (Hackman, 2004). We always assume that the success or failure of a team depends on the leader and sometimes that may be the case, but what if there's more to it than that? It's not just the leader that influences the team; it's the team dynamics that influence the leader. If you take over a team that is not willing to cooperate and collaborate together and the team members do not appear very capable of doing their jobs, then your leadership style may be more hierarchical, command-and-control, project and task oriented, direct, and seemingly less human. In contrast, if you take on a team where the members are open with each other, are great at their jobs, and are communicative and collaborative, then your leadership style may be democratic, open, transparent, and more human. In other words, says Hackman, it's not a one-way street like so many of us assume it is. This is why he argues for this concept of conditions instead of causes. Based on his research, there are five factors: real team, a compelling direction, enabling structure, supportive context, and competent coaching.

More recent research from Martine Haas at Wharton and Mark Mortensen at INSEAD found that another condition is crucial: "shared mindset." This is because, as mentioned above, teams are becoming more dynamic, diverse, and distributed, which means it's tempting to switch to an "us-versus-them" mentality, and it's also crucial to make sure that teams don't have incomplete information. A shared mindset solves these two problems (Haas, 2016). Let's briefly look at these six conditions:

- ◆ **Real team:** clear boundaries, interdependence among members, and at least moderate stability of membership over time
- ◆ **Compelling direction:** a clear purpose that is challenging and consequential, something that focuses on the ends to be achieved rather than just the means to pursue it
- ◆ **Enabling structure:** a structure that enables teamwork, as opposed to hindering it
- ◆ **Supportive context:** resources such as training, rewards, and access to information that enables team members to work effectively

- ◆ **Competent coaching:** someone who can help with mentoring, advice, getting over obstacles and challenges, questions, and the like
- ◆ **Shared mindset:** creating a common understanding and identity; for example, focusing on similarities as opposed to differences

I have a three-year-old daughter and, as any parent knows, raising a child isn't just about feeding them, taking them to school, buying them toys, changing them, and putting them to bed. You must also create an environment where your child can learn, grow, develop, express themselves, and experience new things. For future leaders these enabling conditions are just as important, if not more so, than the tactical applications we are all familiar with. Coach Wooden knew this, which is why he focused on creating those conditions (plays) that enabled his players to succeed. He always said that it takes ten hands to make a basket!

Michel Combes is the CEO of Sprint, the telecommunications company with around 30,000 employees. During our discussion Michel summarized the skill of a coach quite well: "I see my role as a coach. On one side, I need to produce a vision. On the other side, I need to enable people to deliver this vision and to be comfortable in their ability to deliver, and to make sure that I always push them to their maximum."

When it comes to creating effective teams, there is no one best approach to take. Countless studies, books, and reports have been written about teamwork and research keeps changing and evolving. As a leader you must not only be aware of what you do but of the conditions you create for your team to succeed.

How Leaders Can Develop The Skill of the Coach

At the very core of being a great coach is truly believing that your job and your privilege is to help other people become more successful than you. This is an important distinction from simply helping people become more successful because it changes the amount of effort you will put in. Most leaders can typically put in a relatively small amount of effort to help someone grow, learn, or become more successful. But to try to get someone to excel beyond you is a much more challenging task that requires more time and resources. Are you willing to do it?

Another crucial aspect of being a great coach is the ability to connect with the people you work with to truly understand them as human beings instead of just as workers. Try asking yourself a few basic questions about the people you work with:

- What excites them the most?
- What stresses them out or drains them the most?
- What are they most passionate about?
- What are their strengths and weaknesses?
- What are their hobbies or interests outside of work?
- Do they have a family, and if so, do you know anything about them?
- What are their professional and personal goals?
- What do they think of you as a leader?

Of course, the list of questions here can be endless, but the point isn't simply to create a checklist or a survey and have your employees answer them. It's about taking the time and effort to know your people as humans, the same way you would with a potential new friend or significant other.

Many of the skills and mindsets outlined in this book build on top of one another. You will notice that as you embrace the mindsets talked about earlier, doing so will make also make you a better coach.

21
The Technology Teenager

Whenever parents can't figure out a certain technology, the first person they turn to is usually their teenage kids (if they have them). Why is that? It's not because teenagers are technology experts who understand how every piece of technology works and how it was created. It's because teenagers are just technology savvy and digitally fluent. In other words, they understand technology but they don't need to be technology experts. Leaders of the future must be the same way.

Michael Tipsord is the CEO of State Farm, an insurance and financial services company with a workforce of over 90,000 employees and independent contractor agents. He started his career there in 1988. In our interview he highlighted the importance of being tech savvy: "Tomorrow's leaders will need to have a technology fluency that lets them anticipate opportunities and threats, distinguish hype from credible, and embrace transformative possibilities."

Understand How Technology Impacts Your Business

Technology has a dramatic impact on our lives, our organizations, and our world. Most of us rarely think about this because technology has become so ubiquitous that we take it for granted. But from the moment you wake up until the moment before you go to bed, your life is powered by technology. Whether it's the smart assistant you use in the morning to listen to the news, the car you drive to work, the phone or laptop you use to check your email, the plane you fly when traveling, or the TV you turn on when you want to relax, technology is everywhere like air. Of course, technology can refer to many different things: artificial intelligence, machine learning, hardware and software, blockchain, augmented and virtual reality, 3D printing, robotics, quantum computing, and anything and everything in between. It's estimated that by 2030 there will be an average of 9.27 connected devices per person (Safaei, 2017).

Japan recently appointed a new cybersecurity and Olympics minister (responsible for the 2020 Olympic games), 68-year-old Yoshitaka Sakurada. In a recent interview he said, "I've been independent since I was 25 and have always directed my staff and secretaries to do that kind of thing.... I've never used a computer!" This is not something that leaders of the future will be able to get away with, particularly because every aspect of an organization is powered by and dependent on technology (*Irish Times,* 2018).

Robert Dutkowsky is the former CEO and current executive chairman of Tech Data, an information technology and services company with over 14,000 employees. He put this rather simply: "The leader of an organization has to be right on top of technology because virtually every company in the world today is a technology company."

Leaders don't need to understand the details of how the technologies will be deployed, but they do need to understand what impact a particular technology might have on the business. They need to be able to have these conversations and should be able to answer questions like:

- ◆ What does the general technology landscape look like? What are some of the emerging technologies out there today?
- ◆ Which technologies are going to impact your industry?
- ◆ How might your organization use various technologies to improve things like customer satisfaction, employee experience, or productivity?
- ◆ What might happen if the organization doesn't make investments in technology?
- ◆ How are your customers and employees using various technologies?

How Leaders Can Develop The Skill of the Technology Teenager

If you watch how teenagers or even preteens learn how to use technology, you will see that they rarely read an instruction manual. They just pick up or download whatever the technology is and start playing around with it. Leaders must approach technology the same way. A few years ago, if you wanted to learn about a new technology, you would have to sign up for a course, read through a whole instruction manual, or follow the instructions that came on the CD-ROM for whatever device you were trying to learn. Computers today don't even come with CD-ROM drives anymore! Today we have access to learn anything we want, any time, and on any device with platforms such as YouTube, where you can find a tutorial or an overview for any technology you need or want. Even sites like TED are wonderful resources for learning about new technology concepts and ideas. Leaders must take advantage of them.

I get it – lots of new technologies keep emerging. By the time you figure out how to use one of them, another one emerges, so how in the world are you supposed to keep up? We're all used to this idea of something new coming out and then having some time to play around with the shiny toy before a new one emerges. Unfortunately, that world no longer exists. Today shiny toys are being pelted at you and your organization like paintballs in a melee. Instead of thinking, "How do I keep up?" you have to shift your mindset to "This is the new normal." This is the best piece of advice business leaders have shared with me when it comes to technology. You can't control the speed of technology, but you can control your mindset and your response.

By having an overall understanding of the technology landscape, you should be able to determine which tools might have the greatest impact on your business and which ones can wait.

Another useful technique for practicing being a technology teenager is surrounding yourself by people who are more technology savvy than you are. It's not uncommon to hear of business leaders who are mentored by usually younger, more technology fluent employees.

22
How Well Are We Practicing These Skills Today?

The coach, the translator, the futurist, the technology teenager, and Yoda: these are the most crucial skills that leaders of the future must possess in order to be successful over the next decade and beyond. In conjunction with the mindsets discussed earlier, mastering these skills will make you an unstoppable and invaluable leadership force. However, you must remember that your responsibility is to also make sure that those around you master these skills as well.

Let's take a global look at how we are practicing these skills. These numbers are quite consistent with what we saw earlier in the mindsets section. Collectively, respondents believe they are doing a pretty good job of practicing these skills, with the numbers dropping considerably when asked about their managers and senior executives: 57% of all managers and 58% of all senior executives fall into the bottom two categories, respectively. Only 8% of all managers and senior executives were said to be practicing the skills outlined in this book "very well." (See Figure 22.1.)

From this high-level vantage point, we can now break things down by individual contributors (ICs), managers, and senior executives to see where the gaps are and how big those gaps are. ICs put 60% of their managers and 62% of their senior executives in

How Well Are Companies Practicing the Skills for the Future Leader?

	How well do you think you are practicing these skills?	How well do you think your managers are practicing these skills?	How well do you think your senior executives are practicing these skills?
Not well at all	2%	17%	20%
Somewhat well	28%	40%	38%
Reasonably well	48%	29%	29%
Very well	20%	8%	8%

JACOB MORGAN

© thefutureorganization.com

FIGURE 22.1 EVALUATING HOW COMPANIES ARE PRACTICING THE SKILLS FOR THE FUTURE LEADER.

the bottom two categories of "somewhat well" and "not well at all." Managers also put 60% of their senior executives in the bottom two categories. These large gaps can once again be seen across all seniority levels. (See Figure 22.2.)

Mind the Gaps – Again!

When looking at all of the data on skills, we see the same story that we saw earlier when looking at mindsets. Leaders (managers and senior executives) believe they are doing a far better job of practicing these skills than they actually are. This is true when looking at the skills in aggregate and also when looking at each skill separately. There is simply no alignment between how managers and senior executives are practicing these skills when compared to how others less senior believe their managers and senior executives are practicing these skills.

For all leaders, the data shows that they scored quite poorly across the board but individual contributors say that the hardest skill for their managers to practice is Yoda: emotional intelligence. The skill where individuals say their managers are doing the best job is

Practicing the Skills for The Future Leader:
Individual Contributors vs Managers vs Senior Executives

	How well are your managers practicing these skills? (Individual Contributors)	How well are you practicing these skills? (Managers)	Gap between individual contributors and managers	How well are your senior executives practicing these skills? (Individual Contributors)	How well are you practicing these skills? (Senior Executives)	Gap between individual contributors and senior executives	How well are your senior executives practicing these skills? (Manager)	Gap between managers and senior executives
Not well at all	20%	2%	18%	23%	1%	22%	20%	19%
Somewhat well	40%	29%	11%	39%	25%	14%	40%	15%
Reasonably well	29%	49%	20%	28%	50%	22%	30%	20%
Very well	10%	19%	9%	9%	23%	14%	8%	14%

JACOB MORGAN
© thefutureorganization.com

FIGURE 22.2 PRACTICING THE SKILLS FOR THE FUTURE LEADER: COMPARISONS.

that of the translator: listening and communication. When it comes to senior executives, the skill they are practicing the best (according to both individual contributors and managers) is that of the futurist. The skill that senior executives struggle with the most is Yoda.

Around the World

Which countries are doing the best and the worst job of practicing these collective skills? Once again, I looked at the top two categories of "reasonably well" and "very well" along with the bottom two categories of "somewhat well" and "not well at all." In Figures 22.3 and 22.4, you can see the responses across countries to the three questions of "How well do you think you are practicing these skills?" "How well do you think your managers are practicing these skills?" and "How well do you think your senior executives are practicing these skills?"

Collectively, Brazil once again came out on top but this time it was the United States and DACH which came in second place. When we look at managers, Brazil is far and away the highest-scoring country for the top two categories, followed by DACH and the United States. For senior executives, India is not too far behind Brazil, but it's the United States that scores near the bottom of the pack.

Figure 22.4 has a similar chart but instead of looking at the top two categories it looks at the bottom two categories.

Once again we see the respondents from China having the largest percentage in the bottom two categories, followed by Australia and India. For managers, Brazil is clearly ahead of the other countries, followed by DACH. Lastly, when we look at the senior executives, it's Australia that has the highest percentage in the bottom two categories, followed by the United States and the UK.

Are We Future Leader Ready?

Of the almost 14,000 people surveyed, only a third said that their organizations have a policy or program in place to address future leadership requirements in the next ten years. When I asked the 140 CEOs this same question, 86 of them said that they have programs in place to address the future of leadership in the coming ten years. The

**How well are you, your managers, and
senior executives practicing these skills?**

("reasonably well" and "very well")

	US	UK	DACH	India	Brazil	China	UAE	Australia
You	69	67	69	63	80	46	67	64
Managers	38	34	39	34	47	27	36	31
Senior Executives	35	32	37	43	49	39	37	31

JACOB MORGAN
© thefutureorganization.com

FIGURE 22.3 HOW WELL ARE YOU, YOUR MANAGERS, AND SENIOR EXECUTIVES PRACTICING THESE SKILLS? (TOP TWO CATEGORIES).

How well are you, your managers, and senior executives practicing these skills?
("somewhat well" and "not well at all")

	US	UK	DACH	India	Brazil	China	UAE	Australia
You	30	32	29	36	18	50	33	36
Managers	57	59	55	63	47	69	61	64
Senior Executives	61	61	57	56	47	51	60	63

JACOB MORGAN
© thefutureorganization.com

FIGURE 22.4 HOW WELL ARE YOU, YOUR MANAGERS, AND SENIOR EXECUTIVES PRACTICING THESE SKILLS? (BOTTOM TWO CATEGORIES).

remainder are either focusing on leadership in the short-term or were blatantly honest in telling me that they aren't thinking about the future of leadership at all.

While the CEO responses are far more optimistic than the survey responses, we once again see a huge gap between what most employees perceive and believe versus what CEOs are saying they are focusing on. In this instance, it's what employees around the world are perceiving and experiencing, which is more important than what CEOs are saying they are doing. Perception is reality, so if employees are saying that their organizations are not ready for the future of leadership, then they aren't ready, regardless of how optimistic the CEO might be.

There is a tremendous opportunity for us to think about the leaders we want and how we are going to grow them in our organizations and in our society. Throughout this book I have presented my research and that of others, which clearly shows that leaders today are not living up to their potential and that organizations around the world are not ready for the changes we are seeing in the world of work. We simply don't have future-ready leaders. But we can change that – you can change that.

PART 5

BECOMING THE FUTURE LEADER

23
Knowing vs Doing

In today's world it's easy for us to focus on the negative but the most important thing I learned from writing this book is that the future is bright. The CEOs I interviewed identified the Notable Nine as the most crucial mindsets and skills for the future leader, but I want to add one to the list that can be both a mindset and a skill: optimism. As a leader you have to wake up each day believing that the future can be better than it is today and that you can help build that better future. This is not an easy thing to do. You will get caught up in the day-to-day aspects of your job and life, you will switch teams and employers, perhaps you will relocate, and you may even switch careers. Regardless of where your path takes you, you must remain optimistic. The future leader must wake up each morning and ask, "How can I be better and how can I unlock the potential of my people?"

There is a lot of work for leaders and organizations around the world to do. But this also means there is tremendous potential and opportunity, if you take action.

Sheryl Palmer is the CEO of Taylor Morrison, a home building company with over 2,500 employees. A few years ago, she had to do one of the most difficult things in her life and career: write two letters to her team. One of the letters to her team said, "I'll see you in six weeks," and the other letter said, "Make me proud and finish the great work we started." Sheryl had a brain tumor and she wasn't sure if she would make it back from her surgery. The first letter she wrote was the one she wanted her team to receive if the surgery went well and she would expect to be back to work in six weeks. The second letter was the one she wanted her to team receive if it turned out she would not return. The night before the surgery, Sheryl flew back home from Florida, where she had met with the chairman of the board of Taylor Morrison's parent company to finalize the timing and next steps of their UK sale process plans, assuming she returned in a few weeks as planned. It gave her important peace of mind that both the company and the Taylor Morrison team would move forward and be okay. For all Sheryl knew, this could have been her last night on earth and she spent it making sure her people were taken care of. In Sheryl's own words:

Although I always believed I lived life to the fullest and looked for the good in each person and situation, going through this made me realize how precious each life encounter really is. It made me a better leader because I was able to appreciate how important every interaction is, and not to take anything or anyone for granted. Many leaders go through their days fighting fires and not appreciating the golden rule of business: people work for people, not companies. A leader's responsibility is to set the vision and not allow the business just to happen, but rather make relationships and interactions intentional, meaningful, and purposeful. Some may consider it really hard work, but being a leader is a choice, and if you decide that this is who you really are, there is no middle ground – it's all consuming, not two parallel paths. Being a leader can't just be when you show up to the office. It's your natural passion and an eerie intersection in all parts of our lives. But when you really do it, it's the most rewarding life journey in the world.

When Sheryl first told me this story, I got goosebumps. I still do every time I share it with an audience. Perhaps it's no coincidence that both Sheryl as a CEO and Taylor Morrison as a company have almost perfect reviews on Glassdoor, along with many other awards and recognitions. In fact, an astounding 94% would recommend Taylor Morrison to a friend. Sheryl's story and her message underscores the importance of action and leading with intention. I hope you take it to heart.

There's a big difference between knowing and doing. After getting this far in the book, you now know everything you need to become a future leader, but are you going to take the next step and actually do something?

We live and work in a dynamic and rapidly changing world, which means that as leaders we not only need to be able to adapt to the future, but we need to create it. What worked in the past and what works in the present won't work in the future. Some core aspects of leadership – such as creating a vision and executing on strategy – will be just as relevant in the next decade as they are today. However, the majority of the world's top 140 CEOs at leading companies believe that leaders will need to embrace a new array of mindsets and skills in order to lead in the next decade and beyond.

As a reminder, these are the four mindsets: the Explorer, the Chef, the Servant, and the Global Citizen. The five skills are the Futurist, Yoda, the Translator, the Coach, and the Technology Teenager. Leaders who are able to master these Notable Nine and help others around them master them as well will be the most successful and so will their organizations. For leaders, success doesn't just mean creating a more profitable organization. It means creating a place where employees genuinely want to show up to work each day; it means creating an organization that positively impacts society and the world; and it means creating an organization that always puts people first.

One of my recent favorite examples comes from Orbia, formerly known as Mexichem. It's a 22,000-person company with diverse business groups that focus on things like agriculture, building and infrastructure, and polymer solutions. I spoke with their CEO, Daniel Martínez-Valle, to learn more about what they are doing. After their massive rebranding and transformation from Mexichem to Orbia, the new brand is focused on three things: people, planet, and profit – in that order. Everything about the company now is focused on purpose, being human, and positively impacting the world. They publicly defined the organization they want to evolve toward by focusing on six criteria: optimizing their investments, reducing greenhouse gas emissions, evolving to become an innovative solutions provider, reducing waste generated, upskilling their workforce, and increasing women in management roles. The most fascinating part of this new brand, and something I've never seen another company do, is that they developed an ImpactMark. Think of it as an evolving logo that changes every year to show how the company is progressing on their six criteria. The supreme accomplishment would be if their ImpactMark were to become a perfect circle; they acknowledge this can never happen but it is something they strive for. This is how Orbia is transparently committing to make the world a better place.

Leadership used to be a rank or title that was bestowed upon someone and it's still the approach that many of us are used to. For the future leader, this will be something that they must earn, which means this opportunity exists for everyone who wants it. Many of the skills and mindsets outlined in this book are relevant in today's world but will be absolutely essential in the next ten years and beyond. In fact, if leaders don't embrace the skills and mindsets outlined in this book, then they should not be, in leadership positions. We have millions of leaders around the world today, so there is enormous potential for positive change. You need to decide what kind of a leader you want to be, are you willing to step up or will you stand firm in your current ways of doing things?

This book has all of the tools you need to become a future leader. However, like with all tools, they alone don't get the job done. It's the person who wields the tools who does that. The question you must ask is, now that you have the tools what are you going to do with them? When you show up to work tomorrow are you going to be the same person you were before you read this book? I hope not. Here are some practical steps you can take.

Define "Leader" and "Leadership"

How do you define leadership? What does being a leader mean to you? Whom do you consider to be a great leader and why? If you can't answer these questions, how can you possibly lead? Your definition may change over time but you have to start with some kind of a North Star that will ultimately guide who you are as a person, the type of company you want to be a part of, and what kind of leader you are.

THE GOLDEN TRIANGLE OF LEADERSHIP

Who you are as a leader and what kind of leader you will become is shaped by three things that make up what I call the Golden Triangle of Leadership (Figure 23.1): your beliefs, your thoughts, and your actions. A belief is something that you understand or accept as true; it's your North Star and your philosophy on business (and life). Your

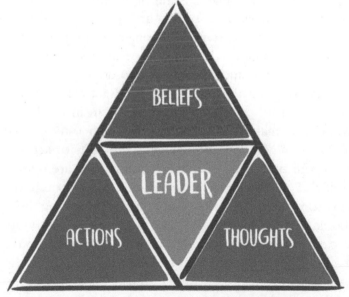

FIGURE 23.1 THE GOLDEN TRIANGLE OF LEADERSHIP.

thoughts are how you think as a result of having that North Star, and your actions are the things you do as a result of your beliefs and thoughts. For example, if one of your beliefs is that people should come before profits, then your thoughts will focus on how you can improve communities, what you can do to make employees more fulfilled at work and at home, how you can take care of your employees during times of business stress, and what you can do to help your people learn and grow as human beings. As a result, your actions might lead you to investing heavily in coaching and mentoring programs, spending more time with frontline employees, dedicating a portion of profits to local community efforts, and even sacrificing your stock price performance or salary so that people who work with you can be taken care of. If one of your beliefs is that leadership is simply about achieving business results, then your thoughts and actions will reflect this accordingly. There are many paths to choose from and I have sought throughout the book to guide you down what I believe is the right one.

Do you know what your beliefs are? Can you see those manifested in how you think? Are your actions reflecting your beliefs and thoughts? These should all connect to one another. This is the absolute core of leadership and requires you to do a bit of introspection. Once you ask yourself these questions and get clarity around these things, it's crucial for you always to keep them in the back of your mind when you make decisions, interact with others, or consider new directions. When you find that your thoughts or actions are not aligning to your beliefs, it's usually a sign that you are not being true to yourself and are being put into a position where you have to compromise who you are. Assuming that you are embracing the concepts in this book, don't compromise – I promise you it's not worth it.

You can think of this process a bit like designing an avatar in a video game. Today, many popular games allow you to pick a character and then customize them with different skills and abilities. As you progress through the game, you have the option to invest your winnings in different areas. For example, you might want to empower your character to wield weapons, use magic, run faster, have more health, be stronger, have greater defensive abilities, and so on. If you were building yourself as a leadership avatar, what kind of character would you be and what areas would you invest in?

As a leader, you must also consider the filters that your organization has in place to grow and create future leaders. Spend some time thinking about what those are currently and what you think they should be. Write them out and talk about them with your peers, your co-workers, and your HR department.

Look at Your Present State

Next, assess which of the skills and mindsets you need to work on most and which ones you have a good grasp of. This isn't easy to do and requires you to look inward. You can follow in the steps of Benjamin Franklin and use his method of assets and liabilities we explored earlier in this book. You should also ask for feedback from your team members. As we have seen, the way leaders evaluate themselves is quite different from how others evaluate the leaders.

To help out with this, I put together an assessment that you and your teams can take to help you understand just how future-leader-ready you are. It will give you a sense of how well you are practicing the skills and mindsets outlined in this book and will provide some further guidance on things you can do. You can find the free assessment at FutureLeaderSurvey.com.

I also encourage you to have open conversations about these skills and mindsets with your team and with your current leaders.

Practice the Skills and Mindsets

The next step is to take all the skills and mindsets you've learned about in this book and make them your leadership operating system. When you turn on your computer, your phone, or another device, it spends a few seconds booting up an operating system that you then use. Each morning when you "boot up," use these nine skills and mindsets as your operating system that gets loaded into your head, heart, soul, and body. This is how you operate from now on – and don't forget that splash of optimism!

As with anything new we learn, it will take time to master it, but you have to start and you have to commit. Benjamin Franklin once said, "Little strokes fell great oaks," meaning gradual and small changes can yield a large impact. If you improve just 1% a day, then you will be 37 times better at the end of the year. For example, you can start spending a few minutes each day reading about a new topic to work on curiosity, take a deep breath before responding in a heated situation to practice empathy, ask for feedback from your team to work on self-awareness, put away technology when having a discussion with someone to work on communication, and look at several possibilities before making a decision to practice thinking like a futurist. Of course, this is just the beginning, but these are relatively simple, basic things you can begin to incorporate in your life that will yield further changes and impactful results.

John Wooden once said, "When you improve a little each day, eventually big things occur. When you improve conditioning a little each day, eventually you have a big improvement in conditioning. Not tomorrow, not the next day, but eventually a big gain is made. Don't look for the big, quick improvement. Seek the small improvement one day at a time. That's the only way it happens – and when it happens, it lasts."

Leadership isn't easy, and becoming a great leader is one of the most challenging things anyone can do. But like all great challenges, they are worth overcoming. If you want complimentary coaching from me during your journey along with access to videos and leadership hacks from the CEOs I interviewed, visit LeadershipReset.com.

Build Your Tribe

Any great leader will tell you that their success and the success of their organization comes as a result of their team. If you want to be a great future leader, you must surround yourself with those who will help you become that leader. Leaders help unlock the potential of those they are leading, but this flows both ways. Your team will also unlock your potential as a leader.

Surround yourself with those who are better than you, smarter than you, and who excel in areas where you struggle. This takes vulnerability and self-awareness, both topics explored in this book. It's easy to surround yourself with those who agree with your ideas and with those who tell you how great and smart you are. It takes enormous courage instead to surround yourself with those who will challenge your ideas and question your assumptions and with those who don't look like you, sound like you, act like you, behave like you, or believe the same things as you.

Build your tribe so that they can make you a better leader.

Avoid a Typical Day

One of the things that I found particularly fascinating when interviewing CEOs, or even business leaders on my podcast for that matter, is that when I asked them what a typical day looks like for them, they couldn't tell me. Their response was always, "I don't have a typical day." However, most of us do have a typical day. We wake up at the same time each day, show up to work at the same time, attend the same meetings, do the same type of work, surround ourselves with the same types of people, eat lunch at the same time, and then go home at the same time. Our days are structured in a very process-centric and, dare I say, robotic kind of way. The more routine and "typical" your job and your day become, the more irrelevant and replaceable you might be.

It's been said that if you want to spark creativity, curiosity, and exercise your brain, you should take a different route to work each day. Doing so allows you to discover new things, deal with new challenges and obstacles, and avoid staying in the doldrums of the familiar; it constantly keeps you on your toes. The same concept applies to what your day actually looks like.

This doesn't mean you can't have some structure or routine in your day; I'm not advocating creating chaos in your life. Instead, I'm encouraging you to change things up when and where you can. Surround yourself with new people and ideas, learn something new, experiment with working on different teams. Avoid having every day look like the one that came before and the one that will come after it.

When you break free from this idea of having a typical day, you will find that you take charge of your life and your career as opposed to just following a script. Not having a typical day puts you into a constant state of learning, growth, and challenging yourself. It also keeps you more engaged in the work that you are doing, helps avoid burnout, creates new relationships, and teaches you to see things from different perspectives. The business leaders I interviewed are involved with diverse projects, meeting with new customers and employees, participating in various team meetings, and doing whatever they can to make sure that their day is atypical. Often leaders can get into the habit of always doing things the same way; creating an atypical day is a great reminder to break out of the box.

What does a typical day look like for you? How can you make it a bit more atypical?

Guide Others

Leadership is a team sport, so what good is it if you are growing and excelling if nobody else around you is? Remember, a lighthouse doesn't exist just to shine a line on itself. The primary purpose of a lighthouse is to guide others. As you think about and embrace the skills and mindsets outlined in this book, ask yourself what you can do to help others do the same, even if it means that they become more successful than you. This is one of the most challenging things for leaders to embrace. It's scary and requires an enormous amount of emotional intelligence and courage.

We can all feel a bit anxious or upset when those around us become more successful than we are, and perhaps we even get resentful. For many leaders, this can be true especially if they are the ones helping make that person more successful. But why? If you have kids, when they are able to do something that you couldn't do or when they do something better than you, you don't yell at them and say, "How dare you? I am your creator!" Instead, you look at them with a sense of pride, joy, and accomplishment, knowing that you had something to do with helping your child succeed. This is how we need to think about leadership.

When you guide others, they in turn will guide you.

Leaders have an enormous responsibility to create an organization where people want to show up to work each day and to build a world that we are all proud to live in. Not only must you embrace and practice the skills and mindsets outlined in this book, but you must also guide others around you to do the same. Being a leader isn't easy, but nothing worth doing ever is. Imagine what our organizations would look like if all leaders practiced the concepts outlined in this book, and imagine what impact this would have on our world. You are a leader, the lighthouse in your organization. Help guide others to success and look out for them.

If this book has helped you become a better leader, please share it with someone else you want to see become a future leader as well.

Lead on!

References

Accenture. "The Promise of Artificial Intelligence: Redefining Management in the Workforce of the Future." 2016. https://www.accenture.com/_acnmedia/PDF-32/AI_in_Management_Report.pdf#zoom=50.

Bailey, Grant. "Nearly Half of British Workers Believe They Could Do a Better Job than Their Boss." *Independent,* November 22, 2017. https://www.independent.co.uk/news/uk/home-news/british-workers-outperform-boss-staff-line-manager-office-politics-onepoll-survey-a8069461.html.

Bailey, Katie. "'Purposeful Leaders' Are Winning Hearts and Minds in Workplaces, Study Finds." University of Sussex. September 7, 2018. http://www.sussex.ac.uk/broadcast/read/40606.

Bariso, Justin. "Google Spent Years Studying Effective Teams. This Single Quality Contributed Most to Their Success." January 7, 2018. https://www.inc.com/justin-bariso/google-spent-years-studying-effective-teams-this-single-quality-contributed-most-to-their-success.html.

Barton, Rachel. "The Power of Brand Purpose." *Accenture.* December 5, 2018. https://www.accenture.com/us-en/insights/strategy/Brand-purpose?c=strat_competitiveagilnovalue_10437227&n=mrl_1118.

Beck, Randall, and Jim Harter. "Managers Account for 70% of Variance in Employee Engagement." *Gallup Business Journal,* April 21, 2015. https://news.gallup.com/businessjournal/182792/managers-account-variance-employee-engagement.aspx.

Bentley. "For Millennials, Does a Big Paycheck Trump Ethical Responsibility?" Bentley University. October 19, 2018. https://www.bentley.edu/news/millennials-does-big-paycheck-trump-ethical-responsibility.

BetterUp. "Workers Value Meaning at Work; New Research from BetterUp Shows Just How Much They're Willing to Pay for It." *BetterUp.* November 7, 2018. https://www.betterup.co/en-us/about/news-press/press-releases/workers-value-meaning-at-work-new-research-from-betterup-shows-just-how-much-theyre-willing-to-pay-for-it/.

Biddle, Matthew. "Moral Leaders Perform Better—but What's 'Moral' Is up for Debate." University of Buffalo. October 22, 2018. http://www.buffalo.edu/news/news-releases.host.html/content/shared/mgt/news/moral-leaders-perform-better.detail.html.

Bloomberg. "Dow CEO Fitterling on Managing Diversity and Inclusion in Corporate America." June 25, 2019. https://www.bloomberg.com/news/videos/2019-06-25/dow-ceo-fitterling-on-managing-diversity-and-inclusion-in-corporate-america-video.

Branson, Richard. "What's the Health of Your Success?" *Virgin* 1178. May 2017. www. virgin.com/richard-branson/whats-health-your-success.

Brené, Brown. "Dr Brené Brown: Empathy vs Sympathy." *Twenty-One Toys*. https://twentyonetoys.com/blogs/teaching-empathy/brene-brown-empathy-vs-sympathy.

Businessolver. "2018 State of Workplace Empathy: Executive Summary." *Businessolver*. 2018. https://info.businessolver.com/empathy-2018-executive-summary#gref.

Catalyst. "List: Women CEOs of the S&P 500." *Catalyst*. June 11, 2019. https://www. catalyst.org/research/women-ceos-of-the-sp-500/.

Çelik, Pinar, Martin Storme, Andres Davila, and Nils Myszkowski. (2016). "Work-Related Curiosity Positively Predicts Worker Innovation." *Journal of Management Development* 35. 10.1108/JMD-01–2016–0013.

Clark, Richard E., and Bror Saxberg. "4 Reasons Good Employees Lose Their Motivation." *Harvard Business Review*. March 13, 2019. https://hbr. org/2019/03/4-reasons-good-employees-lose-their-motivation.

Clifton, Jim. "The World's Broken Workplace." Gallup.com. June 13, 2017. https:// news.gallup.com/opinion/chairman/212045/world-broken-workplace. aspx?g_source=position1&g_medium=related&g_campaign=tiles.

Collins, James C. *Good to Great*. London: Random House Business, 2001.

Cross, Jay. *Informal Learning: Rediscovering the Natural Pathways That Inspire Innovation and Performance*. Somerset: Wiley, 2011.

Cushman. "Futurology: The Pace of Technological Change." Cushman & Wakefield. April 25, 2018. http://www.cushmanwakefield.com.au/en-gb/news/2018/04/ futurology---the-pace-of-technological-change.

Dailey, Whitney. "2016 Cone Communications Millennial Employee Engagement Study." Cone. November 2, 2016. http://www.conecomm.com/research-blog/2016-millennial-employee-engagement-study#download-the-research.

Dartmouth. "Shackleton's Endurance Expedition: A Crewman's View." Dartmouth Library Muse. https://sites.dartmouth.edu/library/tag/ernest-shackleton/.

DDI. "Global Leadership Forecast 2018." https://www.ddiworld.com/DDI/media/trend-research/glf2018/global-leadership-forecast-2018_ddi_tr.pdf?ext=.pdf.

DDI. "Ready-Now Leaders." 2014. https://www.ddiworld.com/DDI/media/trend-research/global-leadership-forecast-2014–2015_tr_ddi.pdf?ext=.pdf.

DDI. "State of Leadership Development 2015." 2015. http://www.ddiworld.com/ DDI/media/trend-research/state-of-leadership-development_tr_brandon-hall.pdf.

De Luce, Ivan. "Researchers Studied the Health of 400,000 Americans and Found That Bad Bosses May Actually Be Giving You Heart Disease." July 9, 2019. https:// www.businessinsider.com/toxic-workplaces-bad-bosses-low-trust-link-to-cardiovascular-disease-2019–7.

Decarufel, Andre. "Four Ways to Become a Global Leader." *Globe and Mail,* May 12, 2018. www.theglobeandmail.com/report-on-business/careers/leadership-lab/what-does-it-really-take-to-think-globally/article17120824/.

Dell. "Realizing 2030: A Divided Vision of the Future." 2017. https://www.delltechnologies.com/content/dam/delltechnologies/assets/perspectives/2030/pdf/Realizing-2030-A-Divided-Vision-of-the-Future-Summary.pdf.

Deloitte University Press. "Global Human Capital Trends 2016." 2016. https://www2.deloitte.com/content/dam/Deloitte/be/Documents/human-capital/gx-dup-global-human-capital-trends-2016.pdf.

Deloitte. "Thinking Global: Global Agility and the Development of a Global Mindset." 2015. www2.deloitte.com/content/dam/Deloitte/uk/Documents/tax/deloitte-uk-global-mindset-nov-2015.pdf.

Deloitte. "Deloitte Global Millennial Survey 2019." May 24, 2019. https://www2.deloitte.com/global/en/pages/about-deloitte/articles/millennialsurvey.html.

Deloitte. "Shift Forward: Redefining Leadership." June 2018. https://www2.deloitte.com/content/dam/Deloitte/us/Documents/about-deloitte/us-shift-forward.pdf

Di Toro, Mark. "Bad Bosses: Glassdoor Survey Reveals Worst Manager Habits: Glassdoor Blog." Glassdoor UK. May 17, 2017. https://www.glassdoor.co.uk/blog/bad-bosses-glassdoor-survey-reveals-worst-manager-habits/.

Diversity Best Practices. "Global Mindset." www.diversitybestpractices.com/sites/diversitybestpractices.com/files/attachments/2017/08/03a_competencies_global_mindset.pdf.

Downes, Larry. "Why Best Buy Is Going out of Business...Gradually." January 2, 2012. https://www.forbes.com/sites/larrydownes/2012/01/02/why-best-buy-is-going-out-of-business-gradually/#48916bcc236c.

Dweck, Carol S. *Mindset: The New Psychology of Success.* New York: Random House, 2016.

Edgecliffe-Johnson, Andrew. "Women Hold Fewer than 5% of CEO Positions in US and Europe." *Financial Times,* December 9, 2018. https://www.ft.com/content/1090105c-fb7b-11e8-aebf-99e208d3e521.

Eisenstaedt, Lee. "Organizational Pace of Change: Thriving in Our Fast Paced World." *Financial Poise,* October 5, 2018. https://www.financialpoise.com/organizational-pace-of-change-surviving-and-thriving-in-our-fast-paced-world/.

Espedido, Juliet BourkeAndrea. "Why Inclusive Leaders Are Good for Organizations, and How to Become One." *Harvard Business Review.* March 29, 2019. https://hbr.org/2019/03/why-inclusive-leaders-are-good-for-organizations-and-how-to-become-one.

Ethics. "Interactive Maps." Ethics & Compliance Initiative. 2018. https://www.ethics.org/knowledge-center/interactive-maps/.

Eurich, Tasha. "What Self-Awareness Really Is (and How to Cultivate It)." *Harvard Business Review.* January 4, 2018. https://hbr.org/2018/01/what-self-awareness-really-is-and-how-to-cultivate-it.

Eurich, Tasha. *Insight: The Surprising Truth about How Others See Us, How We See Ourselves, and Why the Answers Matter More than We Think.* New York: Currency, 2018.

EY. "Global Generations 3.0: A Global Study on Trust in the Workplace." 2016. https://www.ey.com/Publication/vwLUAssets/ey-could-trust-cost-you-a-generation-of-talent/$FILE/ey-could-trust-cost-you-a-generation-of-talent.pdf.

Folkman, Joseph. "5 Business Payoffs for Being an Effective Coach." *Forbes.* February 19,2015.https://www.forbes.com/sites/joefolkman/2015/02/19/5-business-payoffs-for-being-an-effective-coach/#464172a92afb.

Forbes. "Global 2000: The World's Largest Public Companies 2019." *Forbes.* May 15, 2019. www.forbes.com/global2000/#10987b2335d8.

Frankl, Viktor E. *Man's Search for Meaning: An Introduction to Logotherapy.* New York: Simon & Schuster, 1984.

Friedman, Milton. "The Social Responsibility of Business Is to Increase Its Profits." *New York Times Magazine.* September 13, 1970. http://umich.edu/~thecore/doc/Friedman.pdf.

Gallup. "2018 Global Great Jobs Briefing." 2018. https://news.gallup.com/reports/233375/gallup-global-great-jobs-report-2018.aspx.

Gentry, William A., Todd J. Weber, and Golnaz Sadri. "Empathy in the Workplace: A Tool for Effective Leadership." 2016. https://www.ccl.org/wp-content/uploads/2015/04/EmpathyInTheWorkplace.pdf.

Giles, Sunnie. "The Most Important Leadership Competencies, According to Leaders Around the World." *Harvard Business Review.* March 15, 2016. https://hbr.org/2016/03/the-most-important-leadership-competencies-according-to-leaders-around-the-world.

Gino, Francesca. "Why Curiosity Matters." *Harvard Business Review.* September–October 2018. https://hbr.org/2018/09/curiosity.

Glassdoor. "Glassdoor Study Reveals What Job Seekers Are Really Looking for." July 25, 2018. https://www.glassdoor.com/employers/blog/salary-benefits-survey/.

Globoforce. "Bringing More Humanity to Recognition, Performance, and Life at Work." 2017. http://www.globoforce.com/wp-content/uploads/2017/10WHRI_2017Survey ReportA.pdf.

Goleman, Daniel. "What Makes a Leader?" *Harvard Business Review.* January 2004. https://hbr.org/2004/01/what-makes-a-leader.

Goleman, Daniel. *Emotional Intelligence: Why It Can Matter More than IQ and Working with Emotional Intelligence.* London: Bloomsbury, 2004.

Google. "Diversity: Google." https://diversity.google/.

Haas, Martine, and Mark Mortensen. "The Secrets of Great Teamwork." *Harvard Bus iness Review.* June 2016. https://hbr.org/2016/06/the-secrets-of-great-teamwork.

Hackman, J. Richard. "What Makes for a Great Team?" June 2004. https://www.apa.org/science/about/psa/2004/06/hackman.

Hamilton, Isobel Asher. "Facebook Is Going to Start Awarding Bonuses to Employees Who Help the Firm Achieve 'Social Good.'" February 6, 2019. https://www.businessinsider.com/facebook-to-award-employee-bonuses-for-social-good-2019-2.

Harter, Jim, and Amy Adkins. "Employees Want a Lot More From Their Managers." April 8, 2015. https://www.gallup.com/workplace/236570/employees-lot-managers.aspx.

Harter, Jim. "Dismal Employee Engagement Is a Sign of Global Mismanagement." December 13, 2017. https://www.gallup.com/workplace/231668/dismal-employee-engagement-sign-global-mismanagement.aspx.

Holmes. "The Cost of Poor Communications." July 16, 2011. https://www.holmesreport.com/latest/article/the-cost-of-poor-communications.

Horwitch, Mark, and Meredith Whipple Callahan. "How Leaders Inspire: Cracking the Code." June 9, 2016. https://www.bain.com/insights/how-leaders-inspire-cracking-the-code.

IBM. "IBM Leadership, Learning & Inclusion." https://www.ibm.com/case-studies/ibm-leadership-learning-inclusion-manager-engagement.

Imperative. "2016 Workforce Purpose Index." 2016. https://cdn.imperative.com/media/public/Global_Purpose_Index_2016.pdf.

Ingraham, Christopher. "Your Boss Has a Huge Effect on Your Happiness, Even When You're Not in the Office." *Washington Post.* October 9, 2018. https://www.washingtonpost.com/business/2018/10/09/your-boss-has-huge-effect-your-happiness-even-when-youre-not-office/?utm_term=.352176c17846.

Irish Times. "'I've Never Used a Computer,' Says Japan's New Cybersecurity Minister." November 15, 2018. https://www.irishtimes.com/news/world/asia-pacific/i-ve-never-used-a-computer-says-japan-s-new-cybersecurity-minister-1.3698624.

Kashdan, Todd. "State of Curiosity Report 2018." Merck KGaA. 2018. https://www.emdgroup.com/en/company/curiosity/curiosity-report.html.

Kashdan, Todd, et al. "The Five-Dimensional Curiosity Scale: Capturing the Bandwidth of Curiosity and Identifying Four Unique Subgroups of Curious People." *Journal of Research in Personality.* December 2017. https://www.academia.edu/37011226/The_five-dimensional_curiosity_scale_Capturing_the_bandwidth_of_curiosity_and_identifying_four_unique_subgroups_of_curious_people.

Kaufman, Caroline Zaayer. "How to Answer the Job Interview Question: 'What Do You Think of Your Previous Boss?'" Monster. 2018. https://www.monster.com/career-advice/article/former-boss-job-interview.

Keller, Scott, and Mary Meaney. "Attracting and Retaining the Right Talent." *McKinsey & Company*, November 2017. www.mckinsey.com/business-functions/organization/our-insights/attracting-and-retaining-the-right-talent.

Keller, Valerie. "The Business Case for Purpose." *Harvard Business Review.* 2015. https://hbr.org/resources/pdfs/comm/ey/19392HBRReportEY.pdf.

Knott, Anne Marie. "The Real Reasons Companies Are So Focused on the Short Term." *Harvard Business Review.* December 13, 2017. https://hbr.org/2017/12/the-real-reasons-companies-are-so-focused-on-the-short-term.

Kong, Cynthia. "Quitting Your Job." Robert Half. July 9, 2018. https://www.roberthalf.com/blog/salaries-and-skills/quitting-your-job.

Korn Ferry. "Developing Global Leaders." Korn Ferry. August 11, 2014. https://www.kornferry.com/institute/developing-global-leaders.

Korn Ferry. "The $8.5 Trillion Talent Shortage." Korn Ferry. May 9, 2018. https://www.kornferry.com/institute/talent-crunch-future-of-work.

Korn Ferry. "Worried Workers: Korn Ferry Survey Finds Professionals Are More Stressed Out at Work Today Than 5 Years Ago." *Business Wire*. November 8, 2018. https://www.businesswire.com/news/home/20181108005286/en/Worried-Workers-Korn-Ferry-Survey-Finds-Professionals.

Korn Ferry. "From Soft Skills to EI." 2017. http://engage.kornferry.com/Global/FileLib/EI_research_series/KFHG-EI_Report_series-1.pdf.

Kramer, R. "Leading by Listening: An Empirical Test of Carl Rogers's Theory of Human Relationship Using Interpersonal Assessments of Leaders by Followers." Doctoral dissertation. George Washington University, 1997.

Kwoh, Leslie. "When the CEO Burns Out." *Wall Street Journal,* May 7, 2013. https://www.wsj.com/articles/SB10001424127887323687604578469124008524696.

Label Insight. "2016 Transparency ROI Study." 2016. https://www.labelinsight.com/transparency-roi-study.

Lara, Veronica. "What the Internet of Things Means for Consumer Privacy." *Economist,* March 22, 2018. eiuperspectives.economist.com/technology-innovation/what-internet-things-means-consumer-privacy-0/white-paper/what-internet-things-means-consumer-privacy.

Larson, Erik. "New Research: Diversity Inclusion = Better Decision Making at Work." September 21, 2017. https://www.forbes.com/sites/eriklarson/2017/09/21/new-research-diversity-inclusion-better-decision-making-at-work/#4ccc0c4c4cbf.

Lazard. "Levelized Cost of Energy and Levelized Cost of Storage 2018." Lazard. November 8, 2018. https://www.lazard.com/perspective/levelized-cost-of-energy-and-levelized-cost-of-storage-2018/.

Leslie, Jean Brittain. "The Leadership Gap." Center for Creative Leadership. 2015. https://www.ccl.org/wp-content/uploads/2015/04/leadershipGap.pdf.

Levin, Marissa. "Why Great Leaders (Like Richard Branson) Inspire Instead of Motivate." *Inc*. March 30, 2017. https://www.inc.com/marissa-levin/why-great-leaders-like-richard-branson-inspire-instead-of-motivate.html.

LinkedIn Learning. "2018 Workplace Learning Report." 2018. https://learning.linkedin.com/resources/workplace-learning-report-2018.

Lippincott, Matthew. "Effective Leadership Starts with Self-Awareness." April 17, 2018. https://www.td.org/insights/effective-leadership-starts-with-self-awareness.

L'Oréal Group. "Diversity and Inclusion—L'Oréal Group." L'Oréal, www.loreal.ca/group/diversities.

Lorenzo, Rocio, Miki Tsusaka, Matt Krentz, and Katie Abouzahr. "How Diverse Leadership Teams Boost Innovation." January 23, 2018. https://www.bcg.com/en-us/publications/2018/how-diverse-leadership-teams-boost-innovation.aspx.

LRN. "The State of Moral Leadership in Business Report 2018." LRN. 2018. https://content.lrn.com/research-insights/2018-the-state-of-moral-leadership-in-business.

LRN. "LRN Ethics Study: Employee Engagement." 2007. https://assets.hcca-info.org/Portals/0/PDFs/Resources/library/EmployeeEngagement_LRN.pdf.

Maddux, William W., and Galinsky, Adam D. (2009). "Cultural Borders and Mental Barriers: The Relationship Between Living Abroad and Creativity." *Journal of Personality and Social Psychology*, 96, 1047–61. 10.1037/a0014861.

Manpower. "Solving the Talent Shortage." ManpowerGroup. 2018. https://go.manpowergroup.com/talent-shortage-2018.

Matsakis, Louise. "Amazon Pledges $700 Million to Teach Its Workers to Code." *Wired*. July 11, 2019. https://www.wired.com/story/amazon-pledges-700-million-training-workers/.

Maxwell, John C. "Why John Wooden's Teams Won." March 17, 2017. https://www.success.com/john-c-maxwell-why-john-woodens-teams-won/.

Mayo Clinic. "Know the Signs of Job Burnout." https://www.mayoclinic.org/healthy-lifestyle/adult-health/in-depth/burnout/art-20046642.

McChrystal, Stanley A., Tantum Collins, David Silverman, and Chris Fussell. *Team of Teams: New Rules of Engagement for a Complex World*. New York: Portfolio/Penguin, 2015.

McKinsey. "Delivering Through Diversity." January 2018. https://www.mckinsey.com/~/media/McKinsey/Business Functions/Organization/Our Insights/Delivering through diversity/Delivering-through-diversity_full-report.ashx.

McKinsey. "The World at Work: Jobs, Pay, and Skills for 3.5 Billion People." McKinsey & Company. June 2012. https://www.mckinsey.com/featured-insights/employment-and-growth/the-world-at-work.

Mercer. "People First: Mercer's 2018 Global Talent Trends Study." Mercer. May 28, 2018. https://www.mercer.com/our-thinking/career/voice-on-talent/people-first-mercers-2018-global-talent-trends-study.html.

Mindset Works. "Decades of Scientific Research That Started a Growth Mindset Revolution." Mindset Works. www.mindsetworks.com/science/.

Morgan, Blake. "7 Examples of How Digital Transformation Impacted Business Performance." *Forbes.* July 21, 2019. www.forbes.com/sites/blakemorgan/2019/07/21/7-examples-of-how-digital-transformation-impacted-business-performance/#59e090b651bb.

Mosadeghrad, Ali, and Masoud Ferdosi. "Leadership, Job Satisfaction and Organizational Commitment in Healthcare Sector: Proposing and Testing a Model." *Materia Socio Medica* 25, no. 2 (2013). doi:10.5455/msm.2013.25.121–126.

Nyberg A., Alfredsson L., Theorell T., Westerlund H., Vahtera J., and Kivimäki M. "Managerial Leadership and Ischaemic Heart Disease Among Employees: The Swedish WOLF Study." *Occup Environ Med.* 66(1):51–55 (2009). doi:10.1136/oem.2008.039362. Correction published in *Occup Environ Med.* 66(9):640 (2009).

Organisation for Economic Co-operation and Development. "Employment/Self-Employment Rate/OECD Data." https://data.oecd.org/emp/self-employment-rate.htm.

Ou, Amy Y., David A. Waldman, and Suzanne J. Peterson. "Do Humble CEOs Matter? An Examination of CEO Humility and Firm Outcomes." *Journal of Management* 20. 2015. https://createvalue.org/wp-content/uploads/Do-Humble-CEOs-Matter.pdf.

PBS. "Shackleton's Voyage of Endurance." PBS. March 26, 2002. https://www.pbs.org/wgbh/nova/transcripts/2906_shacklet.html.

Predictive Index. "The Predictive Index People Management Study." 2018. https://www.predictiveindex.com/management-survey-2018/.

Puiu, Tibi. "Your Smartphone Is Millions of Times More Powerful Than All of NASA's Combined Computing in 1969." *ZME Science.* February 15, 2019. https://www.zmescience.com/research/technology/smartphone-power-compared-to-apollo-432/.

PwC. "20th CEO Survey." 2017. https://www.pwc.com/gx/en/ceo-survey/2017/pwc-ceo-20th-survey-report-2017.pdf.

PwC. "22nd Annual Global CEO Survey." 2019. https://www.pwc.com/gx/en/ceo-survey/2019/report/pwc-22nd-annual-global-ceo-survey.pdf.

PwC. "Diversity & Inclusion Benchmarking Survey." 2017. https://www.pwc.com/gx/en/services/people-organisation/global-diversity-and-inclusion-survey/cips-report.pdf.

Randstad. "87 Percent of U.S. Workers Say a Multigenerational Workforce Increases Innovation and Problem Solving." August 7, 2018. https://www.randstadusa.com/about/news/87-percent-of-us-workers-say-a-multigenerational-workforce-increases-innovation-and-problem-solving/.

RandstadUSA. "Your Best Employees Are Leaving, but Is It Personal or Practical?" August 28, 2018. https://www.randstadusa.com/about/news/your-best-employees-are-leaving-but-is-it-personal-or-practical/.

RandstadUSA. "4 Ways to Be a Better Boss." https://rlc.randstadusa.com/for-business/learning-center/employee-retention/4-ways-to-be-a-better-boss-1.

Relihan, Tom. "How Going out Can Spur Outside-the-box Thinking." September 18, 2018. https://mitsloan.mit.edu/ideas-made-to-matter/how-going-out-can-spur-outside-box-thinking?utm_campaign=intercultural&utm_medium=social&utm_source=mitsloantwitter.

Reward Gateway. "New Research Reveals Breakdown between Employees and Employer in Recognition, Trust and Communication of Mission and Values." February 5, 2018. https://www.rewardgateway.com/press-releases/new-research-reveals-breakdown-between-employees-and-employer-in-recognition-trust-and-communication-of-mission-and-values.

Reynolds, Alison. "Teams Solve Problems Faster When They're More Cognitively Diverse." *Harvard Business Review*. March 30, 2017. https://hbr.org/2017/03/teams-solve-problems-faster-when-theyre-more-cognitively-diverse.

Robert Half. "Employers Fear 4.5m Workers Could Be on the Move This Year." April 12, 2018. https://www.roberthalf.co.uk/press/employers-fear-45m-workers-could-be-move-year.

Rubenstein, David. "The David Rubenstein Show: Indra Nooyi." November 23, 2016. https://www.bloomberg.com/news/videos/2016–11–23/the-david-rubenstein-show-indra-nooyi.

Safaei, Bardia, Amir Mahdi Monazzah, Milad Barzegar Bafroei, and Alireza Ejlali. 2017. "Reliability Side-Effects in Internet of Things Application Layer Protocols." *International Conference on System Reliability and Safety*. 10.1109/ICSRS.2017.8272822.

SIS International. "SMB Communications Pain Study White Paper." https://www.sisinternational.com/smb-communications-pain-study-white-paper-uncovering-the-hidden-cost-of-communications-barriers-and-latency/.

Smith, Casey. "Promote Ethics and Employee Engagement, Get Smart Training Executive Says." *Tulsa World*. March 24, 2017. https://www.tulsaworld.com/business/employment/promote-ethics-and-employee-engagement-get-smart-training-executive-says/article_f900f41f-16dc-50e4-8485-d7bd8a4c2677.html.

Solomon, Lou. "Why Leaders Struggle with Workplace Feedback." February 11, 2016. http://interactauthentically.com/why-leaders-struggle-to-give-employees-feedback/.

TalentSmart. "About Emotional Intelligence." https://www.talentsmart.com/about/emotional-intelligence.php.

Tanner, Robert. "How Much Does Good Leadership Affect the Bottom-Line?" Management Is a Journey. February 18, 2018. https://managementisajourney.

com/fascinating-numbers-how-much-does-good-leadership-affect-the-bottom-line/.

Udemy. "2018 Millennials at Work Report." 2018. https://research.udemy.com/wp-content/uploads/2018/06/Udemy_2018_Measuring_Millennials_Report_20180618.pdf.

Ultimate Software. "New National Study Conducted by Ultimate Software Reveals Need for Greater Focus on Manager–Employee Relationships." December 4, 2017. https://www.ultimatesoftware.com/PR/Press-Release/New-National-Study-Conducted-by-Ultimate-Software-Reveals-Need-for-Greater-Focus-on-Manager-Employee-Relationships.

Ulukaya, Hamdi. "The Anti-CEO Playbook." TED Talk. May 22, 2019. https://www.ted.com/talks/hamdi_ulukaya_the_anti_ceo_playbook/transcript?language=en.

US Census Bureau. "Older People Projected to Outnumber Children." United States Census Bureau. March 13, 2018. https://www.census.gov/newsroom/press-releases/2018/cb18–41-population-projections.html.

Vesty, Lauren. "Millennials Want Purpose Over Paychecks, So Why Can't We Find It at Work?" *Guardian*. September 14, 2016. https://www.theguardian.com/sustainable-business/2016/sep/14/millennials-work-purpose-linkedin-survey.

Vozza, Stephanie. "Why Employees at Apple and Google Are More Productive." March 13, 2017. https://www.fastcompany.com/3068771/how-employees-at-apple-and-google-are-more-productive.

Walker. "Customers 2020: The Future of B-to-B Customer Experience." 2013. https://www.walkerinfo.com/Portals/0/Documents/KnowledgeCenter/FeaturedReports/WALKER-Customers2020.pdf.

Wellins, Rich. "Global Leadership Development? No Easy Task." Association for Talent Development. June 15, 2016. https://www.td.org/insights/global-leadership-development-no-easy-task.

Wigert, Ben. "Re-Engineering Performance Management." 2017. https://www.gallup.com/workplace/238064/re-engineering-performance-management.aspx.

Wilcox, Laura. "Emotional Intelligence Is No Soft Skill." Harvard Extension School: Professional Development. https://www.extension.harvard.edu/professional-development/blog/emotional-intelligence-no-soft-skill.

Wilson, H. James. "How Humans and AI Are Working Together in 1,500 Companies." *Harvard Business Review.* June–July 2018. https://hbr.org/2018/07/collaborative-intelligence-humans-and-ai-are-joining-forces.

Winkler, Becky. "New Study Shows Nice Guys Finish First." *AMA*. January 24, 2019. https://www.amanet.org/articles/new-study-shows-nice-guys-finish-first/.

Wooden, John. "Motivational Quotes: Success." www.thewoodeneffect.com/motivational-quotes/.

World Bank. "Self-Employed, Total (% of Total Employment) (Modeled ILO Estimate)." https://data.worldbank.org/indicator/SL.EMP.SELF.ZS?view=chart.

Wrike. "Wrike Happiness Index, Compensation." 2019. https://cdn.wrike.com/ebook/2019_UK_Happiness_Index_Compensation.pdf.

Zenger, Jack, and Joseph Folkman. "What Great Listeners Actually Do." *Harvard Business Review*. July 14, 2016. https://hbr.org/2016/07/what-great-listeners-actually-do.

Zenger, Jack, and Joseph Folkman. "The Inspiring Leader." 2015. https://zengerfolkman.com/wp-content/uploads/2019/04/White-Paper_-Unlocking-The-Secret-Behind-How-Extraordinary-Leaders-Motivate.pdf.

Zenger, Jack. "Great Leaders Can Double Profits, Research Shows." *Forbes*. January 15, 2015. https://www.forbes.com/sites/jackzenger/2015/01/15/great-leaders-can-double-profits-research-shows/#3ceea3026ca6.

Zillman, Claire. "The Fortune 500 Has More Female CEOs Than Ever Before." *Fortune*. May 16, 2019. https://fortune.com/2019/05/16/fortune-500-female-ceos/.

Acknowledgments

Each book I've written has been accompanied by a major life event. When I wrote *The Collaborative Organization,* I was engaged; when I wrote *The Future of Work,* I was married; when I wrote *The Employee Experience Advantage,* I had become a dad. Now with, *The Future Leader*, my wife Blake and I are expecting baby number two, a boy!

This book wouldn't have been possible if over 140 CEOs hadn't agreed to be interviewed. I appreciate their time and willingness to share their insights and perspectives with me so that I could share them with you. All these CEOs also have their own teams who had to put in time to coordinate, schedule, and get permission to use the material for this book – a big thank-you to them as well.

Thank you to the team at LinkedIn who believed in this project and agreed to partner with me to survey the almost 14,000 employees around the world: Sophie, Colleen, Suzi, and Dan.

Steve King from Emergent Research, thanks for your advice and guidance on the research for this book.

Thank you, John Wiley & Sons, for helping make this book possible, especially Peter, Jeanenne, Vicki, and Victoria.

To my team who helps me run the business side of things: you are all amazing. Megan, thank you for helping coordinate and schedule everything and for being the best assistant I could ask for! Allen, I've been so fortunate to work with you on all things creative over the years; thanks for the amazing book cover and all the visuals in this book. Vlatko, your designs and creative ideas are always an inspiration in all of my content. Michelle, your assistance with content and research is always a huge help. Abdullah, thank you for your content and data research. Mhyla, thanks for making me look good online! Vlada, thanks for the countless hours you spent with audio and video editing. Drew, thanks for your guidance and support on business strategy. Charlie, thank you for making all my websites look great!

Karen Hardwick and everyone else who made (or attempted to make) introductions to CEOs, thank you for your time and effort.

To my family in LA and Australia, I love you all very much and thanks for your continued support and encouragement.

Lastly, thanks to all of you who keep sharing my ideas, reading my books, attending my talks, and sending me your stories and words of support and encouragement from around the world. You make all of the hard work worth it!

About the Author

After having terrible jobs working for other people, Jacob decided to go off on his own over 15 years ago, with the purpose of creating organizations where people actually want to show up to work. Today, Jacob is a bestselling author and one of the world's leading authorities on leadership, the future of work, and employee experience. He's a highly sought-after keynote speaker and advisor who has worked with organizations such as Microsoft, Disney, PwC, PepsiCo, MasterCard, IBM, and many others. As a professionally trained futurist, his insights are frequently featured in publications such as *Forbes*, *Inc.*, the *Wall Street Journal*, *Fast Company*, and the *Harvard Business Review*. Jacob also created FutureofWorkUniversity.com, which provides educational content, training, and courses on a variety of subjects for the new world of work. He also hosts an award-winning podcast called "The Future of Work with Jacob Morgan," where he interviews the world's top business leaders.

Jacob lives in Alameda, California, with his wife, daughter, and two Yorkie rescue dogs.

To learn more about Jacob and to get access to his content and resources visit TheFutureOrganization.com or email him directly: Jacob@thefutureorganization.com

Additional Resources

The Future Leader Assessment

How many of these skills and mindsets are you practicing effectively today and where do you need to improve? To help you figure that out, I put together an assessment that will evaluate you on the Notable Nine. This will give you a good foundation of what you need to work on. But remember, the assessment only makes sense if you are honest with your answers! To access, visit: **FutureLeaderSurvey.com**

Leadership Reset

Want to get the secret leadership hacks, tips, techniques, and strategies from the world's top CEOs? As a special bonus, I put together a free 31-day coaching and mentoring program with yours truly.

Here's how it works. When you sign up, you will begin receiving a series of videos from me, one a day, for 31 days. Each video will be around 3–5 minutes in length and will share a hack, tip, technique, or strategy from one of the many CEOs I interviewed. This is stuff I couldn't fit into the book but still wanted to share with you as a special thank-you for getting the book.

To get access, visit **LeadershipReset.com** and make sure to use the hashtag **#leadershipreset** on social media so that I can follow your journey and progress!

My Contact Info

Finally, if you want to get in touch, you can reach me via email at Jacob@TheFutureOrganization.com or via my website at TheFutureOrganization.com. There you can also find links to all of my social channels. I hope we get a chance to connect!

Index